Beroul's
Romance of Tristran

Beroul's
Romance of Tristran

by Alberto Varvaro
Professor of the Romance Languages and Literatures
University of Naples

translated by John C. Barnes
Assistant Lecturer in Italian
University of Hull

Manchester University Press
Barnes & Noble Books · New York

Il 'Roman de Tristran' di Béroul
first published 1963 by Bottega d'Erasmo, Turin
This translation © 1972 John C. Barnes
All rights reserved

Published by the University of Manchester
at the University Press
316–324 Oxford Road, Manchester M13 9NR

UK ISBN 0 7190 0474 8

Published in the USA by Harper & Row Publishers Inc
Barnes & Noble Import Division

US ISBN 0 389 04649 3

Printed in Great Britain by
Butler & Tanner Ltd, Frome and London

Contents

Translator's note	*page* vii
Author's note	viii
Introduction: the unity of the romance	1
From Heinzel to Muret	1
Raynaud de Lage	5
The personality and responsibility of the reviser	10

1 The structure of the *Tristran* — 18

Episodes and pauses in the narrative — 18
The episode in the romance — 24
Prophecies and reminiscences — 28
Episode and romance — 32
The chronology of the narrative — 37

2 Narrator and audience — 50

'Seignors, molt avez bien oï' — 50
Solidarity with the protagonists — 58
The chorus — 64

3 The sin of Tristran and Yseut — 73

The love potion: consciousness and responsibility — 74
Ogrin — 81
Marc — 87

4 Feudal forms and human suffering — 95

The theme of the escondit — 95
Yseut's deraisne — 99
The wicked barons — 103
The element of feudal law — 110
The exchange of swords — 112
The Morrois — 117
Adversity and death — 123

5 Narrative technique and figurative patterns — 137

Repetition as a rhetorical device — 138
Remote repetition — 142
Parallel scenes and variations of perspective — 143
Repetition as an element in the narrative rhythm — 146
Dynamic repetition — 148
Narrative parataxis — 151
The narrative rhythm — 153
Figurative psychology and imaginative symbols — 156

6 Beroul and the literary problems of his period — 162

The rendez-vous épié — 164
The lepers — 173
The Blanche Lande — 176
The mingling of styles — 184
Love and the motivation of the action — 186

Postscript, 1971 — 197

Bibliography — 209
Index — 217

Translator's note

I should like to take this opportunity of expressing my gratitude to the late Dr F. Whitehead, who kept a watchful eye on this translation at every stage of its development and made innumerable valuable suggestions for its improvement. I should also like to thank Mr A. F. Kerr and Mr P. R. J. Hainsworth for helping me correct the proofs.

Before the attentive reader comments on the unpardonable liberties I have taken with the original text, I ought perhaps to say that some phrases which were obscure or ambiguous in the Italian have been paraphrased for me by Professor Varvaro, and the corresponding English phrases may therefore contain elements not explicitly present in the original. There were, however, only a handful of such cases, and all other shortcomings are my own responsibility.

In order to make the notes more readable I have excluded from them all publication details of works to which reference is made. This information is now gathered together in the bibliography.

J. C. B.

Author's note

All quotations from Beroul's text follow the Ewert edition, in which the verse numbering is identical to that of the Muret–Defourques edition.

As regards the names of characters in the romance, I have thought it advisable, when discussing Beroul, to adopt the spellings most frequent in his text, and to use the corresponding English forms when speaking of other versions of the legend.

A. V.

Introduction
The unity of the romance

Before beginning the study of any literary text it is necessary to decide whether, and in what sense, it is a unitary work. With many texts, particularly modern ones, the problem is so easily solved that it does not require special treatment, but it is one of considerable difficulty in the case of many medieval works; it certainly cannot be disregarded in a study of the fragment of the Tristram romance preserved in ms Fr. 2171 of the Bibliothèque Nationale. It will perhaps be useful to trace in some detail the history of this old question, in order to understand exactly its present state and to assess the prospects of a solution which is both cautious and satisfactory.

I
From Heinzel to Muret

We must thus go back to Richard Heinzel, who almost a century ago, in a vast enquiry into the sources of Gottfried von Strassburg, set out to examine what he called the 'intrinsic nature' of the extant Tristram texts.[1] Heinzel must have been quite convinced that the *chorizontes* were right to dissect the Homeric poems, or at least that epics were generally formed by the convergence of originally separate episodes, because even in his introduction he immediately spoke of 'parts' which would be found in Thomas and Beroul, without making any attempt to justify his assumption. Accordingly, armed with all his acumen and logical rigour, he embarked on a ruthless vivisection of Beroul's text, 'which soon proves to be a collection and grouping of separate Tristram poems';[2] and since he had no doubt that the octosyllabic couplet had its origins in the two-rhymed tetrastich, he began by isolating twelve fragments which, having piously cut out a few 'clumsy repetitions', he claimed retained more or less extended groups of tetrastich strophes, the remains of earlier versions. But according to Heinzel there must also have existed episodic tales in couplets which incorporated passages of these older compositions, and in fact he thought it possible to identify at least twelve in the Paris manuscript, although—and this is worth noting— the 'collection' did not group them consecutively.[3] Therefore Heinzel was not content with making cuts, but followed his episodic tales through their various interweavings. In other words, Heinzel's 'lays' were not episodes of the extant romance but hypothetical narratives on given themes (No. 4, for example, on the three hostile barons, their treachery and their punishment), the parts of which were not always consecutive, nor were they all preserved in our text, either because some of them had been completely neglected or because they had coincided more or less exactly with parts of other episodes and had been rejected in favour of the latter. Thus the romance was to be broken up not into twelve sections but into a complex mosaic, in which each tessera seemed more or less incomplete.[4] To the twelve episodes[5] were to be added other short passages of various origins, really nothing more than debris after his act of demolition.

One might suppose that it would be difficult to provide the critical argumentation required to justify this complicated dissection; Heinzel, however, did so, and in the most lavish manner. After discussing each episode, he set about proving its independence of all those already examined and excluding the possibility of any interconnection. Where these demonstrations leave something to be desired is not in their quantity but in their extreme captiousness and their ruthless logic, which reaches the point of absurdity. This can be shown by a few examples. The account of the killing of an anonymous baron by Governal was curiously split by Heinzel between two episodes, the sixth and the seventh:[6] the facts adduced to justify this were that in v. 1673 we are told that Tristran is sleeping in the shelter in the arms of the queen, while in v. 1729 we learn only that Tristran is asleep in the shelter, without any mention of Yseut, who does not figure explicitly even in the hero's awakening! The eighth episode, of which Heinzel believed the only remnant to be the barons' counsel concerning Tristran's letter to Marc, was distinct from the sixth, which narrated the preceding events up to the reading of the letter, because the latter featured the three wicked barons, while in the former we read, 'N'i a baron de Cornoualle Ne die: Rois, ta feme pren.'[7] In the mass of such arguments, some really noteworthy contradictions lost the effect they would have had in a more cautious and more measured context.

Thus Muret was in a strong position when he called Heinzel's explanation 'très artificielle', and all the stronger when we consider that Heinzel had completely ignored the undeniable diversity of the

Introduction

traditional forms and the state of the text.[8] But although Muret recognised that the same distinctive stylistic features occurred throughout the fragment, he too thought it was not all the work of a single author: the second part, which 'l'on serait tenté de dire une continuation', began with v. 3011 or a little earlier and differed for the most part not only from Eilhart, who had been followed quite faithfully up to this point, but from all the other versions.[9]

Contemporaneously and independently, Golther[10] too, after rejecting Heinzel's conclusions, noted the remarkable similarity to Eilhart and deduced from this that Beroul's text was bipartite, with the division at v. 2765: vv. 2792–2802 repeated vv. 2707–22 while vv. 2811 *et seq.* established a link between the two parts. An additional argument he used was that the scene of the lovers' judgement and escape, and that of the equivocal oath, were mutually exclusive in the whole tradition.[11] Although the language and style of the second part were similar to those of the first,[12] Golther preferred the view that the fusion had been effected not by Beroul but by the compiler of our manuscript;[13] although doubting whether the contradictions in the story really proved anything, he still thought it a significant fact that after the death of one of the wicked barons they should remain three in number.

In 1897 further arguments were put forward by Röttiger, who put the division back to v. 2754 and declared that the first author, Beroul, was an Anglo-Norman and the continuator a Continental Norman.[14] He believed the fusion to be the work of the copyist, to whom were also to be attributed a few short passages in the first part having peculiar linguistic features.[15]

Röttiger's linguistic evidence was immediately rejected by Muret, who promised to prove nothing less than the unity of the text, with a few interpolations, and also that it was Norman.[16] But by 1903 he had changed his mind and in his edition of the text, even in the title,[17] he remained faithful to the bipartite theory. He now observed that the inconsistency brought about by the reappearance of the dead baron was not explained even if the fragment were not the work of a single author; the episode of the baron's death could have been interpolated, but given its savage barbarity it could not be a chivalric invention.[18] Having then noted the contradictions between vv. 2752–64 and the subsequent narrative, the inconsistencies in the figure of Andret, and one or two other points, he proposed a tripartition, inserting between the first part, consisting of the first

2754 verses plus the supect vv. 2755–64, and the third, from v. 3028 onwards, an intermediate second section, and considering vv. 1656–1746 and 3985–4072 to be of doubtful authenticity.

Little by little, however, the unitarian theory seemed to be gaining ground. When Golther returned to the question he no longer believed in his 1887 thesis: having established the existence of the *Ur*-Tristram, and excluded the possibility of unknown written or oral sources, he then went on to say that all the innovations should be credited to the 'independent inventiveness' of the poet. Beroul's contradictions were similar to those found in the *chansons de geste* and could be explained by oral recitation.[19] Besides, there were contradictions even within each of the two parts, and 'in any case, the hypothetical continuator of Beroul's work would not have taken it over without altering it, but would have made interventions of his own'.[20] Muret too, in his 1913 edition, had doubts about his own distinctions, observing that the link showed considerable skill and that the style of the interpolator or continuator was so similar to Beroul's as to suggest a close relationship between the two—perhaps that of teacher and pupil:[21] the contradictions could be explained by the possibility that the author had composed the work in isolated moments of tranquillity.[22] But there remained the consideration that the second part was to be dated after 1191[23] while the first probably dated from 1165–70, and there were other differences of a more intrinsic nature: the author of the first part, which contained *chevilles* and examples of poetic licence, was a *jongleur* who, as a former clerk, was eager to show off his modest learning and attentive to chivalric forms, who had a taste for moralising and, although not a particularly good psychologist, made judgements on the feelings and actions of his protagonists; the author of the second, on the other hand, although showing a mastery of rhyme and a taste for rhetorical questions, was ignorant of *courtoisie*, portrayed sentiments which were coarse and violent, and had no moral purpose or clerical education. Was this the same author at two different moments? It was made unlikely by the fact that the first part was characterised by archaic declensions, and the second by archaic conjugations. In a word, Muret no longer dared to associate with Beroul's name that of an anonymous continuator, but neither was he convinced of the unity of the work, until in the 1927 edition he admitted that he no longer found the theory of dual authorship satisfactory because it failed to explain away the contradictions, without which no one would ever have thought of doubting the

Introduction

unity of the fragment; it was artificial to emphasise differences of spirit and tone which were differences not between the two parts *en bloc* but between particular passages. The state of the text could be explained by assuming that the original was not a fair copy but a rough draft used both by the *jongleur* for his recitation and by the scribe for his composition of the version in our manuscript.

2
Raynaud de Lage

So a whole period in our account closes with the striking conclusion that the problem is non-existent, a conclusion arrived at by the same critics who had posed it a few decades earlier. Perhaps it is partly for this reason that the unitarian view seemed decidedly to be prevailing,[24] until it was recently disputed again by Raynaud de Lage, in a study which has won a certain amount of authoritative consensus.[25] Raynaud rightly chose to base his deductions on new arguments, dwelling on versification and style rather than returning to the various points already discussed;[26] we shall restate his principal arguments, numbering them for the reader's convenience.

Raynaud said that between the two parts which had already been distinguished well before his time, whatever the explanation, there remained certain contradictions, such as

1 that between Lancïen and Tintaguel as Marc's residence, and
2 that concerning the topography of the Blanche Lande.

Within the second part alone there were in addition

3 that concerning the death of the forester, which in the 'prophetic' passage is effected by Perinis, but is in fact carried out, in a different manner, by Governal, and
4 that concerning Tristran's residence, first with Orri and then with Dinas.
5 Beroul was well acquainted with the places in question, whereas at the end Marc was made to speak as a Continental.[27]
6 Any explanation involving oral composition and a 'brouillon où coexisteraient plusieurs états logiquement incompatibles' was unsatisfactory in that it failed to account for the fundamental modifications of structure and 'altération' of the spirit of the work. The first part was rigorously close to Eilhart, disagreeing

only in details, where the writer 'se désavoue lui-même et s'égare',[28] but v. 2766 marked the beginning of 'un roman tout différent' which repeated the farewell scene, making it pointless because Tristran did not leave, and presupposed in Marc qualities of perjury and perfidy which were psychologically impossible. After the ambiguous oath there remained only the vengeance, and one wondered if the author would have been able to have Tristran leave Cornwall. The ambiguous oath scene itself was treated with humour because the two protagonists were no longer taking any risks. 'Peut-on raisonnablement supposer que l'auteur de la première partie, qui savait bien d'un coup de pouce redresser un détail qui ne lui convenait pas, mais qui s'accommodait de la tradition au point d'en tirer le chef-d'œuvre que nous connaissons, que ce même poète ait procédé d'une façon aussi désinvolte à l'égard du récit traditionnel comme à l'égard de l'action de ses personnages?'[29]

7 In the second part there were many new characters, and above all there was the appearance of Orri, and with him a different picture of life as an outlaw: 'le continuateur de Béroul fait des concessions à un public plus délicat peut-être et moins épris de grandeur . . . on préfère au poème de plein vent une œuvre de salon, on a goûté le *Tristan* de Thomas'.[30]

For the next part of his investigation Raynaud took the first 1500 and the last 1500 verses as samples, and examined the rhymes: he found

8 that in the second group there were twice as many couplets as in the first having a rhyming syllable which did not appear elsewhere in the sample (leading him to conclude that the variation of rhyme was richer in the second part),[31] and
9 that only six pairs of rhyming words occurred unchanged more than once in each sample;[32]
10 in the second group there was a much greater frequency of rich and rare rhymes, many of them involving proper names.
11 The *rejet*, too, seemed to have a different quality, being 'plus brutal' in the second group than in the first.
12 In the first sample fifty-four of the speeches began with a complete, unbroken verse and thirty-three with a verse introduced by an explanatory clause (such as 'Artus dist') or interrupted by an *incise* (such as 'dit il'); in the second group the corresponding figures were respectively thirty-seven and fifty-three.

Introduction

13 The appeal to the public in the first part was not reduced to a fixed formula, while in the second part it 'n'est plus en mesure de susciter le dialogue avec le public et d'appeler les confidences du poète'; in the second sample a very regular formula for presenting characters was 'Atant es vos'.
14 The writer of the first part (whom he called Beroul) had a taste for parenthesis: 'avec ces suspensions du récit, ces intrusions du conteur au milieu de ses personnages, cette façon directe de prendre l'auditeur comme confident, nous sommes en plein dans le style oral, et sans doute plus d'un auteur saura en tirer parti beaucoup plus tard encore. Mais ce n'est pas vraiment le cas du continuateur de Béroul; les parenthèses chez lui sont réduites à peu de chose et se présentent sans cette extrême variété qu'elles ont toujours chez Béroul, qui les invente au lieu de les fabriquer'[33] In the continuation what we found instead was a large number of rhetorical questions introduced by formulas such as 'Que diroie?'; these were indeed parentheses, but did not carry a tone of personal intimacy and remained purely descriptive passages.

Raynaud admitted that none of the arguments advanced was conclusive, but thought that their cumulative weight had the force of proof. The difference, broadly, was between 'celui qui sait jouer de toutes les resources traditionnelles de la *parole* et celui qui est plus un *écrivain* qu'un *diseur*',[34] so that the *Tristran* united the two sides of twelfth-century literature—archaic, oral elements on the one hand, and modern, written elements on the other. The second part remained anchored to the date 1191, whereas the first could be placed twenty or twenty-five years earlier.

Since this thesis depends on an accumulation of minor observations, it is necessary to check them one by one, reviewing them with the same numbering.

1 There is no inconsistency in the references to Lancïen and Tintaguel, since Lancïen is clearly the town in which Tintaguel, the royal castle, is situated.[35]
2 The topography of the Blanche Lande is open to modification to satisfy the demands of narration and fantasy;[36] it would have been more fitting in this connection to exhume Heinzel's observation that after being discovered in their sleep the lovers flee in 'grans jornees' to Wales,[37] whereas later, when the effect of the potion has worn off, they take only a few hours to return to Ogrin.[38]

3 The contradiction concerning the baron's death is certainly plain to see, though
4 the one regarding Tristran's residence shows the same ruthless and excessive logic as (2);

moreover, Raynaud himself gave no explanation of (3) or (4).

5 Vv. 3132–3 have for some years been plausibly explained by the view that communications between Cornwall and Scotland must in fact have been effected principally by sea.[39]
6 We shall return in a moment to the comparison with Eilhart; as regards Raynaud's other observations on the disparity of structure and spirit, the reader is referred to the later chapters of this book. For the time being we shall make only one or two minor observations. The repetition of the lovers' farewells, formerly pointed out by Golther, fits in fairly well with the narrator's general taste for duplication. As for the first author's fidelity to tradition (but what tradition?), it cannot be denied that he in fact took all the liberties that suited him, as is seen in the episode about Marc's ears and in several less important details; but this is one of the points to which we shall be returning. The humour of the oath scene finds a parallel near the beginning in the dialogue between Yseut, Brengain and Marc after the *rendez-vous épié*.[40]
7 The figure of Orri, with all that he implies, is certainly surprising, but it should be realised that once the lovers have been separated there is no reason for making Tristran lead a life of solitary hardship; in other words, whereas hardship is the principal theme of the life in the Morrois, the theme has now changed, and there is no reason why Tristran's situation, which is now of only secondary importance, should not change too. This is a far cry from speaking of an 'œuvre de salon', to be contrasted with a 'poème de plein vent'.
8 A study of the rhymes is undoubtedly of the greatest interest, but it is necessary to note that if we use the data supplied by Raynaud and exclude from each group couplets ending in a syllable not found elsewhere in the sample, the first group is left with ninety-nine different rhyme sounds in the remaining 1420 verses, and the second with ninety-three in the remaining 1340: significantly enough, the average frequency of each repeated pair of rhyming syllables is identical in the two parts,

since it turns out that each one recurs in an average of just over seven couplets in each sample.[41]

9 Raynaud found that it was relatively rare for a pair of rhyming words repeated in the first group to be repeated in the second as well, and spoke of different verbal mechanisms;[42] but it would be considerably more relevant to know how many pairs of rhyming words occur in both groups without necessarily being repeated within one of them. Fortunately Raynaud supplied a complete list of the pairs which are repeated in one of the samples, including those which are not repeated, and those which are not even attested, in the other; thus we find that out of the seventy-nine pairs of rhyming words in question, no fewer than twenty-one are attested in both groups, that is, more than a quarter.[43]

11 The difference in the *rejets* does not seem so great to me, and
14 who can deny the author's participation in the final part of the tale?[44]

Furthermore, it is difficult to see how Raynaud succeeds in reconciling passages such as the crude killings of Denoalan and Godoïne with his description 'œuvre de salon'; and it is striking that Raynaud's view of the second part should be diametrically opposed to those of Muret and Golther mentioned above.[45]

Apart from the impression that there is a difference of tone between the two parts of the romance—an impression which cannot be put into concrete terms and treated objectively—the starting point for all these discussions is basically the relationship of each part with Eilhart.[46] But in the first part there are two episodes, that of Marc's ears and the killing of the traitor baron, which have no counterpart in Eilhart; we have seen that Raynaud, like others before him, proposed to eliminate the latter episode, while sparing the former the same fate only because 'il n'entraîne pas d'incohérence dans la suite'.[47] But the fact is that the two episodes exist and by their very presence discredit the hypothesis that the section faithful to Eilhart's source is the work of Beroul and the independent section that of a second poet. One of the premises for this reasoning is the (perhaps unconscious) conviction that adherence to the German poet's French source extends backwards to cover the whole of the lost first part of the romance, and conversely that all the narrative following Tristran's revenge is independent of the source. But this assumption is neither legitimate nor reasonable: all we know is that in the surviving fragment some parts are more or less similar to Eilhart's source and others are not. That those which are dissimilar should be the last could be an illusion brought about by the fortuitous circumstances which dismembered the manuscript, in the same way as there is no guarantee that the so-called 'real Beroul' was faithful to the source right from the beginning. Moreover, in order to state that where the narrative departs from Eilhart Beroul is disregarding tradition, one would have to be quite sure that the true and only form of the traditional narrative was that followed by the German poet; in fact, if nothing else, the equivocal oath was also known to Thomas.[48]

If we overcome this irrational illusion and realise that the results of Raynaud's stylistic and metrical analysis are really less significant than might have been expected, that the attempt to distinguish between two tastes, two authors and two publics was a failure, there remains no reason for doubting the unity of the romance other than the contradictions of fact. However, a single split into two parts would be insufficient to rationalise these contradictions: it would take an operation similar to Heinzel's, which surely no one would dare repeat today. Nevertheless, part of the criticism striving to disprove the unity of the text is still the fruit of rigorous logic, even if it is shrewder than Heinzel's. It is therefore fitting to repeat the golden words of Joseph Bédier: 'Il est utile, lorsqu'on étudie les faits littéraires, de les considérer comme les plus complexes de tous les faits et les plus délicats: pour les analyser et les apprécier, de pures opérations logiques ne suffisent pas.'[49]

3
The personality and responsibility of the reviser

The *chorizontes* of yesterday and today generally throw little light on the most important aspect of the problem, because they say nothing about what significance and what value they see in the text as we read it today: research into earlier versions is certainly permissible, and even admirable, but it does not exempt the critic from interpreting the version in question as well. Heinzel, for instance, in speaking of a 'collection', meant that for him the author of ms 2171 was no more than a compiler, as seems to be confirmed by his conviction that the text of his 'lays' had been faithfully preserved; but since in literature there exists no gravitational pull drawing 'lays' into 'collections', and since they appear to be so miraculously interwoven, it seems impossible not to recognise that the executant of such a complex task of selection had some literary intention and responsibility. Golther was right when he remarked, 'Supposing we actually had the twelve lays, the explanation of the formation of the surviving text would then create further difficulties: the text is pieced together and dovetailed in an extraordinarily artificial manner, and in order to build it up at all it would have required an almost equal degree of sagacity on the part of the scribe of our manuscript as that with which Heinzel has succeeded in unravelling it again and isolating the individual parts.'[50] Muret was well aware that the hypothetical continuator would have been responsible for all the contradictions, some of which are patently obvious and could therefore have been avoided without any difficulty; it was for this reason that he resorted to the theory of the copy used in both composition and recitation, which Raynaud was right to refute, though he did not give his own view of the extant text.

For various reasons, it seems unlikely that this text can be reduced to a simple combination of two different texts copied one after the other. For one thing, if one or more scenes in the first part were interpolated, did this take place at the last transcription or before? If before, then by the time of the fusion the first text was not such a pure traditional version as it is claimed to have been; if at the time of the fusion, it is clear that this fusion is no longer a simple mechanical juxtaposition. Either way, we cannot say it is a mechanical juxtaposition effected by the scribe of ms 2171—or at least, if it is, then it has not left the slightest trace in the manuscript. Let us suppose, however, that a fusion without active interventions took place at a phase earlier than the manuscript tradition: we must then congratulate the copyist on making such adroit cuts in the two texts as to provoke (let it be admitted) no serious damage. But do vv. 2755-64, which contradict both the first and the second parts, really come from a third source, from which extracts were also copied faithfully and so skilfully integrated as to effect a formal joint of which the exact location can only be guessed at? This seems absurd, and in fact Muret believed that an intermediate passage had been specially written to weld the two principal components together; in general all the *chorizontes* have hinted at the intervention of a reviser. But who could be blind to the way in which this reviser, called to life to justify the existence of these verses 2755-64, did all he could to sabotage the work rather than revise it?

Once we admit the existence of any reviser or continuator, and provided we bear in mind the kind of liberties taken even by scribes, adapting and modifying the texts they copied,[51] only one conclusion can be drawn: that the final 'reviser', in adopting, modifying and adding to the traditional tale as he saw fit, assumed entire responsibility for the text prepared by him, and in every literary respect, contradictions and unevennesses included, he is the author.

Lecoy has pointed out how it is a 'manière de raisonner étrange' to regard one contradiction as a sign of dual authorship, but several contradictions as evidence favouring a single author.[52] We can go further. If we approach the problem from the point of view of the text as it stands, we realise two things: first, it is a fact of cardinal importance that no theory based on multiple authorship can explain all the contradictions in the text and at the same time the psychological and epic unity of the whole;[53] second, the problem itself is turned upside-down, in the sense that if we admit the existence of a reviser we can no longer speak of two or more authors but must talk in terms of the reviser's two or more sources and his treatment of them.

Thus it seems unwise to deny that there are unevennesses or contradictions in the romance, or to maintain that they derive from the work of a single author; the point we must make is simply that towards the end of the tradition culminating in ms 2171 there was a literary individual who accepted them. We can also admit that he had before him, if not Heinzel's twelve lays, then at least Muret's three texts: since the linguistic and metrical character, not to mention the style, of the surviving text is on the whole reasonably consistent, sufficiently so to belie the evidence to the contrary, we must admit that his is a fairly fundamental contribution, at least from the point of view of form; in other words, that he was not only skilful in rearranging his material but a gifted individual capable of giving a uniform stamp to the new text.[54] Thus in the compiler we begin to see an author, assuming that there is no reason to designate otherwise someone whose work is based on more than one source. Luigi Pulci's *Morgante*, derived with numerous cases of unevenness from two sources, is not for this any less the work of Pulci.

It is impossible to ascertain the number or identity of the sources which our narrator had at his disposal. If we could regard as proven the existence of the *Ur*-Tristram and its status as sole prototype of the French tradition, the picture would be reasonably simple; but it seems certain that twelfth-century reality was considerably more complex and varied than this theory claims.[55] So it may be that there were several sources of varied character, and it is certain that they were used with the liberty we have visualised, that is, with a free selection of certain scenes, in which the narrative thread was preserved fairly faithfully, while the tone, perspective and form were freely modified. The research carried out on the source common to our author and to Eilhart shows clearly this capacity for both fidelity and imaginative, emotional reworking of the material.[56] Thus we should regard our narrator as something more than a slave to his sources, something more than a reviser pure and simple; he does modify his sources, but only as far as modification interests him, so that while we can understand how the different origins of the individual episodes left their mark here and there, this partial negligence and all its consequences must be accounted for by a particular narrative taste, which concentrated on certain aspects of the tale and on those alone.

This does not mean that the problem discussed by Heinzel and Raynaud de Lage is meaningless or gratuitous. The mistake made by such critics was one of perspective, in their total lack of interest in the literary personality, great or small, of the reviser. If we are convinced that this personality, which we all feel in the tale of ms 2171, made its appearance not *before* the amalgamation of the various definite or hypothetical texts in the romance, but *at* this amalgamation, then the problem becomes a difficult, subtle, minute search for sources, and, like all enquiries of this kind, provided they consist of more than mere logical alchemy, constitutes a contribution to the history of twelfth-century literature. Anyone who wishes to study the literary character of the Tristram romance in ms 2171 will not be able to by-pass such researches, since this character must be studied partly from the viewpoint of the author's treatment of his sources. But in the last analysis we can justifiably speak, with due circumspection and in the sense we have established, of the text as a unitary work, and thus we can also speak of an author. Is this author Beroul? We have no reason to designate him otherwise, especially since we have no biographical information about him, and since his name has no qualifying function, solely that of an identifying cypher.

Notes

1 *Gottfrieds von Strassburg Tristan und seine Quelle*, p. 289.
2 *Ibid.*, p. 290.
3 *Ibid.*, p. 340.
4 But only rather rarely is the hypothesis advanced that the text of the original episodes was touched up. Heinzel's 'compiler' did not employ the pen, only scissors and paste.
5 *Ibid.*, pp. 298–339.
6 With the division coming between vv. 1728 and 1729; the justification for this is on p. 325.
7 Vv. 2624–5; Heinzel, *op. cit.*, p. 327. Since this observation has been made more than once, it seems necessary to point out that all the barons remain silent because none of them wishes to confront Tristran, least of all the three in question, who are wicked and cowardly.
8 *Eilhart d'Oberg et sa source française.*
9 *Ibid.*, p. 291; in a footnote on p. 334 Muret wondered whether the killing of the anonymous enemy by Governal was an interpolation.
10 *Die Sage von Tristan und Isolde.*
11 It seemed to Golther that the second part of the fragment was derived from a version which differed from both the *jongleurs'* version (Eilhart and the prose romance) and the courtly version (Thomas and imitators).
12 The second part 'is rather rougher, at all events it is the poetry of a *jongleur*' (*ibid.*, p. 88).
13 If it were to be attributed to Beroul, 'then one is all the less justified in believing that Beroul's version follows a number of other poems' (*ibid.*, p. 88).
14 *Der heutige Stand der Tristanforschung.* Röttiger also thought the continuator was younger than Beroul (*ibid.*, pp. 16–21).
15 Röttiger was unable to decide whether a continuator with different intentions had concluded the work left incomplete by Beroul (as occurred in the case of Gottfried) or whether the two parts had been brought together only by the compiler of the manuscript (*ibid.*, pp. 24–5).
16 In his review of Röttiger's book.
17 *Le Roman de Tristan par Béroul et un anonyme.*
18 *Ibid.*, pp. xi–xii.
19 *Tristan und Isolde in den Dichtungen des Mittelalters und der neuen Zeit*, pp. 103–4. Note the perceptive observation, 'Beroul often loses himself in the intuitive painting of details, which sometimes leads him to disregard the coherence and overall outline of the whole' (p. 104).
20 *Ibid.*, p. 104. The opinion that the judgement scene and oath scene cannot exist side by side has been regarded as erroneous since Bédier's reconstruction of the archetype.

21 1913 edition, p. vii.
22 *Ibid.*, p. viii.
23 Cf. v. 3849.
24 For some divergent views cf. Van Dam's 'Tristanprobleme' p. 183 (but Van Dam misunderstands Kelemina's *Geschichte der Tristansage*, pp. 36–7).
25 'Faut-il attribuer à Béroul tout le *Tristan?*' Cf. Lecoy's review.
26 Thus it is admitted without discussion that vv. 1656–1728 are interpolated.
27 Vv. 3132–3.
28 Raynaud de Lage, *art. cit.*, p. 252.
29 *Ibid.*, p. 254.
30 *Ibid.*, p. 256.
31 Eighty rhyme sounds out of 173 in the second sample, as compared with 40 out of 139 in the first.
32 In fact there are only five, since *roïne–gaudine* is found twice in the second group but only once in the first.
33 *Ibid.*, p. 268.
34 *Ibid.*, p. 269.
35 This had already been pointed out by Novati in 'Un nuovo ed un vecchio frammento del *Tristran* di Tommaso', p. 396n.
36 In any case, Novati (*art. cit.*, p. 397n.) had found this description to be precise and detailed.
37 Vv. 2127 *et seq.*
38 V. 2281; cf. Heinzel, *op. cit.*, p. 325.
39 Cf. Loth's *Contributions à l'étude des romans de la Table Ronde*, p. 75. Brugger, in his review of Loth's book, pp. 237–8n., refuted this explanation, preferring to regard the *que* clause, even though it occurs within a speech by Marc, as a piece of information provided by a Continental author; this is also acceptable, but it should be noted that in Wace's *Brut* (vv. 8839–45) Octa and the rebels seem to sail from London to Scotland, and in *Garin le Loheren* (vv. 4216–18) the Bordelais sail from Bordeaux to St Quentin.
40 Cf. pp. 170 *et seq.*
41 The average frequency of repetition for each rhyme is 14·34 verses in the first part and 14·41 in the second.
  After the present pages had been written, Hanoset published his meticulous study 'Unité ou dualité du *Tristran* de Béroul?', in which all the metrical and stylistic arguments of Raynaud de Lage, who had sought to corroborate his thesis in a 'Postscriptum', are shown to be quite valueless.
42 'Faut-il attribuer . . . ?', p. 260.
43 The twenty-one pairs are: *Governal–cheval*, **haut–saut*, **mervelle–conselle*, *feme–regne*, *prendre–pendre*, *terre–querre*, *terre–guerre*,

*merci–ci, *bien–rien, dire–sire, pris–mis, roi–moi, baron–raison, sont–mont, jor–enor, cors–fors/hors, cort–tort, conmune–une, *roine–encline, roine–gaudine, roine–espine.* The five pairs repeated in both groups are marked with an asterisk. Out of a total of ten rich rhymes in the second sample (10) only five involve proper names; in the first group there are two rhymes involving geographical names, the second pair being repeated three times without change.

44 On the appeals to the public (13) cf. chapter 2. Since the events recounted in the first part are generally more dramatic in tone than those in the second, the *rapport* between poet and public will clearly be more intense in the first part. On the formulas mentioned in (13) and (14) cf. Hanoset, *art. cit.*, pp. 529–30.

45 As regards the reappearance of the dead baron and similar contradictions, besides referring the reader to chapter 1 we should mention how in the *Pèlerinage Charlemagne* Charles leaves with 80 000 men in the first band alone; these then disappear completely, with the result that no one notices the emperor's arrival at Jerusalem and Constantinople. As the editor rightly remarks, 'they were no longer needed for the rest of the narration' (p. xxxv). In the *Aspremont*, on the other hand, the pagan Synagon definitely dies at v. 5678, having been decapitated by Naimon; but he speaks again at v. 6366 as one who has not even been in the battle, while this is again contradicted in v. 6877. Note the observations of Tobler in Grober's *Grundriss*, vol. 1, p. 329, and of Menéndez Pidal in his *Poema de mio Cid*, pp. 70–3.

46 This was openly recognised by Golther in his *Tristan und Isolde*, p. 104.

47 'Faut-il attribuer . . . ?' p. 250n.

48 According to Fourrier (*Le Courant Réaliste dans le roman courtois en France au moyen âge*, vol. 1, p. 79), this episode was in fact in the *version commune*. Some doubts have been advanced about the thesis supported principally by Schoepperle (*Tristan and Isolt: a Study of the Sources of the Romance*), for example those expressed by Le Gentil in 'La Légende de Tristan vue par Béroul et Thomas', p. 117, and more recently by Legge in her review of Jonin's *Les Personnages Féminins*, p. 511 ('Qu'Eilhart représente le dérivé le plus fidèle de la tradition est une hypothèse impossible à prouver . . . il n'est probablement qu'un remanieur comme les autres'). Hofer, in *Die Komposition des Tristanromans*, p. 288, went so far as to say that it was Eilhart who had departed from Beroul.

49 *Les Légendes Epiques*, vol. 1, p. 462.

50 *Die Sage von Tristan und Isolde*, p. 76.

51 This was openly admitted by a scribe-reviser of the *Roman de la Rose*, quoted by Tobler (*Grundriss*, vol. 1, p. 327): 'Si ai en maint lieu moult ostees De paroles et adjoustees, C'on puet bien vëir et

Introduction

savoir.' Rychner's *Contributions à l'étude des fabliaux*, vol. 1, chapter 2, is outstanding on this point.

52 *Art. cit.*, p. 88.

53 Cf. Ewert, 'On the text of Beroul's *Tristran*', pp. 89–90.

54 Thus Pope's hypothesis that Beroul was 'a *remanieur*-poet . . . who scorned not to adapt old material when it lay before him, but was equally ready to invent freely when the old material failed or did not satisfy him' ('Note on the dialect of Beroul's *Tristan* and a conjecture', p. 191) seems to be correct (which was also what Ewert thought, *art. cit.*, p. 89), but should be seen in conjunction with the vindication of Beroul's psychological and poetic treatment, most recently emphasised by Le Gentil in 'La Légende de Tristan' and 'L'Episode du Morois et la signification du *Tristan* de Béroul'.

55 We cannot linger here on such a complex problem. I refer the reader to the perceptive and distinguished pages of Pauphilet, *Le Legs du moyen âge*, pp. 107–25, to Fourrier, *op. cit.*, pp. 32 *et seq.*, and to my study on 'La teoria dell'archetipo tristaniano'.

56 Cf. the numerous comparisons which have been made between Beroul and Eilhart, from Muret's 'Eilhart d'Oberg' to Jonin's *Les Personnages Féminins*, pp. 17–34. Le Gentil wrote, on p. 111 of 'La Légende de Tristan', 'Le diseur, lui, accepte un canevas préétabli, dont il se soucie peu de modifier les lignes générales, se réservant au contraire une large initiative dans le travail de mise en œuvre: il ajoute, retranche, contamine au besoin plusieurs sources, au risque de se contredire, docile à toute image, à toute émotion qui le sollicite au passage.' On the basic problem we should recall Castro's remark in *La realidad histórica de España*, p. 7: 'If in a writer of quality . . . one finds something which has been taken from another writer, before saying it does not belong to him one must determine the function of the borrowing in the work as a whole and see how it links up with the rest of the worthy activities of the author. Plagiarism occurs when something is transplanted into human soil which is barren.'

I
The structure of the Tristran

1
Episodes and pauses in the narrative

Every reader of Beroul's tale will certainly have noticed those frequent pauses or—one might almost say—hiatuses in the flow of the narrative, after which the author seems to get a second wind and begin again as though he were just starting, with a voice clearer and more refreshed than would seem possible in view of the ceaseless succession of eight-syllable couplets on the written page. For instance, when the poet has told of the death of the dwarf Frocin, he continues:

> Seignors, molt avez bien oï
> Conment Tristran avoit salli
> Tot contreval, par le rochier,
> Et Governal sor le destrier
> S'en fu issuz, quar il cremoit
> Qu'il fust ars, se Marc le tenoit.
> Or sont ensenble en la forest,
> Tristran de veneison les pest.
> Longuement sont en cel boschage;
> La ou la nuit ont herberjage,
> Si s'en trestornent au matin.   [vv. 1351-61]

This passage serves to introduce the account of the lovers' first meeting with Ogrin,[1] but with the exception of the last two verses it contributes nothing to the progression of the narrative, since we have just heard everything else it contains in the passage ending at v. 1305:[2] as this new beginning occurs less than fifty verses later, it cannot seriously be maintained that it is intended to remind the listener of events recounted some time earlier and that the poet is thus satisfying a need for clarity. This passage obviously has a different function: in fact we have come to a pause in the flow of the narrative. The reference to the situation which has developed in the course of the preceding narrative, although superfluous because the intervening episode is very short, acquires significance if we accept the hypothesis of such a pause, allowing thus a degree of autonomy to the following block of narrative and relating the verses in question to it, not in the function of a *rappel* to the body of a unitary narrative, but rather as an introduction to this quasi-autonomous episode.

If we continue reading we shall find confirmation of our hypothesis. After recounting the chance meeting with Ogrin and the conversation between the three, the narrative sweep becomes quite broad again for a moment, and after a very precisely defined passage of time,[3] duration once again becomes indeterminate:

> Au matinet s'en part Tristrans;
> Au bois se tient, let les plains chans.
> Li pain lor faut, se est grant deus.
> De cers, de biches, de chevreus
> Ocist asez par le boscage.
> La ou prenent lor herbergage,
> Font lor cuisine et lor beau feu,
> Sol une nuit sont en un leu. [vv. 1423-30]

It is clear that the 'moment', chronological and narrative, of the meeting gives way to a presentation devoid of both events and precise indications of time, as was briefly suggested by vv. 1357-1361, quoted above, which, immediately following the *rappel*, do in fact introduce the encounter with Ogrin. Finally, if we note the similarity between

> La ou la nuit ont herberjage,
> Si s'en trestornent au matin [vv. 1360-1]

and

> Sol une nuit sont en un leu, [v. 1430]

the correspondence between the two passages can be clearly seen. Thus, just as the former served to build up tension again after a pause in the narrative, so we can expect the latter to be leading up to another pause; and in fact we immediately read:

> Seignors, oiez con por Tristran
> Out fait li rois crïer son ban—
> En Cornoualle n'a parroise
> Ou la novele n'en angoise—
> Que, qui porroit Tristran trover,
> Qu'il en feïst le cri lever.
> Qui veut oïr une aventure,

> Con grant chose a an noreture,
> Si m'escoute un sol petitet!
> Parler m'orez d'un buen brachet ... [vv. 1431–40]

These verses have all the characteristics typical of an *exordium*. The appeal to the listeners ('Seignors, oiez') is repeated and amplified in a traditional *jongleurs*' formula in vv. 1437–9; in v. 1440 we find the announcement of the theme to be developed in the following verses, while its deeper *senefiance* is indicated immediately before this, in v. 1438. It is certainly no coincidence that in the first verses we find a *rappel* of a type completely identical with that in the preceding episode and at first sight equally functionless, since all that is said here we have just learned, with a few variations, from the lips of Ogrin.[4]

We have thus found in the body of the narrative two points of lesser force which isolate a moment of high dramatic tension, establishing strongly marked pauses before and after, in such a way that this cannot have happened by chance but must be intentional. We must now examine the extent of this practice so that we can make a suitable appraisal of its importance in the structure of the romance.

If we recommence our reading from the beginning, which, as we know, occurs *in medias res*, owing to the loss of several pages of the only manuscript, our attention will be arrested by the verses around v. 573. The episode of the *rendez-vous épié* ends at v. 572 and its consequences and the developments arising out of it have been indicated:

> Acordez est Tristran au roi.
> Li rois li a doné congié
> D'estre a la chanbre; es le vos lié!
> Tristran vait a la chanbre et vient,
> Nule cure li rois n'en tient. [vv. 568–72]

Clearly we are here passing from the account of a precise event to that of a situation: while the present tense of v. 568 and the perfect in v. 569 obviously have only a momentary value, we pass on through the 'es le vos lié' to the last two verses, with their durative and frequentative presents. Thus we are transported from the vividness of the foreground to the indistinct background lighting of the intervals.

And the following verses are these:

> Ha! Dex, qui puet amor tenir
> Un an ou deus sanz descovrir?

> Car amors ne se puet celer:
> Sovent cline l'un vers son per,
> Sovent vienent a parlement,
> Et a celé et voiant gent;
> Par tot ne püent aise atendre,
> Maint parlement lor estuet prendre.
> A la cort avoit trois barons . . .   [vv. 573–81]

At first we are still in 'durative time', which the 'un an ou deus' of v. 574 renders still more vague, but at v. 581 we notice a definite break, which violently ends the standstill to which the narrative has come. Moreover it is not only this momentary weakening of the narrative tension which has caused us to pause: despite the absence of striking features such as those of vv. 1431 *et seq.*, this too is obviously an *exordium* conforming to the technical requirements of the *sententia* (v. 575), which is amplified in the following verse.[5] The process is saved from rhetorical coldness by the impassioned interrogative of vv. 573–4 (which could of course be classified, in a frigid stylistic analysis, as just another rhetorical trimming) and by the way in which the maxim unobtrusively fits in with, and in fact seems to spring directly out of, the affairs of the lovers, so that it is not an abstract aphorism to which the narrative serves as a gloss but an active comment on the narrative. In fact we are at a turning point in the romance, since here the poet starts his account of the ruse of the flour on the floor, by means of which the lovers will be caught red-handed.

Equally obvious is the break at v. 1306, where the poet leaves the lovers in the wood and makes a rapid but clear transition to the episode of Marc's horses'-ears, which is clearly not essential to the narrative:

> . . . Longuement *sont* en cel desert.
> Oiez du nain com au roi sert:
> Un consel sot li nains du roi . . .   [vv. 1305–7]

The end of the episode also comes abruptly (v. 1350). There follows the *exordium* of the first encounter with Ogrin, upon which we have already commented, and we have also looked at the opening verses of the next episode (*Husdent*). Here too the last verse establishes, within the time span of the episode, the narrative result attained (here the dog's new-found disposition for hunting) and the episode ends with a general observation:

> Molt sont li chien de grant servise!   [v. 1636][6]

The following episode, the killing of an anonymous traitor baron, is introduced in an equally direct manner:

> Seignors, *molt* fu el bois Tristrans,
> Molt i out paines et ahans.
> En un leu n'ose remanoir;
> Dont lieve au main ne gist au soir:
> Bien set que li rois le fait querre
> Et que li banz est en sa terre
> Por lui prendre, quil troveroit . . .
> . . . Un de ces trois que Dex maudie,
> Par qui il furent descovert,
> Oiez conment *par un jor* sert!   [vv. 1637–43 and 1656–8]

This time the *exordium* is a particularly long one[7] and the initial 'Seignors' is appropriately taken up twenty-one verses later by means of the 'oiez'. Here too, as in the other cases, there is a clear switch from 'durative' time to the narration of a particular event, as is indicated in the passage by 'molt' (v. 1637) and 'par un jor' (v. 1658). It is equally interesting to note that these verses take up motifs with which we are already familiar from previous *exordia*: vv. 1360 and 1430, already quoted, correspond to v. 1640, and the proclamation has already been spoken of in vv. 1431 *et seq*. These are certainly not fortuitous parallels, but are part of a subtle play of echoes, and at the same time of a routine technique of the author, who seems to have created certain constant patterns for beginning and ending an episode.

The next clearly identifiable link passage closes the episode of the traitor's death, which is closely bound up with the rapid mention of the 'arc qui ne faut', and opens that of the discovery of the lovers asleep in their shelter:

> *Longuement* fu en tel dechaz.
> Mervelles fu de buen porchaz:
> De venoison ont grant plenté.
> Seignor, *ce fu un jor d'esté*,
> En icel tens que l'en aoste,
> Un poi aprés la Pentecoste.
> Par un matin, a la rousee,
> Li oisel chantent l'ainzjornee;
> Tristran de la loge ou il gist,
> Çaint s'espee, tot sol s'en ist . . .   [vv. 1771–80]

Here again the preceding episode fades away in a *longuement* which establishes a pause, without notable events, in the lovers' extremely stormy existence. Then, the 'Seignor' marks a direct approach to the next section, immediately placing the action in time with a wealth of detail which would surprise us were it not in fact traditional material in *exordia*.[8] The episode closes with vv. 2131-2 ('Trois anz plainiers sofrirent peine, Lor char pali et devint vaine'), which are followed by the well known *exordium* on the limited duration of the love potion, justifying the second encounter with Ogrin and Yseut's subsequent return to court. Here there is no clearly marked pause in the narrative until v. 3027. By then another stable situation has been established: Yseut is living with Marc, and Tristran has moved in with Orri the woodman, without losing contact with the queen:

> O Tristran [Orri] ert la sejornanz
> Priveement en souterrin.
> Par Perinis, li franc meschin,
> Soit Tristran noves de s'amie.
>
> Oiez des trois, que Dex maudie:
> Par eus fu molt li rois malez,
> Qui o Tristran estoit meslez.
> Ne tarja pas un mois entier
> Que li rois Marc ala chacier,
> Et avoc lui li traïtor.
> Or escoutez que font cel jor . . .   [vv. 3024-34]

It is no longer necessary to stop and comment on stylistic habits with which we are by now quite familiar. This is the beginning of the oath on the Blanche Lande, which ends more than a thousand verses later:

> Li uns de l'autre s'est sevrez,
> Chascun s'en veint a son roiaume;
> Li rois Artus vient a Durelme,
> Rois Marc remest en Cornoualle.
> Tristran sejorne, poi travalle.   [vv. 4262-6]

—an ending as typical as any of the others, with a systematic statement of the protagonists' situation *after* the events narrated. And equally typical are the following verses, which begin the last episode which has come down to us, the deaths of Denoalan and Godoïne:

> Li rois a Cornoualle en pes,
> Tuit le criement et luin et pres;
> En ses deduiz Yseut en meine,

> De lié amer forment se paine.
> Mais, qui q'ait pais, li troi felon
> Sont en esgart de traïson.
> A eus fu venue une espie... [vv. 4267-73]

This time there is no chronological reference to mark a clear dividing line between the two moments in the narrative, and yet the impression is that there is a substantial distance between v. 4266 and v. 4267; this is precisely because the latter forms a kind of echo to v. 4265.

2
The episode in the romance

We have thus identified nine passages in which we can clearly see the narrator's intention to indicate a pause, and we can legitimately conclude that the structural unit of the romance is the episode. But this cannot be regarded as a point of arrival in our research, rather as a first finding which requires further qualification and probing. In the meantime, are there in fact ten episodes in the romance?[9] We should be unable and unwilling to say categorically that these are the correct divisions; vv. 320, 909 and 2765, for instance, could be regarded as *exordia* to independent episodes.[10] But since our task is not one of dissection like that of Heinzel or his more moderate followers, we shall be well advised to limit ourselves to what seems obvious and certain; we shall immediately see that this is sufficient to allow us to approach the most important problem, that of the structural function of the episode.

Undoubtedly the experienced reader will already have been reminded of the old thesis energetically put back into circulation by Rychner, who maintains that the *chansons de geste* can sometimes be divided into episodes corresponding to sessions of recitation.[11] If the same were to be found with respect to our episodes, we should find ourselves dealing with a structure principally, or at least originally, dictated by practical considerations, arising out of the fact that the poem was meant for recitation by *jongleurs*. It is true that formulas such as that of vv. 1437–9 ('Qui veut oïr une aventure, Con grant chose a an noreture, Si m'escoute un sol petitet!') are quite typical of the manner in which narratives are presented by *jongleurs*, and that with 'un sol petitet' the *jongleur* seems to be openly announcing that he is about to relate a brief episode.[12] But if this were so we should expect the various episodes to be of equal length, whereas Beroul varies between the forty-four verses of the account of Marc's horses'-ears and the 1238 verses devoted to the oath at the Blanche Lande. A quick calculation makes it clear that there is no constant length, nor even an average length: the episodes of Husdent and the deaths of Denoalan and Godoïne are the only two of comparable length, with 205 and 218 verses respectively, but even this is a deceptive parallel because the Godoïne–Denoalan episode, which is the last one of the story, is incomplete. Finally, apart from the evidence of the formula we have mentioned, which is anything but conclusive, there is not a single hint of a real division into sessions, despite the fact that these are found in the epic. Even the appeals to the audience, which we have found in so many of the *exordia*, would not be sufficient proof; in any case they are also found in other situations, and, besides belonging to a commonplace rhetorical tradition, they meet poetic demands which we shall investigate later.[13]

So we can leave this hypothesis and follow another line of investigation, suggested by a few verses in the first episode:

> Des estoiles le cors [Frocin] savoit,
> Les set planestres devisoit;
> Il savoit bien que ert a estre:
> Qant il oiet un enfant nestre,
> Les poinz contot toz de sa vie.   [vv. 323–7]

This description of the dwarf's astrological arts, which, if not exactly detailed, is certainly not concise, here seems superfluous: certainly these same arts allow him to foresee that Marc, convinced by the lovers' deceptive speeches which he heard when he was up in the pine tree, will direct his anger towards Frocin ('Bien set li rois fort le menace, Ne laira pas qu'il nu desface', vv. 333–4); but we can also be sure that his astrological abilities must have been well known to the audience, who in the course of the romance must have already seen them in action on other occasions. Thus it seems that the narrator wishes to render the episode in some way autonomous, by repeating information which is wasted on anyone who happens to know the whole romance but necessary for those who are hearing this episode for the first time. Further on we read:

> Par Perinis, *un suen prochain*,[14]
> Avoit mandé que l'endemain
> Tristran venist a lié matin.   [vv. 4347–9]

Here Perinis is presented as unknown to us although he has already been mentioned seventeen times in our fragment alone, and indeed at the last mention it was assumed that we knew him quite well:

> son mesage a fait
> Perinis qui tant mal a trait
> Por le servise a la roïne. [vv. 3553-5]

So it seems that at least in these two cases the episode is regarded as a complete and autonomous narrative unit, capable of an independent existence. Thus we seem to be returning by a different path and perhaps in a different sense to the thesis of the *chorizontes*, that is, to regarding Beroul's romance as a collection of more or less independent episodes. But this is neither necessary nor provable. In considering the passage about Frocin we must remember that his astrological talents must have been mentioned not only in earlier episodes (the existence of which is not certain) but already at the beginning of this same episode, since it is Frocin who discovers the lovers' rendezvous at the fountain, and he does it by reading the stars.[15] Therefore even someone who happened to be listening to this episode without knowing the earlier ones could not be ignorant of these talents: even for him vv. 323 *et seq.* would be superfluous.

There is no doubt that, of our ten episodes, the one most loosely connected with the tale as a whole is that of Marc's horses'-ears, which is absent from all the other versions of the romance, which is not referred to elsewhere in the version, and which makes no reference to other episodes. Nevertheless, even this episode is not an independent *lai*, which the story-teller was able to insert into the loose structure of the Morrois scenes. Almost inevitably the barons to whom the dwarf reveals Marc's secret are three in number, just as there are three *felon* who hate and persecute the lovers; but no link is established between these two groups; rather is the 'fringe' episode inevitably assimilated into the general framework of the romance. It is linked to this, openly and consciously, by its closing verses, which comment on the dwarf's death:

> Molt en fu bel a mainte gent,
> Que haoient le nain Frocine
> Por Tristran et por la roïne. [vv. 1348-50]

It should be noted that this episode is worked into the general pattern of the narrative not only by its form but also by its substance. The tale of the king's ears is not simply included among the events affecting the fortunes of Tristran and the queen; the emotional tone of the episode, which shows passionate hatred for the dwarf, also reflects the aversion the poet feels for all the lovers' enemies.

But even if there is no allusion to Marc's ears at any point in the romance, it must nonetheless be admitted that the dwarf's death has already been foreshadowed. When Marc, still in the tree, alters his opinion about the lovers' guilt, he directs his anger against Frocin, who told him the opposite and persuaded him to hide where he could overhear their conversation:

> De mon nevo me fist entendre
> Mençonge, porqoi ferai pendre;
> Por ce me fist metre en aïr,
> De ma mollier faire haïr;
> Ge l'en crui et si fis que fous.
> Li gerredon l'en sera sous:
> Se je le puis as poinz tenir,
> Par feu ferai son cors fenir . . .
> . . . Or ne laira q'au nain ne donge
> O s'espee si sa merite
> Par lui n'iert mais traïson dite. [vv. 269–76 and 292–4]

These threats have no direct connection with Frocin's later death, which occurs for other reasons, while on this occasion he evades the king's wrath by fleeing (vv. 331–6). Marc's very indecision as to the method of putting him to death[16] turns these threats into a mere outburst of anger rather than a deliberate and direct anticipation of the dwarf's death. Yseut's words as she is about to be led to the pyre are in a different tone:

> Bien sai que li nains losengier
> Et li felons, li plain d'envie,
> Par qui consel j'ere perie,
> En avront encor lor deserte. [vv. 1060–3]

Here hatred for the traitors and the prediction that they are doomed to death are transformed from an impassioned invocation by the queen into a promise and pledge by the narrator to his audience, who are assured of the final rendering of accounts, of the just vengeance which must inevitably overtake the villains, since earthly events reflect the working out of a consistent plan of justice. Thus in a respect other than that of pure content an episode which in all probability was originally independent[17] can be given significance for the ethical structure of the romance and merged into a deeper and firmer unity than that which is purely external.

3
Prophecies and reminiscences

To the subject of narrative prophecies, however, we shall have to give much fuller treatment, especially since it is precisely the well known prophecy of the traitors' deaths which has provided a solid basis for all the arguments of the *chorizontes*. It will therefore be fitting to study this stylistic device as a whole, still from the standpoint of the structure of the narrative.

It is necessary to make an immediate distinction between prophecies made by the author and those put into the mouth of one of the characters, because, as we have just seen, the latter type, although they can also in a sense commit the author, generally remain the entire responsibility of the individual character. An example of an extremely personal prediction is Governal's oath to Tristran when it seems that Yseut is about to end up on the pyre:

> Ja, par Jesu, le fiz Marie,
> Ne gerrai mais dedenz maison
> Tresque li troi felon larron,
> Par quoi'st destruite Yseut ta drue,
> En avront la mort receüe. [vv. 1000-4]

But although Governal's promise[18] does not subsequently have to be fulfilled, since Yseut is saved, and although it does not in the least commit the narrator by foreshadowing the deaths of the wicked barons, it is still not without a wider significance in the structure of the narrative, because by involving Governal in the work of vengeance it constitutes an obvious basis for the subsequent deaths at his hands of the anonymous baron and the forester.

Other references by characters to future action have no structural function,[19] but we do hear one striking prediction from Marc. After Yseut's return to court and the beginning of Tristran's exile the three wicked barons are still not satisfied and ask the king for a formal *escondit* by the queen; Marc flushes with rage and indignation at this new threat to his domestic tranquillity and later erupts before Yseut in a violent piece of invective against the barons:

> Et je lor ai trop consentu;
> N'i a mais rien del covertir.
> Par lor parler, par lor mentir,

Ai mon nevo de moi chacié;
N'ai mais cure de lor marchié.
Prochainement s'en revendra,
Des trois felons me vengera;
Par lui seront encor pendu. [vv. 3192-9]

Although in the whole scene Marc has expressed deep regret for the banishment of his nephew ('Par vos est il hors du païs', v. 3065; 'Cent dehez ait par mié la cane Qui me rova de lui partir!', vv. 3068-3069; 'G'en ai por vos chacié Tristran', v. 3136) and violent anger against the barons ('Vos me sorquerez, ce me poise', v. 3071; 'O vos ne puis plus avoir pes', v. 3075, etc), to whom he has made a threat to recall Tristran ('Ge ferai le baron venir Que vos aviez fait fuïr', vv. 3085-6), this time not only is what Marc says even more violent in tone and more partial to the lovers, seeming for the moment to transfer him into the group of characters engaged in a relentless struggle against the wicked barons, but it also has a tone of objective certainty[20] which seems better suited to the narrator than to one of the characters. And indeed the narrator is always careful to presage the traitors' final downfall, as if to reassure the public of the lovers' inevitable triumph. When the forester runs off to inform Marc that he has discovered the lovers sleeping in each other's arms in the hut of leaves in the Morrois, the poet says:

Mex li venist son cors conduire,
Qar puis morut a si grant honte
Con vos orrez avant el conte. [vv. 1918-20]

And when Yseut, about to return to Marc, takes her leave of Tristran and begs him to stay hidden with Orri until it is quite clear how the king will behave towards him, we find again:

Li trois qui erent de moleste
Mal troveront en la parfin,
Li cors giront el bois, sovin. [vv. 2822-4]

Without for the moment discussing predictions which are fulfilled within the same episode and precede the prophesied event by only a few verses, we are still left with v. 386. After overhearing the lovers' protestations of innocence the king looks for the dwarf in order to punish him, but cannot find him because Frocin, abreast of events, thanks to his astrological learning, has fled in good time. The poet comments:

Dex! tant ert a Tristran sordois!

—a verse which can refer only to the subsequent 'flour on the floor' episode.

Finally, we return to the most controversial passage in the whole romance:

> Tuit quatre [li felons] en orent tels soudees:
> Li dui en furent mort d'espees,
> Li tierz d'une seete ocis,
> A duel morurent el païs;
> Li forestier quis encusa
> Mort crüele n'en refusa;
> Quar Perinis, li franc, li blois,
> L'ocist puis d'un gibet el bois.
> Dex les venga de toz ces quatre,
> Qui vout le fier orguel abatre. [vv. 2755-64]

There can be no doubt that these verses contradict not so much the earlier episode relating Governal's killing of the traitor in the wood, since the author is not very specific as to the dead man's identity, but the later account of the forester's death, again at the hands of Governal (vv. 4045 *et seq.*). But is there any greater accuracy in Marc's prediction when he promises that the three 'seront encor pendu'? Is it really true that the forester's death, when it is actually narrated, occurs 'a si grant honte', as the author promised? Is not Yseut's curse equally inaccurate when she says the three men's corpses 'giront el bois, sovin'? Moreover, just as we have considered the situations from which the other prophecies arise, so it must not be forgotten that those of vv. 2755-64 are pronounced at a highly dramatic moment, not long before the day of the lovers' meeting with Marc at the Gué Aventuros, when they are still uncertain of the king's attitude, and therefore not long before what may prove to be their final separation and the climax of their misfortunes.

The true value and significance of these forebodings may perhaps be suggested or confirmed by the opposite device, the evocation of events which have already happened. We shall not consider the frequent references to the duel with the Morholt, which serves as an example of Tristran's valour and also of the barons' wickedness and cowardice,[21] or the rapid *résumé* of past events with which Tristran opens his letter to Marc in order to recall his services (vv. 2556 *et seq.*), or other similar passages.

When Yseut begs Tristran to take refuge with Orri she has

recourse to the persuasive force of a pleasant memory, which for us is enigmatic:

> Por moi sejorner ne t'ennuit!
> Nos i geümes mainte nuit,
> En nostre lit que nos fist faire.[22]   [vv. 2819-21]
>
> El buen celier, soz le boron,
> Seras entrez, li miens amis.   [vv. 2828-9]

Further on, when Tristran goes to Orri's,

> Par l'entree priveement
> Le mist Orri el bel celier.   [vv. 3016-17]

The tone, and particularly the use of the definite article, seem to indicate that the cellar is well known. When Tristran later tells Perinis what to relate to Yseut, his words are:

> A la roïne puez retraire
> Ce que t'ai dit el sozterrin
> Que fist fere si bel, perrin,   [vv. 3350-2]

—from which we learn that the *celier* was constructed by Yseut's order. The theory that all this refers back to episodes narrated in the lost beginning of the romance is a very weak one, since we possess the whole of the story of the life in the Morrois, and in it the *celier* is never mentioned, though there is just one fleeting reference to a forester whom Governal visits:

> Quar Governal, ce m'est avis,
> S'en ert alez o le destrier
> Aval el bois au forestier   [vv. 1832-4]

But these verses, instead of explaining the others we have quoted, create a similar problem, since here we again find the use of the definite article for a completely unknown character. Tristran's words are sufficient to characterise and summarise the circumstances of life in the forest:

> Et poise moi de la roïne,
> Qui je doins loge por cortine;
> En bois est, et si peüst estre
> En beles chanbres, o son estre,
> Portendues de dras de soie.   [vv. 2179-83]

In this picture the *celier* has no place and its comforts are in contrast with the hardship of life in the forest. But if we continue our reading, Yseut surprises us again when she speaks to Perinis of the disguise to be adopted by Tristran at the Blanche Lande:

> Di li qu'il set bien un marchés,
> Au chief des planches, au Mal Pas;
> G'i sollé ja un poi mes dras. [vv. 3294-6]

When and how this happened is completely unknown to us, and we know even less of the relations between Yseut and Artu to which they both allude, Yseut when she asks Marc to invite him to the *escondit*:

> Et li mien cors est toz seürs,
> Des que verra li rois Artus
> Mon mesage, qu'il vendra ça;
> Son corage sai des piça, [vv. 3273-6]

and Artu, in greater detail, when he says to Perinis:

> Menbre li [to Yseut] de l'espié lancier,
> Qui fu en l'estache feru;
> Ele savra bien ou ce fu.
> Prié vos que li dïez einsi. [vv. 3546-9]

There still remains to note Gauvain's statement:

> Li plus coverz est Guenelons,
> Gel connois bien, si fait il moi:
> Gel boutai ja a un fangoi,
> A un bohort fort et plenier [vv. 3462-5]

and the corresponding assertion of Evain:

> Asez connois Dinoalen...
> ... Se je l'encontre enmié ma voie,
> Con je fis ja une autre foiz,
> Ja ne m'en tienge lois ne fois,
> S'il ne se puet de moi defendre,
> S'a mes deus mains ne le fais pendre. [vv. 3484-92]

4
Episode and romance

The theory that all or some of these references would find an explanation in the lost parts of the romance is weakened not only by the case in which, as we have seen, we are in a position to check for ourselves, but also by the absence of corresponding episodes in other Tristram texts. Thus even those scholars most inclined to see the principal interest of these passages in the glimpses of sources and relationships which they afford have been unable to get a great deal out of them.[23] This seems to justify us in restricting ourselves to Beroul's extant text and in regarding these passages not as mere vestiges, meaningless if considered as isolated references to otherwise unknown episodes, but rather as something—call it a vestige if you will—which is preserved for a purpose of which the author was at least to some extent conscious, and which is thus not without its value and significance in the extant context. In fact even if we suppose that there is little deliberate purpose behind these references, we shall nevertheless be entitled to look for a possible structural function that they perform.

We shall thus confine ourselves to noting that there have been preserved or inserted in the romance a number of allusions to well known episodes (such as that to Frocin's astrological powers), prophecies, some more detailed than others, of events which later occur in a different manner, and references to circumstances in all probability unknown to all the listeners. These phenomena are not to be interpreted one by one, searching for the key to each particular passage within its own isolated context, but must be considered together. In my opinion it is through a consideration of the particular relationship between the episode and the romance as a whole that we find their simplest explanation, which carries deeper conviction from being based not on accidents happening in the course of a self-perpetuating tradition but on the poetic talents and imaginative formulation of the last narrator.[24]

The theory of the independence of the individual episodes, which we have already proposed to investigate, can be considered, despite a few points that seem to favour it, as indubitably erroneous when we look at verses such as 386, where there is a reference in the first episode to the second; or particularly, such as 1920 ('Con vos orrez avant el conte'), which also refers to a later episode; or, finally, such as the well known verses 2755-64, which in spite of their inconsistencies imply that the romance is a unitary work; and above all when we look at the narrator's constant effort, already noted, to give effect to his own ethical code by awarding the wicked barons the punishment they deserve. This sentiment, so powerful that it must be considered a *leitmotiv* of the work, not only permeates all the episodes and colours them with a unifying passion, but on the narrative plane constitutes an extension of the plot beyond the limited confines of the episode, within which the poet could never settle all the accounts which he regards as open, or pay off all the debts which sooner or later must fall due.

Leaving aside the extreme view which would make all the episodes independent and so leave us with no narrative, but only a series of episodes of single or multiple authorship, it remains to be seen how the episode, which we have isolated as a structural unit consciously chosen by the author, is nonetheless framed in the overall unity of the narrative. Having disposed of the idea that in Beroul's case the division into episodes might be necessitated by functional considerations, such as the needs of recitation, we are left with only one way out, which in my view is the key to this intricate problem: for Beroul the episodic system—that is, the concentration of the narrative into a series of pictured scenes so clearly conceived, so imaginatively moulded as to create between them areas of deep shadow (all the more obvious the more vivid is the light illuminating the episodes)—this episodic system is really a mental structure, an essential mode of poetic composition, a category of the imagination. With him it is not that the equilibrium which is always set up between the centripetal force represented by the unity of the narrative and the centrifugal force determined by his passionate liking for detail is constantly maintained despite all the difficulties; the truth is that the latter force, which is particularly powerful, at certain moments exerts itself almost to the point of overthrowing the cohesion of the whole, alternately subsiding into a pause of lesser intensity and returning to exert itself with renewed vigour. The result is a broken line, taut in places and slack in others, continuous but precariously so. Thus for Beroul the episode is not a moment in the narrative, it is a 'station', and, as was the case later, in the Way of the Cross, each station, although presupposing a total unity and forming a part of it, nevertheless seeks a completeness of meaning, and above all of expressiveness, of its own.

The concept of expressiveness, achieved in the narrative moment and not in the whole, is the key to understanding Beroul. At a fairly naïve level it leads to prolixity, as in the repetitiveness of the account of Frocin's astrological powers, or worse still to crudity, as with the verses put into Marc's mouth when he threatens the hated dwarf with death:

Par moi avra plus dure fin
Que ne fist faire Costentin

> A Segoçon, qu'il escolla
> Qant o sa feme le trova.
> Il l'avoit coroné' a Rome,
> Et la servoient maint prodome;
> Il la tint chiere et honora;
> En lié mesfist, puis en plora.   [vv. 277–84]

This painstaking *résumé* of Constantine's conjugal misfortunes,[25] attributed to Marc when he is burning with anger and still perched in the tree, is in all respects extremely inopportune. But even this corresponds, at a rather elementary level, to the need for a completeness which will make the detail fully and almost autonomously expressive, and which emerges as such a marked characteristic of our narrator. But this requirement, precisely because it concerns the detail and not the whole, sometimes makes itself felt unexpectedly and after the event, not appearing until the unfolding narrative arrives at a difficulty which a more expert narrator, more skilled in construction, would have surreptitiously obviated earlier.[26] After Tristran's flight Yseut exclaims:

> 'Dex,' fait elë, 'en ait bien grez!
> Or ne me chaut se il m'ocïent
> Ou il me lïent ou deslïent.'
> Si l'avoit fait lïer li rois,
> Par le conmandement as trois,
> Qu'il li out si les poinz estroiz
> Li sanc li est par toz les doiz.[27]   [vv. 1048–54]

If we now consider the prophecies or the reminiscences we have studied, they will all seem to be at least justified, if not conditioned, by the context and fully meaningful within it, without there remaining elements which are inexpressive or arouse curiosity without satisfying it. All the references to the inevitable punishment hanging over the traitors, including the most detailed and the most controversial, are made when the lovers' situation seems most tragic, and when certainty of the legitimate vengeance to come is thus most needed. Conversely, v. 386 ('Dex! tant ert a Tristran sordois!') expresses regret that the malignant dwarf has not already been put to death. The same thing happens with references to the past. Yseut's mention of the *celier* (vv. 2819 *et seq*.) is not only meaningful in that through its reference to their mutual passion it impels Tristran to fulfil her wish: it also surrounds Yseut's farewell with a gentle and extremely human melancholy, together with a persistent, invincible nostalgia for their troubled but happy life as outlaws ('Nos i geümes mainte nuit, En nostre lit que nos fist faire'). In this atmosphere of separation the memory of the *celier* becomes an expression of Yseut's tormented and divided spirit. And when Tristran later reminds her through Perinis of 'el sozterrin Que fist fere si bel, perrin', this is a reminiscence not of a past event, but of a past emotional situation, of the happy days of exile. So that it could even be rather boldly suggested that, since it would have been inconsistent for the poet to select the hut of branches and the bed of leaves as symbols of these happy memories, he forged this new, unexpected image, taking it from some different traditional version. Thus Yseut's reminiscence regarding the Mal Pas ('G'i sollé ja un poi mes dras') seems a happy anticipation, right from the earliest moments, of the theme of the muddy ford, which dominates all the first part of the episode of the Blanche Lande, and the reminiscence which associates Yseut and Artu serves to confirm that element of sympathy and almost of complicity between the two, by projecting it into an unspecified and for this very reason more distant and yet, as it were, enduring past. Gauvain's and Evain's reminiscences have an identical effect: they are in both cases deliberately contrived in order to give duration and a broader justification to their hatred for the wicked barons, almost as a symbol of the permanence of the struggle between good and evil and the conscious certainty of this permanence which comforts the virtuous. In fact in Beroul every feeling, every impulse of the spirit or of the heart, at the moment in which it is generated or comes to the surface of consciousness and is expressed, needs to be accepted as eternal, to create a duration for itself; and this it achieves by this fictitious projection in time. This is the real reason why the narrative is organised in episodes, each one trying to overpower the impression made by the narrative as a whole, by asserting itself as a lasting, coherent, self-contained entity, not a transitory moment in a larger totality.[28] Thus an explanation of the structural peculiarities of Beroul's narrative not only gives a rational reason for the numerous apparent irrationalities in the romance by tracing them back to a deep source, the nature of the poet's imagination and his way of looking at reality in as far as it serves as material for the romance, but also points to a deep constant of Beroul's poetry, which, as we shall see, is manifest in other aspects of his work. One is tempted to say that they have carried us straight to the core of his personality as a narrator.

I do not claim thus to have solved all the problems connected with this aspect of the text or to have settled questions dealing with the prehistory of the romance or its divisions and its allusions to otherwise unknown episodes. These questions are important, but require to be treated along different lines. The problems upon which I hope to have shed some light are those of Beroul's text as it stands, of the text as an object of literary analysis in its own right. The two approaches do not exclude each other in the overall context of literary historiography, but pursue different objectives: a text such as Beroul's is studied either to trace the links in the chain of tradition preceding it,[29] or in its own right and in its extant form, including a study of the literary use the poet makes of anything surviving from, or referring to, an earlier stage of development. This is the approach I have selected and it is in this light that I wish my suggestions to be read; these suggestions do not seek to provide a convenient but illusory way of avoiding critical controversies concerning the development of the Tristram tradition, but simply to fit in with a different way of approaching the problem. To what extent this shift of viewpoint can prove fruitful is not for me to judge.

5
The chronology of the narrative

The reader will probably want further confirmation of the singular relationship which I have postulated between the episode and the narrative whole. If I am correct about the nature of this relationship, then it ought to be reflected in the chronological arrangement of the romance. I have already pointed out that the passing from one episode to another corresponds to a slackening off of event, to the insertion of a period of empty and hence vague time between the close-textured periods of the episodes. An example was the end of the sentence scene and of the flight into the wood:

> Seignors, eisi font *longuement*
> En la forest parfondement,
> *Longuement* sont en cel desert   [vv. 1303–5]

The episode of Marc's ears, which follows immediately, is in no way connected chronologically with the preceding scene. The only temporal element it contains is:

> S'en vint *un jor, aprés disner*,
> Parlout a ses barons roi Marc,
> En sa main tint d'auborc un arc.   [vv. 1336–8]

'Un jor, aprés disner': it is easy to see the total autonomy in time of the individual episode, its independence of the chronological framework of the romance. In exactly the same way the episode immediately following, the first meeting with Ogrin, although the poet could not leave it totally unconnected with earlier events (i.e. the episode, not of Marc's ears, but of the flight to the forest), can nevertheless make do with a 'Longuement sont en cel boschage' (v. 1359), providing an antecedent which can here again be taken up by:

> En l'ermitage frere Ogrin
> Vindrent *un jor, par aventure*.   [vv. 1362-3]

'Un jor' (v. 1658) is again the generic temporal determination of the episode concerning the death of the anonymous baron. But in other cases the degree of indeterminacy is still greater, or perhaps we should say less attempt is made to avoid vagueness. When Marc has restored the lovers to favour after the *rendez-vous épié* episode, the three wicked barons[30] hasten to rekindle his suspicions. However, it is never stated in what chronological relationship this new episode, which will lead to the condemnation of the lovers, stands with respect to the preceding one; but it was none the less necessary to link up the barons' discussion, which precedes their meeting with the king and thus marks the beginning of a new and fast-moving action, with the discovery that brings about their intervention:

> Qar, en un gardin, soz une ente,
> Virent *l'autrier* Yseut la gente
> Ovoc Tristran en tel endroit
> Que nus hon consentir ne doit.   [vv. 589-92]

At the beginning of the final episode of the story a spy comes to inform the three barons that Tristran has not left Cornwall and refers to the moment in which the king became angry with them for pressing him to subject his wife to an *escondit*;[31] this moment is also indicated by 'l'autrier':

> Li rois vos sout *l'autrier* malgré
> Et vos en acuelli en hé,
> Por le deraisne sa mollier.[32]   [vv. 4277-9]

Even temporal indications which seem more precise really express the same lack of interest in the appropriate arrangement of the romance in time. When the episode of the Blanche Lande begins, with the barons' renewed request for the trial of Yseut, there is a reference to Tristran's restitution of the queen a short time previously:

> Ne tarja pas *un mois entier*
> Que li rois Marc ala chacier,
> Et avoc lui li traïtor.
> Or escoutez que font *cel jor*. [vv. 3031–4]

The second temporal indication ('cel jor') is introduced as if the overall chronology had already been completely fixed, but the first, on account of its negative form, is not an accurate indication of the passage of time.

Only twice in passing from one episode to another do we find the chronological relationship more carefully stated. We have already quoted[33] the opening verses of the episode of the discovery in the forest. But it should be noted that the indications of time ('un jor d'esté, En icel tens que l'en aoste, Un poi aprés la Pentecoste. Par un matin') are all quite general, and that although they place the action in an idealised literary time sequence they do nothing to fix its place in the development of the story.

However, the same cannot be said of the episode immediately following. Here we are at the turning point of the romance, which hinges on no less than the expiry of a fixed temporal duration, that is to say, on the changed effect of the *lovendrinc* after three years, so that greater precision is inevitable:

> Seignors, du vin de qoi il burent
> Avez oï, por qoi il furent
> En si grant paine lonctens mis;
> Mais ne savez, ce m'est avis,
> A conbien fu determinez
> Li lovendrins, li vin herbez:
> La mere Yseut, qui le bolli,
> A trois anz d'amistié le fist.
>
> Tant con durerent li troi an,
> Out li vins si soupris Tristran
> Et la roïne ensenble o lui
> Que chascun disoit: 'Los m'en fui'.
> L'endemain de la saint Jehan
> Aconpli furent li troi an
> Que cil vin fu determinez.
>
> 'Ha! Dex,' fait il [Tristran], 'tant ai traval!
> Trois anz a hui, que riens n'i fal,

> Onques ne me falli pus paine
> Ne a foirié n'en sorsemaine.   [vv. 2133-40, 2143-9, 2161-4]
>
> Trois anz a bien, si que n'i falle,
> Onques ne nos falli travalle.'   [vv. 2303-4]

It should be added that in this case the narrator takes the trouble to prepare for this event as early as the end of the preceding episode (the discovery in the forest):

> Trois anz *plainiers* sofrirent peine,
> Lor char pali et devint vaine.   [vv. 2131-2]

But this exception only serves to prove the rule, because it is an exception fully justified by the narrative and structural value which a temporal detail here assumes, and above all because even this element, hidden in an unconvincing manner until this moment, is sprung upon the reader. Naturally, Beroul has already mentioned the potion, at least in one scene when the lovers drank it ('du vin de qoi il burent avez oï'), but he did not take the slightest trouble at that stage to anticipate that which, together with its erotic powers, is its unique characteristic, namely its limited duration. He was well aware what were to be the consequences of this essential piece of information later in the romance, but since it did not affect the narrative as it was being imaginatively and emotionally developed *at that stage*, he disregarded it, once again providing clear—indeed, striking—confirmation of his indifference towards the overall chronological structure of the romance, or rather—and it is this that concerns us more directly—of his view of the romance as a succession of completely moulded moments which do not depend for their completeness on insertion into the whole.

We need not have been afraid of discovering a defect in our findings; rather we seem to have come upon the most unexpected and most convincing confirmation of them. All that remains is to complete our investigation by examining the use of chronological indications in the body of the episodes. Here again we do not always find a great measure of precision; when Tristran decides to teach Husdent to hunt silently he says:

> Et a ce metrai je ma paine
> Ainz que ja past *ceste semaine*.   [vv. 1597-8]

And instead we soon learn:

> Ainz que *li premier mois* pasast,
> Fu si le chien dontez u gast
> Que sanz crïer suiet sa trace.   [vv. 1621-3]

The structure of the *Tristran*

After the end of the *rendez-vous épié* episode Yseut runs into her chamber and relates everything to Brengain, while Tristran confides in Governal. And what of Marc, who is in a violent rage with the dwarf?

> Ne pout son nain trover li rois;
> Dex! tant ert a Tristran sordois!
> A sa chanbre li rois en vient;
> Iseut le voit, qui molt le crient:
> 'Sire, por Deu, dont venez vos? . . .' [vv. 385–9]

This is immediately followed by the dialogue between the two, during which Yseut says, 'A ton nevo parlai *ersoir*' (v. 432) and Marc then relates how *le soir* (v. 474) the dwarf had him climb into the pine tree. Thus we learn that a night has passed, and since Brengain is immediately afterwards asked to recall Tristran to court, the prophecy made by Marc in the tree is verified:

> Buen virent aprimier *cest soir*!
> Au parlement ai tant apris
> Jamais jor n'en serai pensis.
> *Par matinet* sera paiez
> Tristran o moi, s'avra congiez
> D'estre a ma chanbre a son plesir. [vv. 312–17]

So it is clear that within the confines of this episode the chronological framework is quite precise and that it was only the search for dramatic effect which suggested the idea of leaving the overnight pause barely hinted at, in order not to interrupt the onrushing flood of events. In point of fact this more precise consciousness of time generally obtains in the body of the episodes. When Tristran and Yseut are caught red-handed the furious Marc enjoins:

> Certes, Tristran, *demain*, ce quit,
> Soiez certains d'estre destruit [vv. 781–2]

And sure enough:

> Or vient li jor, la nuit s'en vait.
> Li rois conmande espines querre
> Et une fosse faire en terre.
> Ja estoit bien prime de jor. [vv. 866–8 and 873]

Tristran thinks of personally carrying his letter to Marc:

> Et anevois, *en tens oscur*,
> Qant li rois dormira seür,
> Ge monterai sor mon destrier. [vv. 2441–3]

This he proceeds to do and:

> Anuit, aprés solel couchier,
> Qant li tens prist a espoisier,
> Tristran s'en torne avoc son mestre. [vv. 2449-51]

The mission is completed and finally:

> Tant ont erré par le boschage
> Q'*au jor* vindrent a l'ermitage.[34] [vv. 2481-2]

In short, this obvious, though perhaps unconscious, attention to chronology, which is lost in the linking of separate episodes, is generally maintained within the individual episode, and can even lead to a high degree of accuracy, with a view, of course, to a particular effect:

> Par saint Tresmor de Caharés,
> Ge vos ferai un geu parti:
> Ainz ne verroiz *passé marsdi*—
> *Hui est lundi*—si le verrez. [vv. 3076-9]

Here it is an impatiently decisive reply that Marc is giving to yet another of the barons' demands.[35] This result of our enquiry into the chronological outlines of Beroul's romance fits together with our earlier findings and crowns them with yet another confirmation.

There seems to be no further reason for delaying our conclusion. It emerges then, that the structure for the romance is built round a succession of 'stations', which, although they are obviously part of a larger whole, do develop as individual units of action and of poetic significance, as expressive wholes, momentarily deadening the listener's awareness of preceding and following episodes by virtue of their dazzling abundance of imaginative effect. And we are given a clue to this phenomenon, a clue which also serves as a tangible proof: just as the action coagulates round certain fixed points and crystallises into episodes, remaining static and in addition seeming to become more tenuous in the gap between these episodes, in the same way the chronological framework of the romance becomes positively flimsy as far as interrelation of the various scenes is concerned, while re-acquiring its normal solidity within the confines of each taken individually. It is in the context of this particular mode of narrative composition that one should consider those details regarded as anomalous when examined in the context of the romance as a whole. All Beroul's technical habits—that of mentioning facts or objects only when necessary for an understanding of the action, that of recalling earlier episodes which are unknown but allusion to which serves to underline particular expressive effects, that of passionately and imprecisely anticipating future events—all these have a precise and recognisable significance within the context of the single narrative moment and therefore must all be related to the fundamental quality of Beroul's imagination: the technique of composing in scenes, of representing reality as a succession of static, emblematic moments, where the operative phrase is not 'succession' but 'static, emblematic moments'.

This style is not, of course, exceptional in medieval French literature. Writing of the lack of chronological continuity in the accounts of battles in the *Chanson de Guillaume*, Frappier has observed: 'Ces ellipses n'ont rien de très surprenant: si certaines semblent dues à l'intervention maladroite du remanieur, la plupart résultent probablement d'un mode de composition qui sacrifie volentiers les liaisons narratives au mouvement des tableaux et des images, à la suite rapide et souvent contrastée de scènes essentielles au gré de l'auteur.'[36] The epic poets generally feel free from any precise concern with chronology and tend to synthesise the action into an unrealistic and purely narrative temporal structure.[37] But their lack of realism is dissimilar from Beroul's in that they have no notion of episodic concentration nor of relatively clear chronological structure within the episode, and eliminate the empty intervals between passages of narration, usually by resorting to certain unskilful formulas;[38] Beroul, on the other hand, often turns these pauses to account as descriptive moments summarising the situation established during the rapid succession of the preceding events. Nor is Beroul's narrative similar to the courtly romance, even though Chrestien may not pay any greater attention to chronology;[39] the romance with which we are concerned is not in fact episodic in the same sense as the courtly romance[40] because the significance of the separate moments is not that they are elements in the total *Weg* of chivalry; they are not stages in a 'courtly education', they are adventures more in the modern than in the medieval sense. Echoing an observation by Bayrav,[41] we could compare the technique of epic chronology and other similar techniques with those medieval paintings which present within the same frame a multiplicity of non-simultaneous events; Beroul's technique, on the other hand, would be closer to that of juxtaposed scenes, of presentation in rigorously distinct and internally homogeneous pictures, where the distance in time between two consecutive scenes is filled in by the observer on the basis of their distance in content, assuming the situation established in the one to be extended in time until it is modified by the new events of the next.[42] This technique, or rather this relationship between phases of action and phases of inertia, must be referred back to a particular conception of reality, which is indifferent to moods and to stable situations but reacts vigorously to events. Beroul certainly thought it superfluous to linger over anything other than turning points in the action, because only in a character's actions, not in any sustained immutability or any abstract modification in time, whether caused by a dynamic personality or by the influence of events or of what others hear of him, can that character be defined and qualified.[43]

Notes

1 Cf. Kelemina's *Geschichte der Tristansage*, p. 38. Something has probably been omitted in this passage, since the subjects of *sont* in v. 1357 must include Yseut, who is not, however, mentioned until now. The possibility that the poet is referring only to Tristran and Governal is excluded by the words 'Tant s'entraiment de bone amor' (v. 1365), which follow still without any specific mention of Yseut.
2 And vv. 1351–61 contain verbal reminiscences of this earlier passage. Cf.

> Mais or oiez de Governal:
> Espee çainte, sor cheval,
> De la cité s'en est issuz;
> Bien set, se il fust conseüz,
> Li rois l'arsist por son seignor   [vv. 965–9]

with

> Et Governal sor le destrier
> S'en fu issuz, quar il cremoit
> Qu'il fust ars, se Marc le tenoit.   [vv. 1354–6]

And again,

> Seignors, eisi font longuement
> En la forest parfondement,
> Longuement sont en cel desert   [vv. 1303–5]

with

> Longuement sont en cel boschage.   [v. 1359]

3 Vv. 1420-3:
> Et saciez de voir, sanz dotance,
> *Cele nuit* jurent chiés l'ermite;
> Por eus esforça molt sa vite.
> *Au matinet* s'en part Tristrans.

4 Vv. 1370-6:
> Sire Tristran, grant soirement
> A l'en juré par Cornoualle,
> Qui vos rendroit au roi, sanz falle
> Cent mars avroit a gerredon.
> En ceste terre n'a baron,
> Au roi ne l'ait plevi en main,
> Vos rendre a lui o mort ou sain.

For the exact meaning of *lever le cri*, cf. Jonin's *Les Personnages Féminins*, p. 75, with the correction by Lejeune in 'Les "Influences Contemporaines" dans les romans français de Tristan au XIIe siècle', p. 146n.

5 Cf. Geoffroi de Vinsauf's *Poetria nova* (ed. Faral in *Les Arts Poétiques*, pp. 194-262), vv. 126 *et seq*.

6 Both Matthieu de Vendôme in his *Ars versificatoria* (ed. Faral, *op. cit.*, pp. 106-93), IV, 49, and Geoffroi de Vinsauf in his *Documentum de modo et arte dictandi et versificandi* (*ibid.*, pp. 263-320), III, recommend the use of general ideas or proverbs for a conclusion.

7 The various *exordia*, precisely because they remain outside the quickly moving episodes, lend themselves, as in this case, to a calmer description of the protagonists' spiritual and moral situation, which is otherwise rare. Cf. also chapters 3 and 4.

8 There is nothing strange about a descriptive parenthesis such as this, which is after all of moderate length and almost essential to the tale, since it must be explained why the lovers should fall asleep in broad daylight. Suffice it to note that scenes like this, of an even more decorative nature but still serving the purpose of dramatic suspense, are not absent from the epic. Cf. *Charroi de Nîmes*, ed. Perrier, vv, 14-18: 'Ce fu en mai, el novel tens d'esté: Fueillissent gaut, reverdissent li pré, Cil oisel chantent belement et soé. Li cuens Guillelmes reperoit de berser D'une forest ou ot grant piece esté' (cf. the Lange-Kowal edition of ms D, with some amplification and the mention of Pentecost); or the almost identical passage in the *Prise d'Orenge*, vv. 39-43; or again *Garin le Loheren*, vv. 289-93. As can be seen, the mention of Pentecost as a 'moment of destiny' also makes an early appearance in the epic.

9 These would be the following: (1) the *rendez-vous épié* (vv. 1-572); (2) the discovery, sentencing and escape of the lovers (vv. 573-1305);

(3) Marc's ears (vv. 1306–50); (4) the first encounter with Ogrin (vv. 1351–1430); (5) Husdent (vv. 1431–1636); (6) the death of one of the traitors (vv. 1637–1773); (7) the lovers' hut of leaves (vv. 1774–2132); (8) the second encounter with Ogrin, leading to a peace treaty with the king (vv. 2133–3027); (9) the oath on the Blanche Lande (vv. 3028–4266); (10) the death of the traitors (vv. 4267–4485).

10 Respectively the flight of Frocin, the leap from the chapel, and the Gué Aventuros.

11 Cf. Rychner's *La Chanson de Geste*, pp. 48–54. But cf. Delbouille's 'Les Chansons de Geste et le livre'.

12 I have already mentioned a similar formula, from the *fabliau* of the *Trois Boçus*, in 'I *fabliaux* e la società, p. 280. On introductory formulas of the type *Qui veut oïr* cf. Langfors's *Les Incipit des poèmes français antérieurs au XVIe siècle*, pp. 338–41. On the epic *exordia* cf. Gautier's *Les Epopées Françaises*, vol. 1, pp. 372 *et seq.*

13 Cf. chapter 2.

14 *Prochain:* 'close companion' (Ewert); '*familier*' (Muret, first edition).

15 Here as elsewhere the parallels established by Bédier (edition of Thomas, vol. 2, p. 246) emerge as extremely fallacious to anyone who reads the variants. In *R* it is Andret who discovers the lovers, without the assistance of astrology; in *T* there is a dwarf but he is not an astrologer. But for us the confrontation with Eilhart is sufficient.

16 Hanging (v. 270), burning (v. 276), death by the sword (v. 293).

17 Cf. most recently Loomis's 'Breton folklore and Arthurian romance', pp. 290–1; Bolelli's 'La leggenda del Re dalle Orecchie di Cavallo in Irlanda'; Foulon's 'Le Conte des oreilles du roi Marc dans le *Tristan de Béroul*'; Newstead's 'King Marc of Cornwall'; and Giese's 'König Markes Pferdeohren'.

18 A similar vow is made by Aimer le Chetif in the *chansons* of the Monglane cycle (cf. Hofer's *Die Komposition des Tristanromans*, p. 276). There are other epic vows in the *Couronnement de Louis*, v. 669, the *Charroi de Nîmes*, vv. 1367–71, and the *Prise d'Orenge*, vv. 282 *et seq.* and 350 *et seq.*

19 Cf. vv. 2358 *et seq.*, 2441 *et seq.*, 2556 *et seq.*, and 2830 *et seq.* We must not be surprised at the repetition of the contents of Ogrin's letter to Marc (the first and third of these passages); in the *Couronnement de Louis*, for instance, the Pope's message to Galafre is first communicated by the Pope to the barons (vv. 439–44) and then delivered in almost identical form to the recipient (vv. 455–60); the same thing happens with the message from Gui d'Alemagne to Loois (vv. 2370–80 and 2392–2402).

20 'Prochainement s'en revendra' as compared with the earlier 'Ge ferai le baron venir'.

21 As early as v. 28 Yseut refers to it, and in the same scene at v. 136 it is again mentioned by Tristran. At v. 844 it is the townsfolk of Lancïen

who recall it. Marc's allusion to it at v. 2038 is made with reference to the sword and not to Tristran.
22 It should be mentioned that immediately after this at least two verses are missing, since we find nothing to correspond with this rhyme in -*aire*, and the rhyme -*este* of v. 2822 also remains isolated.
23 Only the mention of the *celier perrin* seems to preserve a confused recollection of Thomas's version of the life in the forest.
24 Bearing constantly in mind that we are dealing with oral poetry, hence Golther's observation on p. 77 of *Die Sage von Tristan und Isolde*: 'The *jongleur* recites the individual parts, and is thus fully conscious of their connection with the whole story, but not entirely aware of their detailed relationship with each other' (cf. also Kelemina's *Geschichte der Tristansage*, p. 38). See also Rychner's *La Chanson de Geste*, pp. 46 et seq.
25 On these cf. Graf's *Roma nella memoria e nelle immaginazioni del medio evo*, pp. 108-10.
26 It seems to me that Beroul goes much further than Jauss implies in his accurate observation that 'in oral poetry, which depends on immediate effects, one must not expect to find motivation which is perfectly consistent throughout, or compositional techniques prepared for well in advance' (*Untersuchungen zur mittelalterlichen Tierdichtung*, p. 158), and that with him certain tendencies in composition originally determined by systems of diffusion of literary works have become completely intrinsic, and strengthened into modes of invention.
27 The most striking case of such lack of narrative foresight is that of the limited duration of the love-potion, on which see below.
28 On a lower level this imaginative process coincides with an elementary system of description to which we can relate the sudden appearance of a forester in v. 1834. In order to explain how the lovers could have been left alone and how it was possible to take them by surprise, it was necessary to get rid of Governal; but there is nothing easier—he is sent *au forestier*, of whom we know nothing. More examples could easily be given, but the conclusion is always the same: the background to the action comes into the limelight to satisfy occasional necessities, without any organic plan.
29 And owing to our fragmentary knowledge of the preceding period, even an enquiry of that nature, if it is not abstract and mechanical, can acquire real value from the point of view of literary history.
30 On whom cf. chapter 4.
31 Cf. vv. 3031 *et seq*.
32 Between the two events there must have passed more than fifteen days, since when Marc and Yseut decide to organise the *deraisne* we read: 'Atant est li termes baniz A quinze jorz par le païs.' And more time has certainly passed since the oath.

33 Cf. p. 22.
34 Where Yseut had stayed behind and 'pus li soir qu'il en issirent Tresque l'ermite et el les virent, N'out les eulz essuiez de lermes' (vv. 2491-3). Note the anticipation contained in the verses assigned to Tristran: 'Roïne de parage, Tornon arire a l'ermitage; Encor *enuit ou le matin*, O le consel de maistre Ogrin, Manderon a nostre talent Par briéz sanz autre mandement' (vv. 2279-84).
35 An attentive reading reveals that the episode of the *deraisne*, which follows, is also rich in chronological indications. As we have seen, 'Atant est li termes baniz A quinze jorz par le païs' (vv. 3278-9). Yseut immediately sends Perinis to Tristran (v. 3288) and the messenger carries straight on to Artu's court (v. 3357). 'Toz les degrez en puie a orne, El chaceor monte et s'en torne, N'avra mais pais a l'esperon, Si ert venu a Cuerlion' (vv. 3365-8), and when he finally arrives he announces the forthcoming oath and states precisely: 'D'hui en huit jors est pris le termes' (v. 3447). So Perinis must have taken seven days to travel to Artu's court, and certainly the verses describing his return seem to indicate a fairly long period: 'Conme plus puet, et il chemine; Onques un jor ne sejorna Tant qu'il vint la don il torna' (vv. 3556-8). Strangely, he returns not to Tintaguel but to Dinas (vv. 3562-3; is the 'lune dime' simply the tenth day of the lunar month or the tenth night after his departure? In either case not much time remains before the *escondit*—'li terme aprime' (v. 3564)—which is in fact narrated immediately afterwards).
36 *Les Chansons de Geste du cycle de Guillaume d'Orange*, vol. 1, p. 168.
37 Thus one fine morning in the *Prise d'Orenge* Guillaume hears tell of Orable, immediately falls in love with her and says not only that he cannot bear this love but 'Ne puis dormir par nuit ne someillier, Ne si ne puis ne boivre ne mengier, Ne porter armes ne monter sor destrier, N'aler a messe, ne entrer en moustier' (vv. 371-4); at once the hero goes in disguise to Orenge, arriving there before King Arragon has got out of bed (v. 425). Later, it is only at the end that we learn that Guillaume was besieged in Gloriete for seven days, without this being even hinted at in the account of the siege. Schürr, in *Das altfranzösische Epos*, pp. 133-4, sees a correlation between these jumps in time and space and the abstraction prevailing in the arts at that time.
38 The author of the *Moniage Guillaume II*, to shorten journeys, uses 'De lor jornees ne vos sai conte rendre' (v. 3181; cf. vv. 5475 and 5054-5, as well as Curtius's *Gesammelte Aufsätze*, p. 169).
39 Cf. Frappier's 'La Composition du *Conte du Graal*', pp. 80 *et seq.*
40 Cf. Nolting-Hauff's *Die Stellung der Liebeskasuistik*, pp. 22 *et seq.*
41 *Symbolisme Médiéval*, p. 59.
42 Cf. Auerbach's *Mimesis*, pp. 100-1: 'The *Chanson d'Alexis* is a string of autonomous, loosely interrelated events, a series of mutually quite

independent scenes from the life of a saint, each of which contains an expressive yet simple gesture.... It is a cycle of scenes. Each one of these occurrences contains one decisive gesture with only a loose temporal or causal connection with those that follow or precede. Many of them are subdivided into several similar and individually independent pictures. Every picture has, as it were, a frame of its own. Each stands by itself in the sense that nothing new or unexpected happens in it and that it contains no propulsive force which demands the next. And the intervals are empty. But it is with no dark and profound emptiness, in which much befalls and much is prepared, in which we hold our breath in trembling expectation, the emptiness sometimes conjured up in the style of the Bible, with its intervals which make us ponder. Instead, it is a colorless duration without relief or substance, sometimes only a moment, sometimes seventeen years, sometimes wholly indefinable.

'The course of events is thus resolved into a series of pictures; it is, as it were, parceled out. The *Chanson de Roland* taken as a whole is more compressed; the coherence is clearer; the individual picture sometimes displays more movement. But the representational technique (and this means more than mere technical procedure, it includes the idea of structure which poet and audience apply to the narrated event) is still exactly the same: it strings independent pictures together like beads. ... The scenic moment with its textures is given such power that it assumes the stature of a moral model. The various phases of the story of the hero or the traitor or the saint are concretized in gestures to such an extent that the pictured scenes, in the impression they produce, closely approach the character of symbols or figures, even in cases where it is not possible to trace any symbolic or figural signification.'

43 The archaic character of such a conception and of its effects on structure is to be understood in an ideal rather than an absolute chronological sense; cf. a similar observation by Kelemina in his *Geschichte der Tristansage*, p. 38.

I was able to acquaint myself with Robson's study 'The technique of symmetrical composition in medieval narrative poetry' only when it was too late to take account of it in the text. However much Robson strives to be cautious, his method, at least in Beroul's case, is extremely questionable and completely devoid of the objectivity he claims for it; his findings seem totally unacceptable, if only because they presuppose absolutely gratuitous interpolations and displacements.

2
Narrator and audience

In the preceding chapter we asked whether the episodic structure of the romance is due to the distribution of the narrative in several sessions of recitation, and we believed it possible to exclude this explanation. Even if this hypothesis had been confirmed we should still have singled out one particular way in which the external structure of the poem is affected by the relationship between poet and audience; but the external structure is not the only aspect of the work where it is possible for this relationship to be a decisive factor in our characterisation of the romance: it is enough to substitute a different approach for our interest in the influence exerted on the work of literature by the audience or by the conditions under which poet and audience came together, and to enquire how the narrator intended to direct the audience's reaction to the work. So the object of our enquiry will be not so much the poet–audience relationship in itself, as the position and function which the author gives to the narration in the context of this relationship. This is not to say that for us the work remains a pretext for substantially marginal research but rather that we shall make every effort to characterise its qualities and its aims; and since these are here characterised not abstractly but in a context which is by definition historical, in view of the historical existence of both the poet and the public for whom he narrates, the result will be a contribution towards establishing the identity of the work in the full context of its concrete reality.

I
'Seignors, molt avez bien oï'

On even a superficial reading, one can see that Beroul neither evades nor conceals his relationship with his audience, but stresses and parades it. In fact it becomes immediately evident that for him 'narration' means 'immediate communication', emotional co-participation of narrator and audience in the uncertain vicissitudes of the protagonists.[1]

Almost all the episodes examined in chapter 1 contain at the outset a direct address to the audience, such as 'Seignors, molt avez bien oï Conment Tristran . . .' (vv. 1351–2).[2] Sentences of this kind obviously served to attract the audience's attention at the beginning of the recitation, in the case of episodic recitation, or more simply, as in this particular passage, to encourage renewed concentration when a short pause in the narrative tension was followed by a return to the full flow of the narrative. Thus it does not seem that in Beroul this habit of appealing to the audience is altogether negligible even from a non-functional viewpoint, because since in a continuous recitation of the work there is no need to keep establishing fresh contact with the listeners, claiming their attention from their various other interests, it must certainly be related to a need for human contact which is renewed every time the narrator comes to a new episode in his dramatic tale. And yet such formulas in this legitimate context could be regarded as lacking in any value other than humble and perhaps voluntary acceptance of a traditional usage and therefore in themselves insignificant, or even as evidence of meagre originality and limited awareness in the poet of his relationship with his public; and for this reason alone I propose to ignore them, contenting myself with noting their existence.[3]

Passages where the audience is addressed sometimes appear in forms similar to those of these introductory formulas. In the much discussed passage foretelling the fate of the traitors and closing with the verses

Dex les venga de toz ces quatre,
Qui vout le fier orguel abatre, [vv. 2763–4]

the poet reaches a climax of feeling after which there seems to be a moment of silence. The narrator's voice now begins again more quietly, as if he has had a moment to get his breath back:

Seignors, au jor du parlement
Fu li rois Marc o molt grant gent. [vv. 2765–6]

In precisely the same way, when Yseut is about to be led to the stake she curses the traitors, convinced that they will be punished, and concludes with the exclamation: 'Torner lor puise a male perte!' (v. 1064), whereupon the narrator continues: 'Seignor, au roi vient la novele Q'eschapez est par la chapelle Ses nies . . .' (vv. 1065–7). Still earlier, when the lovers are about to be burnt, Yseut exclaims:

Qui m'oceïst, si garisiez,
Ce fust grant joie, beaus amis;
Encor en fust vengement pris. [vv. 906–8]

This is followed by:

> Oez, seignors, de Damledé,
> Conment il est plains de pité ... [vv. 909-10]

Shortly afterwards, when Tristran obtains permission to enter the chapel alone and reaches the window:

> A soi l'en traist a sa main destre,
> Par l'overture s'en saut hors;
> Mex veut sallir que ja ses cors
> Soit ars, voiant tel aünee. [vv. 944-7]

It should be noted how the narrator, having arrived at the point of greatest dramatic tension ('s'en saut hors'),[4] intensifies rather than weakens it by not putting the desperate reasoning of the following verses into Tristran's mouth but expressing it in the third person, thus showing that he himself participates in the mortal risk of his hero. Now the poet must describe the leap and explain how Tristran saved himself:

> Seignors, une grant pierre lee
> Out u mileu de cel rochier;
> Tristran i saut molt de legier.
> Li vens le fiert entre les dras,
> Quil defent qu'il ne chie a tas. [vv. 948-52]

In all these passages we can clearly see how such pseudo-introductions serve the needs of literary expression, and it cannot, therefore, be objected that they are gratuitous. The narrator has led us to a very high degree of feeling or tension, which the demands of the tale render impossible to sustain; so he makes a sort of pause, continuing in a calmer, more direct narrative tone. But he wishes to prevent this sudden drop in intensity from confusing the spectators and undermining his control over them; it is for this purpose that he addresses them directly.[5]

At other times the address to the spectators is used in a way that seems to approximate even more closely to its use in the introductory passages: in fact, however, it serves a very different purpose. In the 'flour on the floor' scene the nature of the plot against the lovers is at first indicated only in the vaguest way: Marc orders Tristran to leave early the next morning for Artu's court. The trap is now about to be sprung: 'Tristran fu mis en grant esfroi' (v. 693) and measures the distance between his bed and the queen's, intending to leap across as soon as the king is asleep. 'Dex! quel pechié! trop ert hardiz!' (v. 700), comments the narrator, with passionate participation, and then he proceeds:

> Li nains la nuit en la chanbre ert;
> Oiez conment cele nuit sert:
> Entre deus liez la flor respant,
> Que li pas allent paraisant. [vv. 701–4]

Apparently we have here nothing more than a warning not to let the dwarf's action escape our minds. The imperative is not here used as a link between the passionate tone and the narrative tone, but is a part of the latter. And in fact its purpose is not to mark a change of style; this time it serves directly to heighten the tension.[6] The audience now knows the data of the situation and the lines along which the action will presumably develop. The moment has come. An extremely suggestive verse ('Li nains la nuit en la chanbre ert') has set in motion the course of events which will inexorably bring the two lovers to their downfall. The next verse announces nothing unexpected, nor is it made necessary by a possible loss of concentration, either previous or subsequent. It both delays for another moment the clear description of the dwarf's trap (vv. 703 et seq.) and binds the attentive circle of listeners more closely to the narrator.

As if to confirm what we have said, an almost identical verse occurs later in a similar situation. The episode relating the death of the wicked baron in the forest begins with the description of the lovers' sufferings; immediately after this begins the new narrative motif:

> Un de ces trois que Dex maudie,
> Par qui il furent descovert,
> Oiez conment par un jor sert!
> Riches hom ert et de grand bruit ... [vv. 1656–9]

The difference is that here the verse is used at a moment of low tension, to increase it right from the start.[7]

This reinforcement of tension can also be found elsewhere, for instance in the episode of the discovery in the forest. After a short initial scene, the heat overcomes the lovers, who lie down on the leafy ground, separated by Tristran's unsheathed sword.[8] Silence reigns:

> N'avoit qu'eus deus en cel païs;
> Quar Governal, ce m'est avis,

> S'en ert alez o le destrier
> Aval el bois au forestier. [vv. 1831–4]

And in this deep silence the note of tragedy suddenly rings out:

> Oez, seignors, quel aventure:
> Tant lor dut estre pesme et dure!
> Par le bois vint uns forestiers,
> Qui avoit trové lor fulliers
> Ou il erent el bois geü ... [vv. 1835–9]

Beroul does not make the woodman's footsteps in the forest the only sign of peril; he also raises his own voice, and again it is not purely a question of commanding the attention of inattentive listeners. The two verses in the mouth of the narrator and directly addressed to the audience, while powerfully colouring even the first stages of the adventure with drama, unite poet and audience in passionate suspense.[9]

The verse 'Oez, seignors, quel aventure!' recurs a second time, identical and in a similar situation, in the final episode, which is already well past its beginning, though it is only now that the decisive part begins. Yseut

> Avoit mandé que l'endemain
> Tristran venist a lié matin;
> Li rois iroit a Saint Lubin.
> Oez, seignors, quel aventure!
> L'endemain fu la nuit oscure;
> Tristran se fu mis a la voie
> Par l'espesse d'un'espinoie.
> A l'issue d'une gaudine
> Garda, vit venir Gondoïne. [vv. 4348–56]

Comment appears superfluous. It will perhaps be more profitable to pass on to an examination of a still more impassioned use of such verses. When, in the early part of the story, Marc wishes to send Brengain to fetch Tristran back to the court, she protests that the hero has a profound hatred for her and pushes her lie to its conclusion: 'Sire, por Deu, acordez m'i, Quant il sera venu ici' (vv. 517–18). The narrator does not remain insensitive to this consummate skill in deception, and comments

> Oiez que dit la tricherresse!
> Molt fist que bone lecherresse:
> Lores gaboit a esscïent
> Et se plaignoit de maltalent. [vv. 519–22]

And in order to underline her virtuosity and exploit the effect to the maximum, he continues:

> 'Rois, por li vois,' ce dist Brengain,
> 'Acordez m'i, si ferez bien.'
> Li rois respont: 'G'i metrai paine.' [vv. 523-5]

And this is still not all; with extreme skill and an insight not only into psychology but into narrative possibilities, when Brengain finally goes, he makes his own comment, which expresses simultaneously his amusement, his sarcasm and his admiring joy at the trick seen on the level both of its ingenious inventor and of the character fooled by it, in the verse:

> Yseut s'en rist, et li rois plus. [v. 527]

The narrator's explicit comment has been made earlier, in vv. 521-2; now the scene closes with a verse which does not break the narrative texture, which on the contrary is full of meaning, and which has a swift sparkle like the end of an act in a comedy.[10] In a passage which is so shrewdly calculated and polished, v. 519 must have a precise value, formulistic though it may be. Note, too, that it is not inserted at the beginning of the scene, in an introductory function, but rather in the central pause and adjacent to the author's assessment of Brengain and his explanation of her behaviour. All this serves to identify a well placed narrative pause calculated to reinforce the effect. Here, when the narrator makes his personal intervention—and it is an enthusiastic intervention ('Molt fist que bone lecherresse')—he feels the need to associate the listener with himself by means of an admiring, amused comment which, in view of its form, one might say is meant to be shared by the audience ('Oiez que dit la tricherresse!'). Between the verse addressed to the audience and that which concerns the narrator alone there is therefore a fusion of sentiments which is precisely that which the author is patently seeking.[11]

Thus the appeal to the listeners for attention is not an expedient of *jongleurs'* rhetoric, but indicates a moment of intense emotional communication with the audience. In the silence of the night the dwarf has sprinkled flour on the floor of the royal bedchamber and Tristran has realised this. Shortly afterwards the king gets out of bed and goes out with the dwarf.

> Dedenz la chanbre n'out clartez,
> Cirge ne lanpë alumez.

> Tristran se fu sus piez levez.
> Dex! porqoi fist? Or escoutez!
> Les piez a joinz, esme, si saut,
> El lit le roi chaï de haut. [vv. 725-30]

The exclamation and the interrogation of v. 728, followed as they are by the 'Or escoutez!', obviously take on a tone of their own; it is almost as if they were uttered by the audience, to whom the narrator replies with the invitation to listen to the next part of the tale.[12] In actual fact, at the instant when the narrator–audience duality comes to the surface in the tale, it is already fused into a unity; since the narrator's emotional response has the same direction and intensity as the audience's, a firm emotional solidarity has been established between the two. The author does not allow the listeners' reactions to be unforeseen, neglected or unused, but rather he cleverly directs them and expresses them collectively in a single vibrant voice. This voice is echoed in the enthralling course of events, which thus acquire a background of human concern, and which are tempered and enriched by this same emotional force. In short, the three elements, the narrator with his reactions, the audience with theirs, and thirdly the narration itself, do not remain separate from each other, they are not kept apart by the contemptuous discipline, distrustful of any effusion, of a high literary culture, but are united and carried before a single vibrant flood, which, through being concentrated, acquires a grandiose force. But to explain the poet's behaviour as the result of fully conscious, premeditated calculation would be to distort the facts. It should be understood, not so much as the consummation of a long experience as a writer, but as the innate feeling for the audience which is characteristic of the best dramatic actors; and it is undoubtedly not an acquired quality. This seems to indicate that the author was not a man of letters writing in the silence of a *scriptorium* for professional reciters, but was himself experienced in meeting the audience face to face, and was frequently at the centre of that warm emotional familiarity which is conveyed to us even today by his verse.[13]

If this conclusion is correct it must be possible to test it on a larger scale, precisely because it is not a simple external characteristic we are discussing but an intimate feeling in the poet himself for the atmosphere of narration. In fact, in the course of the romance we shall not fail to come upon more than one direct attempt to refer

Narrator and audience

matters to the listeners, beginning with apparently general forms such as

> D'Iseut n'estuet pas demander
> S'ele out poor d'eus [Tristran and Governal] encontrer.
> [vv. 2489–90]

But here already, with the use of 'demander', the presence of an audience and the possibility of an intervention on their part is hinted at. On the other hand, a verse such as 'Atant estes vos Pirinis' (v. 3393) is openly addressed to the audience but remains clearly formulistic, as does the 'que vos diroie?' or 'que diroie?' which recurs four times.[14] And the parenthetical 'sachiez' interrupting the following passages are no innovation of Beroul's own:

> Tristran, sachiez, une doitie
> A un cerf traist, qu'il out visé,
> Par les flans l'a outrebersé. [vv. 2152–4]
>
> D'Iseut grant joie demenoient,
> De lui servir molt se penoient;
> Quar, ce saciez, ainz n'i ot rue
> Ne fust de paile portendue:
> Cil qui n'out paile mist cortine. [vv. 2965–9]

Or, a little differently:

> A la cort avoit trois barons,
> Ainz ne veïstes plus felons. [vv. 581–2]

The absence of any individual intonation does not, however, mean that on the whole these formulas have no weight, because while originating in clearly defined types of literary expression, giving us much assistance when we come to put the romance in its historical setting, they also emphasise that spontaneous need for a relationship with the listener, of which we have seen the importance for the poetic tone of the narrative. Besides this they are not always formulas devoid of individual expressive value. The forester discovers the lovers sleeping in the Morrois and hastens to inform the king:

> Et li rois Marc en son palais
> O ses barons tenoit ses plaiz;
> Des barons ert plaine la sale.
> Li forestier du mont avale
> Et s'en est entré, molt vait tost.

> Pensez que onc arester s'ost
> Desi que il vint as degrez
> De la sale? Sus est montez. [vv. 1863-70]

In this case the very animated interrogative has the specific function of showing how the poet shares the listener's disgust at the contemptible forester's eagerness to betray the lovers, which nothing can curb, not even the grandeur of the royal court. And here again it is not by chance that the poet's need to assure the audience that his sentiments are identical with theirs comes to the surface; the pace of the whole episode has been set by the forester's breathless sprint, underlined by the contrast with lovers' oblivious slumber ('Du bois [li forestier] s'en ist, cort a mervelle. Tristran avoc s'amie dort', vv. 1850–1).

So the narrator is able to reinforce the close contact which he has created between himself and his audience, whose emotional reactions he constantly controls, attuning them to his own and always keeping them at the highest tension permitted by the narrative. Although these direct incursions of the narrator into the tale are, of course, frequent in the literature of the time, as are also the conventional appeals to the audience, it is the *quality* of these features in Beroul which makes them so characteristic of the author, because in other texts these stylistic devices play a less prominent part and above all produce a literary effect which is less intense, often going no further than the quasi-elegiac lament of verses such as 'A, Deus, quel duel quant li vassal chet'.[15]

2
Solidarity with the protagonists

To think that Beroul uses these stylistic devices for a purely utilitarian purpose, making them merely a manifestation of consummate professionalism, would be to misunderstand their true significance, as well as much of the tone and meaning of the romance. In fact they correspond to an essential characteristic of the relating and the representation of life; they are the effect of a conscious or unconscious refusal to narrate for the egoistic delight of the narrator who, either physically alone or isolating himself by means of wishful thinking, takes a pleasure in his own narrating and loses himself in it. We can only regret that the unsatisfactory way in which the romance has been handed down has deprived us of the beginning and end, and with them perhaps explicit declarations by the author concerning his intentions in narrating; but our regret is tempered by the extreme clarity with which the poet's position *vis-à-vis* his work is revealed in every verse. It may be that he wished to make his work into a commentary based on those ethical and social ideas which certainly are reflected in the romance and which we shall investigate. But his didactic intentions do not for a moment induce him to take a detached attitude to his narrative, as they should; in this way he differs from a master of painting, who, although referring to a figure he has himself created, stands back from it and passes judgement on it. It may also be that he intended to divert his listeners and make them forget reality for an hour or so; but diversion for him has lost its etymological meaning[16] and is constantly transformed into participation. If this were participation in the narrated tale seen as a succession of adventures, of alternating moments of anxiety and relief, this would not exclude any moral purpose or desire to entertain he may have had, nor even relegate it to second place, but would on the contrary contribute towards its more effective realisation. In fact, however, the object of the poet's impassioned participation is not primarily the vicissitudes of the narrative: what leaves him breathless is the human suffering of his protagonists, their very existence, with its charms and tribulations. Every event is evaluated and passionately felt from the point of view of the protagonists, to whom every tremor of emotion is related. And here an essential transformation necessarily comes about: what seems to be a form of narrative hypnosis, a psychological link between narrator and narration quite unaffected by the human quality of the latter and determined exclusively by the possibilities of involvement implicit in it, becomes in reality a sharing in the protagonists' suffering and for this profoundly altruistic reason alone gives rise to hypnosis. What involves the narrator in the romance is the tragic destiny of his characters, that is to say, his feeling that their sufferings are also his sufferings, his isolation of them as examples of a situation in life which is not exclusive to them but potentially common to everyone. Furthermore Beroul, in his enthusiastic solidarity and sympathy, experiences a feeling which, because of its altruistic nature, has no reason to confine itself to an isolated *rapport* but can and must be common to all, must be felt in all its emotive force throughout the circle of listeners and return to the narrator as a token of comforting communion. So that beneath his constant appeals to the audience, beneath the hackneyed formulas and even more beneath those which are renewed and vibrant, there is a profoundly human root, a tragic, intimate feeling for life.

But this is still not all. Participation of this nature is obviously not peculiar to Beroul: all the great story-tellers have been endowed with it and it could well be said to be absolutely essential to great poetry. So we must not only identify it but define it, qualify it with its characteristic forms. To this all the observations we have so far made will contribute, but they are not enough.

Let us for a moment consider Marie de France, a contemporary of Beroul and herself a great narrator. Who could say that in the dramatic climb up the hill in the *Douz Amanz* or in the lady's long journey in search of her wounded lover in *Yonec* the poetess's heart does not participate in the protagonists' drama? But Marie's participation is always discreet, inherent in the very tone of the language, in the swift, skilful turns of phrase; it is expressed more in the emphasis of the narrative than in explicit interventions by the narrator, and when it is more openly expressed it tends towards the nostalgic tone of elegy, as in *Le Chaitivel*. In the *Douz Amanz* the only direct intervention is a subdued, 'Mes jo criem que poi [ne] li vaille' (v. 176); in *Yonec* we find a stronger outburst when the jealous husband fixes the iron prongs to the window through which the lover will have to pass: 'Deus! qu'il ne sout la traison Que aparaillot le felun!' (vv. 295–6). But this is an exception.

On the other hand, Beroul's distinguishing characteristic is first and foremost the extroversion which impels him to seek contact with feelings which are in accord with his own, to share with others his sorrowful intuition of life. But the key to the difference between him and Marie lies in his complete repudiation of the elegiac attitude, of inactivity and passive participation. Beroul is unable to contemplate in silent sorrow, to be tacitly compassionate. His sense of solidarity incites him to some form of action, to an explicit manifestation which will both give vent to his sorrow and vindicate it. His devotion to the protagonists' cause is absolute and without light and shade; the antagonism between the protagonists and the traitors is so uncompromising as to permit no one to hesitate or remain uninvolved. The inevitability of a decision, which at the same time fixes the character of him who takes the decision, is truly one of the features of the medieval *aventure* such as Eberwein characterised it, making *Lanval* her starting-point: 'From the king and queen down to the lowest courtier, all must here take sides and take a stand on Lanval's mysterious adventure, the mystery of which is all the more essentially and deeply linked with him the less they all know what it is they are taking a stand on, and the less they can get direct access to the phenomenon itself, instead of seeing it only indirectly *via* Lanval and seeing its effect on him';[17] and 'a totality of feelings—respect, admiration, love, envy and hatred—is awakened around him and towards him'.[18] The only difference is that what normally applies only to the characters Beroul has extended to the listeners as well, compelling them too, with his passionate enthusiasm, to take sides. Tristran's *aventure*, besides serving as a reference point for judging the characters in the romance, is thus also a touchstone for the qualities of the audience.

It is rare for Beroul to speak of the barons without breaking off for a moment to utter a violent malediction against them:

Un de ces trois que Dex maudie.	[v. 1656]
Fors des felons que Dex cravent!	[v. 2754]
Enfer ovre, qui les tranglote!	[v. 2826][19]
Mal aient il, trop sont engrés!	[v. 2891]
Oiez des trois, que Dex maudie.	[v. 3028]
Li troi felon, qui mal feu arde.	[v. 3788][20]

Nor is the dwarf treated any better:

| Dehez ait il conme boçuz! | [v. 640] |

And the treacherous forester also gets his share:

| Male gote les eulz li criet, Qui tant voloit Tristran deztruire! | [vv. 1916–17] |
| Li forestier, qui vergonde ait.[21] | [v. 1972] |

But the hatred for the traitors is only a reflection of the poet's impassioned sympathy for the protagonists, whose every action he follows with trepidation. They are conceived as being in a hostile world fraught with dangers, and every step, every gesture, seems to place their very destiny at stake; they move over such treacherous ground that even when they take considered risks they seem to be acting imprudently. But the poet's anxious voice constantly accompanies them, as we have already seen many times:

| Dex! quel pechié! trop ert hardiz! | [v. 700] |
| Dex! porqoi fist? or escoutez! | [v. 728] |

In the night Tristran jumps onto the queen's bed, soiling it with
blood which he loses from a wound reopened by the effort; the king
returns and he jumps back again:

> Au tresallir que Tristran fait,
> Li sans decent—malement vait—
> De la plaie sor la farine.
> Ha! Dex, qel duel que la roïne
> N'avot les dras du lit ostez!
> Ne fust la nuit nus d'eus provez;
> Se ele s'en fust apensee,
> Molt eüst bien s'anor tensee.   [vv. 747-54]

But instead the two lovers are caught and Tristran allows the
three barons to bind him:

> Ha! Dex, porqoi ne les ocist?
> A mellor plait asez venist.   [vv. 825-6]

Later, when the forester tells the king of Tristran and Yseut's
hiding-place, Marc prepares to go there:

> S'il les trove, molt les menace,
> Ne laira pas ne lor mesface.
> Molt est li rois acoragiez
> De destruire; c'est granz pechiez.   [vv. 1949-52]

Now Marc stands in the depths of the Morrois before the two lovers
sleeping side by side:

> Li rois en haut le cop leva,
> Iré le fait, si se tresva;
> Ja decendist li cop sor eus:
> Ses oceïst, ce fust grant deus.   [vv. 1991-4]

When the barons discover that Tristran, banished from the kingdom, has stayed in hiding near Tintaguel and is coming to visit
Yseut, they decide to spy on the meeting, and Yseut, who knows
nothing of this, gives her lover a rendezvous for the following
morning:

> Dex! la franche ne se gardoit
> Des felons ne de lor tripot.   [vv. 4345-6]

Each time it seems that the poet realises the mistake his characters are making, and is unable to withhold a stifled cry of regret or anxiety.

His solidarity with the lovers seems unlimited, but it is not as blind as it sometimes appears. Let us consider the only two passages where the narrator names himself, thus providing the extreme case of a participation which brings into action not merely an anonymous human person but a clearly identifiable individual—everything, in fact, implied by the name of one who names himself. Although this has not previously been pointed out, it is not by chance that these passages are linked with the feeling of solidarity between the poet and the *dramatis personae* which we are discussing; two essential reasons for such solidarity are crystallised in these very passages, and again this is no coincidence.

When Tristran and Governal attack the group of lepers as they are taking Yseut away:

> Li contor dïent que Yvain
> Firent nïer, qui sont vilain;
> N'en sevent mie bien l'estoire,
> Berox l'a mex en sen memoire:
> Trop ert Tristran preuz et cortois
> A ocirre gent de tes lois. [vv. 1265–70]

Thus the poet insists, with all the weight of his authority, on the hero's perfect prowess and chivalry, and frees him from his defects by modifying the narrative in order to restore what he calls the true version, thus making him act in a manner worthy of the passionate sympathy which he entertains for him.[22] In short, the circle appears to be closed: the protagonist must be perfect to merit the narrator's affection, and he modifies him in such a way as to make him perfect.

But the second passage is considerably more important, though this is not generally realised. Here the poet really does state the most intimate reason for his emotional position:

> Fu ainz mais gent tant eüst paine?
> Mais l'un por l'autre ne le sent,
> Bien orent lor aaisement.
> Ainz, puis le tens que el bois furent,
> Deus genz itant de tel ne burent;[23]
> Ne, si conme l'estoire dit,
> La ou Berox le vit escrit,
> Nule gent tant ne s'entramerent
> Ne si griment nu conpererent. [vv. 1784–92]

This time the *auctoritas* invoked is twofold, the *estoire*[24] and the poet who has read it. And what is it that he is seeking to authenticate?

> Nule gent tant ne s'entramerent
> Ne si griment nu conpererent.   [vv. 1791-2]

The affairs of Tristran and Yseut acquire their emblematic value precisely because they represent the most extreme projection of the common experience of love and of the sufferings of love. And here we can discern another not inconsiderable difference from other contemporary literary forms, because although the two lovers' affairs merit and are sometimes given the name of *aventure* they emerge from the comparison as a good deal more human than the usual medieval *aventure*.[25] Despite the love potion Tristran and Yseut's love never seems in Beroul to be the manifestation of some supernatural power, let alone of divine grace; its religious awe is directed towards greatness in suffering, and thus remains on a totally human level. In this way their love becomes an emblem of a general, perennial condition, but this does not mean that the interest it arouses is a didactic interest, as the fact of its being an example would seem to suggest. The poet's emotion is occasioned not by the sin but by the suffering, the innumerable troubles they endure. This constitutes as specific a confirmation as one could wish of our earlier contention, and an open affirmation, all the more convincing for being so solemnly pronounced and so formally documented, of the unselfish human reasons for the emotions which germinate exuberantly in the narrator and infect and overwhelm the audience, giving warmth to the tale with their intense fervour, and uniting narrator, audience and narration in a single circle of sympathies.

3
The chorus

We have seen how this circle of sympathies finds expression either in phrases which the narrator sometimes addresses to his audience and sometimes attributes to it, or directly in the narrator's exclamations. We could add that in the preceding chapter it seemed that in certain prophecies put into the mouths of the protagonists, and once even into Marc's mouth, the narrator's feelings showed through, barely screened by the camouflage. But there is yet another medium, which is rather more remarkable and more frequently employed.

Narrator and audience

When Yseut has been handed over to the lepers and they flock round her, their wish fulfilled: 'Qui ot le brait, qui ot le cri, A tote genz en prent pitiez' (vv. 1226–7). When Marc kills the dwarf: 'Molt en fu bel a mainte gent, Que haoient le nain Frocine Por Tristran et por la roïne' (vv. 1348–50). When the proclamation is made ordering the capture of Tristran, who has fled to the wood: 'En Cornoualle n'a parroise Ou la novele n'en angoise' (vv. 1433–4). When everyone eagerly assembles to watch Yseut being given back to Marc: 'N'i remest chevalier ne dame Qui ne vienge a cel'asenblee. La roïne ont molt desirree; Amee estoit de tote gent, Fors des felons que Dex cravent!' (vv. 2750–3). Her return to the city is celebrated with the same common enthusiasm: 'Tote la gente ist de la vile, Et furent plus de quatre mile, Qu'omes que femes que enfanz; Que por Yseut, que por Tristranz, Mervellose joie menoient' (vv. 2957–61).[26] And just read this passage:

> Li criz live par la cité
> Q'endui sont ensenble trové
> Tristran et la roïne Iseut,
> Et que li rois destruire eus veut.
> Pleurent li grant et li petit,
> Sovent l'un d'eus a l'autre dit:
> 'A! las, tant avon a plorer!
> Ahi! Tristran, tant par es ber!
> Qel damage qu'en traïson
> Vos ont fait prendre cil gloton!
> Ha! roïne franche, honoree,
> En qel terre sera mais nee
> Fille de roi qui ton cors valle?
> Ha! nains, ç'a fait ta devinalle!
> Ja ne voie Deu en la face,
> Qui trovera le nain en place,
> Qi nu ferra d'un glaive el cors!
> Ahi! Tristran, si grant dolors
> Sera de vos, beaus chiers amis,
> Qant si seroiz a destroit mis!
> Ha! las, quel duel de vostre mort!
> Qant le Morhout prist ja ci port,
> Qui ça venoit por nos enfanz,
> Nos barons fist si tost taisanz
> Que onques n'ot un si hardi
> Qui s'en osast armer vers lui.
> Vos enpreïstes la batalle

> Por nos trestoz de Cornoualle
> Et oceïstes le Morhout.
> Il vos navra d'un javelot,
> Sire, dont tu deüs morir.
> Ja ne devrion consentir
> Que vostre cors fust ci destruit.'
> Live la noisë et li bruit;
> Tuit en corent droit au palés.   [vv. 827–61]

These highly emotional words of the citizens of Tintaguel are at no point lacking in verisimilitude; not a single phrase sounds unsuited to those to whom it is attributed. On the contrary they contain an extended motivation of the citizens' respectful affection for Tristran, whose best known exploit is recalled, that undertaking which once and for all set him apart from the group of wicked barons, and made their settled antagonism an inevitable outcome: 'Qant le Morhout prist ja ci port . . . Vos enpreïstes la batalle Por nos trestoz de Cornoualle.' But although this motivation can be attributed only to those who actually utter it, there is not in this speech a single feeling which the narrator does not share: the premonition of imminent tragedy ('Tant avon a plorer'), the necessity to side actively and openly with the hero ('Ja ne devrion consentir'), the admiration for Tristran ('Tant par es ber') and for Yseut ('Roïne franche, honoree'), the hatred for their enemies ('Cil gloton', 'Ha! nains, ça fait ta devinalle!').

The *planctus* is repeated when Yseut is led out of the royal palace on her way to the stake:

> Qant la dame lïee virent—
> A laidor ert—molt s'esfroïrent.
> Qui ot le duel qu'il font por li,
> Com il crïent a Deu merci!
> 'Ha! roïne franche, honoree,
> Qel duel ont mis en la contree
> Par qui ceste novele est sorse!
> Certes, en asez poi de borse
> En porront metre le gaain;
> Avoir en puisent mal mehain!'   [vv. 1073–82]

We must not overlook the way in which v. 837 recurs like a *leitmotiv* at v. 1077, or the coexistence and parallel development of the lament for Yseut and the hatred for the traitors, which we know to be a characteristic feature of the narrator's participation in the romance.

We find identical developments in the reactions of this 'chorus' of the people to Husdent's refusal to remain separated from his master (vv. 1452 *et seq.*); these bring about the chorus's direct entry into the action, their request to the king to free the dog. But this outcome is effective only in appearance, for in reality three barons make the same request to the king immediately afterwards (v. 1473) and only then is it granted.

Since it is clear that the chorus speaks first and foremost as a character in its own right, we must not exaggerate the importance of its role as the narrator's spokesman. Even so, our conclusion remains unaltered. The creation of the chorus is the expression of a constant factor in the poet's imagination which we have come across before and shall come across again, a constant which could be defined as an urge to identify and make concrete. Thus the anonymous feelings of the crowd, which at first remain abstract ('A tote gent en prent pitiez'), or are only beginning to be individualised, as in the expressions of jubilation which welcome Yseut's return, find a far more perfect mode of coagulation, which in a sense succeeds in transforming the abstract into the tangible, the psychologically analysable into the concrete sense impression, feeling into vocal expression, multiplicity into unity.

This process is widespread in Beroul. When Tristran asks for permission to enter the chapel, 'Or l'a l'un d'eus [meneors] dit a son per: "Bien le poon laisier aler"' (vv. 939–40). When Marc asks the barons whether he should countenance the reinstatement of Yseut the poet does not say, 'The barons' counsel was that the queen should be received but that Tristran should be sent into exile', but 'N'i a baron de Cornoualle Ne die: "Rois, ta feme pren . . ."' (vv. 2624–5). The impression made by Yseut sitting on the shoulders of the bogus leper (vv. 3941–8) and by her oath (vv. 4217–31) is conveyed in the same way. However, in this case also, we are not dealing with something peculiar to Beroul. Frappier, for example, noted that in the *Chanson de Guillaume* there are few characters and the warriors express themselves in unison 'à la manière d'un chœur'.[27] There is a sort of chorus of townsfolk in one scene of the *Moniage Guillaume II*,[28] and many further instances could be cited. But these choruses voice only the opinion of their members; for example, in the first of the two passages in the *Moniage* the divergent opinions of the townsfolk are incarnated in two speakers. Beroul's chorus, on the contrary, expresses feelings which are also those of the narrator and the audience; thus his objective is almost always to give the action of the protagonists a wider reverberation, to broaden and crystallise the circle of solidarity. This circle of solidarity within the romance is always in harmony with that created without by the narrator and audience; it duplicates it, strengthens it and establishes an additional link between the inner plane of the romance (situated in a distant narrative time) and the external plane (re-lived in a twelfth-century hall or market-place). The listener, with his individual effective participation, being already fortified by the support of the narrator, can now regard himself as part of the 'chorus', one of the townsfolk of Lancïen, and his feeling of participation is intensified in this new and unexpected fellowship. This destroys the clear-cut distinction between the narrative plane and the plane of reality, which has already been blurred by the narrator himself, whose lively participation has constantly ignored it; now it no longer exists even for the audience. Just as the action of the romance has been entirely transfused into the audience's consciousness, so does it absorb, in a manner of speaking, their own real existence. The magic circle which the narrator uses to establish an alliance between himself, the romance and the audience fulfils its purpose by making real for everybody this exemplar of human passion, this train of events which involves these characters who loved each other as much as any couple ever loved each other, and for their passion paid as great a tribute of suffering as any couple ever paid.

Notes

1 This is how Waremann, in his 'Spielmannsdichtung', p. 153, concludes a brief comparison between Eilhart and Beroul: 'What characterises Beroul's poem as the work of a *jongleur* is neither the motifs, nor the ideas, nor the formal technique, but simply the stylistic effects of a constant habit, on the part of the author, of addressing his audience.' This is a conclusion which we can accept and develop, even if we refuse to regard these as characteristics of the *jongleur* (cf. *infra*).
2 It is clear that the romance was intended for recitation and not for reading.
3 Some recent critics, starting from the conclusions of Curtius in his classic *European Literature and the Latin Middle Ages* and exaggerating them with the extremism characteristic of imitators, seem intent on reducing the study of medieval works of literature to a systematic examination of commonplaces and formulas, so that these works are

made to lend themselves to evaluation in terms of geometry rather than of literary criticism, with the author's individuality being assessed in quantitative terms, since he is turned into a meeting point for specific and analysable quantities of *topoi* and *formulae*. To counteract such extreme conclusions it is indispensable to return to the vigorous *mise au point* by Menéndez Pidal (in 'La épica española y la *Literaturästhetik des Mittelalters* de E. R. Curtius' and 'Fórmulas épicas en el *Poema del Cid*', from which I quote: 'Let us not allow the *topoi* to obscure our view of the poem. If the *topos* is commonplace, insignificant and counterfeit, the poet is imitating no one and he is the only person responsible for the way in which he develops a spontaneous and natural function of the mind, working out, for example, a contrast, as in the case of *Mio Cid*, the *Roman de Thèbes* and the *Orlando Furioso*. If, however, the *topos* is literary and shows signs of being derived from elsewhere, the poet must still never be forgotten, because besides seeing in the adoption of the theme the durability of a literary tradition, in the study of which Curtius deploys such erudition and achieves such success, it is necessary to bear in mind constantly and *above all else* the inventive, creative side, which serves, much more than the theme, to place each writer who adopts it' [p. 254]) and to the sober judgement of Battaglia in *La coscienza letteraria*, p. 107: 'It is true that the signs of active spontaneity can subsequently be transformed into an orderly scheme of *topoi* and *tropoi*, but the opposite is also true, that real living feeling can return even to old and worn-out themes, imbuing them with genuine contemporary experience and restoring their truth to life.'

4 It should be borne in mind that a little earlier we find: 'S'uns escureus de lui sausist, Si fust il mort, ja n'en garist' (vv. 923–4). Cf. Waremann, *diss. cit.*, p. 152.

5 At least one other case seems to be similar. The three wicked barons finally get out of the mud at the Mal Pas and this satirical parenthesis closes:

> Voiant le pueple, se despollent,
> Li dras laisent, autres racuellent.
> Mais or oiez du franc Dinas,
> Qui fu de l'autre part du Pas . . .   [vv. 3863–6]

See also a passage very soon after this: when all the knights have crossed the Mal Pas, only Yseut remains, watching for an opportunity to have herself carried across by the disguised Tristran:

> De l'autre part fu Yseut sole.
> Devant le gué fu grant la fole
> Des deus rois et de lor barnage.
> Oiez d'Yseut com el fu sage!

> Bien savoit que cil l'esgardoient
> Qui outre le Mal Pas estoient.
> Ele est au palefroi venue ...   [vv. 3879-85]

6 Waremann, *diss. cit.*, p. 151, asserts that through Beroul's use of the word 'oiez' 'a degree of tension is created'. This seems to be true only in a few cases, and in any case a rather generic observation.

7 The following passage should also be taken into consideration; here, since the climax is more distant the effect is intentionally less pronounced, but underlined by the alliterations and by the etymological word-play:

> Tristran l'estent [l'arc], si s'apensa,
> Oiez! en son penser tensa;
> Prent s'entente, si tendi l'arc.   [vv. 4441-3]

This is the scene of Godoïne's death, and Tristran does not yet understand why Yseut is asking him to bend his bow.

8 Before minutely describing the way in which the lovers are lying, the narrator says: 'Oez com il se sont couchiez' (v. 1816), which in this instance really is a formula for calling attention to details the importance of which will be understood only later.

9 Another formula in the accepted sense is 'Mais or oiez des endormiz' (v. 2063), which in the same episode marks the shift from the narration of Marc's action to that of Yseut's dream and the awakening of the lovers.

10 For this scene cf. *infra*, pp. 170 *et seq*.

11 The same kind of amused participation in the heroes' clownish feats (and of extension of this participation to the audience) is found in the episode where the disguised Tristran makes the three wicked barons fall into the mire of the Mal Pas: 'Oiez du ladre com il ment' (v. 3812), 'Oiez del ladre, du desfait, Donoalen met a raison' (vv. 3838-9).

12 Compare this with the following passage, taken from the beginning of the flour-episode. The barons are speaking:

> 'Mandez le nain, puis soit asis.'
> Et il i est molt tost venuz;
> Dehez ait il conme boçuz!
> Li un des barons l'en acole,
> Li rois li mostre sa parole.
> Ha! or oiez qel traïson
> Et confaite seducion,
> A dit au roi cil nain Frocin!
> Dehé aient tuit cil devin!
> Qui porpensa tel felonie
> Con fist cist nain, qui Dex maudie?   [vv. 638-48]

Narrator and audience

13 To conclude our examination of these formulas, it should be noted that they are twice used by the characters of the romance, in the scene where Tristran's letter is read at Marc's court (v. 2532, where Dinas is speaking, and v. 2552, spoken by the chaplain). There is no doubt that these are pure introductory formulas.
14 Cf. vv. 2884, 3564, 3991 and 4098.
15 *Chanson de Guillaume*, v. 2075.
16 Latin *diverto*, 'I turn aside'.
17 *Zur Deutung mittelalterlicher Existenz*, p. 46.
18 *Ibid.*, p. 48.
19 In this case it is Yseut who is speaking.
20 In addition to v. 3788, Yseut also indulges in the following imprecations: 'Deu pri qu'il soient vergondé' (v. 3206) and 'Aient il male maudiçon!' (v. 3215); there is also Marc's 'Dex vos destruie' (v. 3082).
21 When Yseut is bound and led to the pyre: 'Par Deu, trop firent que vilains!' (v. 900).
22 It is a well-known fact that Eilhart allows Tristran to kill the leader of the lepers. It could be objected that at other times the narrator does not seem to require perfection in his protagonists, whom he allows to behave quite badly. But, in the first place, as we have been obliged to assume in assessing individual passages, there is a judgement on the lovers' conduct within the episode, as well as an overall judgement applying to the poem as a whole. Furthermore, elsewhere the lovers have to save themselves from extreme disasters, while here, with such disparity of strength and social status, lack of restraint would have been gratuitous cruelty. Besides, our contempt for the lepers comes out strengthened rather than weakened by this modification. For a number of reasons, which will become clear as we proceed, the lepers cannot be put on the same level as the traitors. The fastidious disgust of protagonist and narrator is the adequate response to their instinctive action, while for the malice of the wicked barons there can be nothing short of a cruel, implacable vengeance. Pauphilet, too (*Le Legs du moyen âge*, p. 127), writes of Tristran's restraint: 'Pourquoi? Non par pitié, puisqu'un autre va l'assommer; mais par ce que la lutte ne serait pas égale et que lui, Tristran, ne courrait pas assez de risques.' Besides, Beroul's affection for his protagonists is due not to any exemplary perfection in them, as is the case with the protagonists of so many courtly romances, but simply—as we shall show a little further on—to the complex and tormented, but extremely human, greatness of their passion. On this scene cf. also pp. 173 *et seq.*
23 Cf. O. Schultz-Gora's 'Zur französischen Metapher', pp. 225 *et seq.*
24 Note that the *estoire* is here the tale and not the book.
25 Eberwein wrote (*op. cit.*, p. 51): 'The conception of "chance" current in this world-picture is one of miracle, grace, revelation of the forces of

the Beyond and the truth here below, and is thus always "religious",
even when it appears to be "secular".'
26 Cf. up to v. 2971.
27 *Les Chansons de Geste* . . ., vol. 1, pp. 172–3.
28 Vv. 1770–84 and 1873–84.

3
The sin of Tristran and Yseut

The emotional circle which binds the narrator and audience together is justified by the fact that at its heart there is a human, moral problem. It is thanks to this that mere technical skill is surpassed; the skill of a narrator able to bind the audience to himself through the various resources of his consummate artistry is an external skill but in this text it is clearly transcended by a deep passion. From narrative technique we are taken directly to social and moral reality as divined by the narrator and corporately felt by the audience.

Right at the heart of the tale of Tristran and Yseut there seems to lie a moral problem. This is not a narrative which relies for its fascination on a succession of unexpected developments, or for its dramatic effect on the pleasing interweaving of the various adventures: it is, as has been said, entirely based on the struggle between love and social laws. Tristran has been brought up by his uncle Marc, with whom he is connected by both family and feudal ties, and loves Marc's wife. Thus the hearts of the three protagonists are forced into an insoluble dilemma: Tristran is torn between knightly duty and almost filial affection on the one hand and love on the other; Yseut, between conjugal duty and love; and Marc, between affection for his wife and nephew and justifiable anger because of the unwarrantable wrongs they have committed against him. Within this pre-arranged framework, in which the only things that are not already fixed are the nature of the love between the two and the way it began, the only possible attitude for the narrator, and therefore for the audience, suggested by the situation would seem to be a feeling of human pity which would embrace all the protagonists without making any moral judgement. But instead, as we have already seen many times, Beroul separates the good from the bad with vigorous, impassioned zeal; he is a partisan rather than an objective narrator, disposed to grant his sympathetic understanding only to certain characters and to withhold it from others right up to their dying day.

This enables us to formulate more clearly the terms of our enquiry: how does the moral and social drama of the romance take shape in Beroul, bearing in mind that his view of things is definitely polarised? Unfortunately, owing to the fragmentary state of the text, many features that would contribute towards a solution are absent and we must bear in mind how fragile arguments are which lack a secure textual basis. In order to understand the nature of Tristran and Yseut's love with the material available, we must study the references to the love potion and the two encounters with the hermit Ogrin, where the author faces up to the problem fairly and squarely.[1]

I
The love potion: consciousness and responsibility

It is obvious that Beroul attributes the origin of the love to the potion, but his assessment of its effects does not seem to be consistent throughout the romance. As we know, the overall coherence of the narrative is broken up by his preference for completeness within the individual narrative 'moments', and one consequence of this is that Beroul did not even deem it appropriate to state right from the outset that the effect of the potion is of only limited duration.[2] But Beroul differs from what we read elsewhere[3] in that the effect of the potion on the lovers does not appear to have been prepared by any reciprocal affection nor, on Yseut's side, by the first promptings of love. Indeed, the allusion to the first effects of the *vin herbez* mentions a sudden subjection:

> Tant con durerent li troi an,
> Out li vins si soupris Tristran
> Et la roïne ensenble o lui
> Que chascun disoit: 'Los m'en fui.' [vv. 2143-6]

Moreover in their confession to Ogrin, the potion is the only reason that the lovers allege for their adultery:

> Tristran li dit: 'Sire, par foi,
> Que ele m'aime en bone foi,
> Vos n'entendez pas la raison:
> Q'el m'aime, c'est par la poison.
> Ge ne me pus de lié partir,
> N'ele de moi, n'en quier mentir.' [vv. 1381-6]

And Yseut speaks still more plainly:

> Sire, por Deu omnipotent,
> Il ne m'aime pas, ne je lui,
> Fors par un herbé dont je bui,
> Et il en but.[4] [vv. 1412-15]

So the potion is interpreted not as a moment, however decisive, in a psychological development, but as the beginning and root cause of everything. Here again Beroul's imagination does not go in search of nuances or barely perceptible progressions, but forcibly juxtaposes two diametrically opposed emotional conditions, indifference and irrevocable love, between which the only hinge is the potion; the potion is not a symbol nor an emblem of the lovers' passion, but the reason for it. Thus an essential role is assigned to the potion, and for this very reason it seems to become a tangible instrument of a fate which is indifferent to man, and pitches him around like straw ('Out li vins si soupris Tristran Et la roïne ensenble o lui Que chascun disoit: "Los m'en fui" '). This is a singularly powerful and even barbaric idea, at least in the sense of something violent, simple and ultimate, which pervades the whole romance because the overwhelming violence of the first effects of the *lovendrinc* is constantly renewed during the three years of its action and unwaveringly robs the lovers of any power to resist or seek a compromise.

This fundamental theme of the romance has never been overlooked by scholars, especially since it is thrown into sharper relief by its contrast with the analytic, rationalist psychologising of Thomas, who investigates with scrupulous and as it were merciless attention the secret movements of the heart (and more particularly of the mind) and seeks to arrange them in an order representing a plausible, or at least clear and conscious, course of development. Here, on the contrary, the love is accepted as something which exists, involving passion and suffering, something unfathomable and unquestionable, and which envelops everything in its unalterable irrationality. Nor is this justified, as in other twelfth-century cases, by one of those age-old maxims such as *omnia vincit amor*, which express the abandonment of the desire to analyse when confronted by an obstinate residue which evades comprehension. Beroul rejects both this compromise between rationality and irrationality and the possibility of cloaking it with some traditional authority, because his narrative is—or at least seems to be—not carefully contrived with a definite aim in view, but directly and sympathetically heard and comprehended. This way of looking at things is very much facilitated by the concrete, objective presence of the potion, which exempts the narrator from any other justification arising out of the nature of love itself and at the same time determines the course and the nature of the love as he intuitively apprehends it. In this way both tradition and a physical object serve to spare the poet, as well as the *dramatis personae,* a different and more searching analysis, which could not help but impair the element of inscrutability in the passion of love, thus diminishing its sublimity and, one might almost say, its *numen*.

So if we reject the interpretation of the potion's function as symbol of a love conceived in psychological terms, it would seem that the potion tends rather to represent a tangible intervention of destiny, a mysterious and therefore disturbing incursion by some will extraneous to the world of human beings. This is an attractive and powerful conception, but as far as we can say today Beroul does not seem to have adhered to it consistently. To prove the point, let us for a moment consider into what terms, assuming that he were consistent, the whole action would have been transposed. First and foremost, what would be the significance of destiny in a world which is, and cannot help but be, Christian? We must exclude the possibility of its here being identified with Providence, given the consequences to which it leads. It could in theory be understood as an intervention of the devil, but there is not a hint of the problems arising from the struggle between good and evil and the necessity of deciding the outcome, which on the religious level have no real significance in the development of the romance. The Middle Ages had yet another kind of destiny not necessarily bound up with a precise religious framework, identified in the image of *Fortuna labilis*, but its operation was concerned rather with a man's material prosperity and not his spiritual state.[5]

And yet, without being conceptually clear, without even a name and perhaps hardly distinguishable from pure chance, the blind force made concrete in the love potion is not all that different from the Fate of the classical world. It explains man's actions without justifying them and without exonerating him from his individual responsibility. When Tristran and Yseut invoke the potion it is not their moral state that they are seeking to clarify and justify. In the verses we have quoted phrases such as 'Los m'en fui' could seem to refer only to the situation in which the lovers actually find themselves, to their suffering, their misfortunes, their tribulations and their dishonour. But Ogrin, who knows about the potion, is not the only one to describe their situation as 'pechié' (v. 1390) and 'folie' (v. 2297), which is the same thing, and themselves as 'pecheor' (v. 1392); Yseut herself speaks of 'pechié' (v. 2264) and 'folie' (v. 2323). In the same way Oedipus did not regard himself as innocent of the crimes he unwittingly committed by the decree of destiny, and punished himself by putting out his own eyes. Although man is as straw in the hands of destiny, he preserves his dignity by recognising his responsibility even for that which he is unable to avoid.

Tristran and Yseut do not curse the force which masters them, but only Brengain, who involuntarily became its handmaid. Their reaction does not go beyond elegiac nostalgia for their lost tranquillity and felicity (vv. 2157 *et seq.*). Nor could it be otherwise, for since their suffering is caused by their love, it has the same source as their happiness. This situation is a long way from that of the heroes of antiquity, to whom destiny brings only cause for lament, so that the hero's moral detachment can be total. Moreover, an essential characteristic of our romance is that the lovers are constantly aware of the fate which has struck them, while more often than not the Greek hero's destiny was revealed to him only in a blinding flash of light after the event, as a new and dramatic insight into his own past and therefore unredeemable actions. On the other hand, for Tristran and Yseut the intervention of fate is entirely limited to the initial drinking of the potion, which suddenly alters the emotional elements in the situation, and for ever; it is not an invisible hand of iron controlling events unknown to man until the moment when he is called to account but a mechanism through which a single impulse has been transmitted, a hand which on a single occasion has rearranged the pieces on the board. All the subsequent action will be determined by this impulse, by this rearrangement, but it will still be left to the initiative and in a sense to the choice of the characters. And this is not an insignificant difference, because it is precisely at this point that the Christian inheritance of the world in which the legend grew up and in which our poet shaped it becomes an operating factor.[6] In fact it is worth noting that the existence and action of the love potion are unknown to everyone except Tristran, Yseut, Brengain and, later, Ogrin. It has often been wondered why this should be so, and the keeping of the secret has been seen as a sort of surreptitious means of keeping the tale on its feet, since otherwise it could have come to a reasonable solution.[7] But the real reason for keeping the mistake about the potion a secret, which seems ridiculous at first sight, is to be found at a deeper level, below that of narrative convenience. The apparent contrast between those in the secret and those outside it then emerges as the only means of preserving the balance of moral responsibility in the individual characters. If the action of the potion were unknown to all, for a medieval narrator the lovers' fault would be relatively slight: they would be blindly thrown into each other's arms and quite free from responsibility. To fulfil Beroul's concept of human nature, which is certainly more limited and rigid than that of the classical writers, awareness of the fault is a necessary requirement for responsibility, even if it is not sufficient to influence the action; a fatal, unconscious love would undoubtedly strike him as the work of the devil. If, on the other hand, everyone knew of the potion, degrees of responsibility would again be unequal because the lovers would remain bound in their actions by an inevitable irrationality while the other characters would be obliged and able to act in a clearly rational manner. Instead, as we can now see, all the characters are given an equal share of mystery and fear, all the actions lie in that grey zone between moral awareness and unconsciousness which is a feature of reality. Each character acts according to his own nature and his own will and bears the responsibility for his behaviour, but the course of events does not unfold on a stage where everything is clearly lighted. Everywhere and for everyone there is to be sensed a residuum of mystery and irrationality which increases the dignity and the responsibility of human action, a residuum which for the lovers is the potion, and for the others is ignorance of the potion. The apparent incongruity is thus nothing other than substantial congruity and enables the poet to colour the events with a mixture of lucid will and apprehensive doubt, of conviction and uncertainty (or chance—in effect the same thing); a mixture of rationality and absurdity, precariously blended together.

All this is obviously a feature of the legend in general, but in Beroul it is turned to better account than in other versions because here the hazardous and perplexing uncertainty of human life and actions is so keenly felt. This will emerge more clearly later.

Even though, through its vagueness, or rather through the poet's refusal to investigate it, the nature of the power embodied in the potion escapes definition and thus in this respect simplifies the lovers' position, they cannot thereby, as we shall see, escape moral responsibility. This aspect of the romance seems peculiarly involved, or—what comes to the same thing—seems to be treated by the poet only on the surface. Let us first look at the passages relevant to this point. When Yseut tells Brengain of the risks she has run in the rendezvous at the fountain, the servant comments:

Granz miracles vos a fait Dex,
Il est verais peres et tex

> Qu'il n'a cure de faire mal
> A ceus qui sont buen et loial. [vv. 377-80]

Later, when the lovers are found out, the poet feels the need to reassure the listeners about the outcome:

> Molt grant miracle Deus i out,
> Quis garanti, si con li plot. [vv. 755-6]

This evidently refers to the leap from the chapel and the subsequent rescue of Yseut. And in fact this episode is introduced by the following verses:

> Oez, seignors, de Damledé,
> Conment il est plains de pité;
> Ne vieat pas mort de pecheor:
> Receü out le cri, le plor
> Que faisoient la povre gent
> Por ceus qui eirent a torment. [vv. 909-14]

Eventually the success of Tristran's leap is accompanied by the comment 'Bele merci Dex li a fait!'[8] and the tone is no different when we are told that Tristran allows himself to be captured because he is confident that there will be an *escondit*:

> Mais en Deu tant fort se fiot
> Que bien savoit et bien quidoit,
> S'a escondit peüst venir,
> Nus n'en osast armes saisir
> Encontre lui, lever ne prendre;
> Bien se quidoit par chanp defendre. [vv. 813-18]

When we look at these passages it cannot surprise us that divine mercy should be invoked to save the condemned lovers, or that it should actually intervene in their favour. The verse 'Ne vieat pas mort de pecheor' could be glossed by far more extreme examples taken from any collection of *miracles*; but while in these divine intervention saves from the clutches of the devil even the most hardened sinner who still has that spark of faith necessary to invoke it, here it permits, not the lovers' permanent salvation (i.e. that of their souls), but only that of their bodies. Thus a return to sin is permitted, especially since the divine intervention has no effect, not even as a warning against persisting in their course, on the hearts of the lovers, who accept it almost as a right. This is a far cry from the conception of divine grace and its effects which we find in the *miracles*, particularly when divine aid is called upon to support decidedly immoral actions, from the base deception of Marc when he is hiding in the pine tree to the request for an *escondit* to prove that what actually happened did not happen.[9] In short, directly or indirectly, God insures the lovers against the consequences of their every action, but their life is nonetheless adjudged to be sinful.[10]

If we look at these verses again we shall not be able to help noticing an emphatically juridical tone in the language, with the use of words and phrases such as 'loial' (v. 380), 'garanti' (v. 756),[11] 'recevoir le cri' (v. 912) and 'se fier' (v. 813). However unusual this may seem, for Beroul the relationship between the lovers and God does not seem to coincide with the relationship between the lovers and moral law. In other words, for him the offence against moral law, of which the lovers are undeniably guilty, certainly does not determine their position in the eyes of God. If we premise that the relationship with God is obviously understood in the strictly feudal, juridical sense, we can only say that it does not seem to be compromised by the sin of the lovers, who are still called *loial*. And this can be explained only by admitting that the lovers are guilty on account of their adultery but never seem to have offended God in person. The text leaves us in no doubt on this point but the fact that it is incomplete denies us the opportunity of choosing between two possible interpretations: it could be that since the potion is drunk unwittingly Beroul takes it that in the adultery it causes there is no intention to sin; or it could also be that in the poet's *simpliste* and rather unorthodox mental picture the contradiction is not even noticed, and that we have on the one hand a tendency to personify God which goes as far as identifying Him with a feudal lord, and on the other the impossibility of conceiving moral law simply as the tyrannical will of this lord, because if everything had to be traced back to Him even the potion would in the last analysis come from Him.

Our uncertainty could undoubtedly be resolved in favour of the former hypothesis if we were to accept that Beroul stuck rigorously to the well known theory of sin which Saint Augustine had formulated with crystalline clarity: 'Voluntas quippe est qua et peccatur, et recte vivitur', and 'Non igitur nisi voluntate peccatur'.[12] This theory had later been developed to its logical extreme by Abelard, who had removed all significance from the sinful act, since the sin is already present in the *consensus* to a desire recognised to be wrong, and hence there would be no sin if *consensus* were not given.[13] If this were so, it would be quite clear that God protects the lovers from the hostile acts of their uncomprehending fellow beings because he knows them to be innocent while Ogrin, himself a man, cannot but remain sceptical of the excuse of the potion and demands a repentance which would here have no sense. Thus there would be no embarrassing distinction between God and morality but simply a God who knows the hearts of men, and man who is bound to judge by appearances.

But if this were Beroul's reasoning it would be most strange that in the second conversation with Ogrin the lovers do not speak of the potion or say that their will has been liberated; and it would be quite unnecessary for Yseut to arrange the deception at the Mal Pas and the equivocal oath because at any time she could simply have sworn that she had never wished to sin with Tristran, or even that she had never sinned with him, which would have been the same thing. Instead she feels the need to take advantage of an ambiguity of fact rather than a distinction of moral philosophy, and it never emerges, as it certainly should, that the lovers become adulterous when they continue to meet secretly after the effect of the potion has worn off.

Besides all this, we must not forget that in these arguments we are only developing to logical extremes elements which are not given any particular importance in the text. This does not mean that Beroul vacillated between more than one notion of sin or that he adopted one of his own, but simply that this set of problems was in the long run largely a matter of indifference to him. In other words, Beroul constructed the relationship between God and the lovers in a manner which is by now familiar to us and for the reasons which we have seen, but since he was not particularly sensitive to the religious aspects of the situation he used these moments to widen still further the vast circle of sympathy for his heroes, by including God in it.

2
Ogrin

But let us return to the meetings with Ogrin. The first comes about 'par aventure' (v. 1363), while the lovers are wandering through the wood. Ogrin is not introduced in any way, as if he were already known, and at first the episode seems to have a decidedly secondary function, because all the hermit appears to do is to warn Tristran of the proclamation and of the price on his head. But after a very short pause Ogrin passes on to the most important issue:

> Ogrins li dit molt bonement:
> 'Par foi! Tristran, qui se repent,
> Deu du pechié li fait pardon,
> Par foi et par confession.'
> Tristran li dit: 'Sire, par foi,
> Que ele m'aime en bone foi,[14]
> Vos n'entendez pas la raison:
> Q'el m'aime, c'est par la poison.
> Ge ne me pus de lié partir,
> N'ele de moi, n'en quier mentir.' [vv. 1377-86]

The dialogue continues, but this initial misunderstanding prevents any progress, let alone any agreement between the hermit and the lovers. While Ogrin quite properly asserts that only repentance can annul sin and goes on to show that *foi* and *confession* are the means by which divine pardon may be obtained, Tristran maintains that they are free from responsibility because of the potion. Since Ogrin shows no signs of yielding and the lovers can see no possibility of liberating themselves from the action of the potion, all the ways out seem to be closed. Ogrin again speaks of 'repentir' (v. 1394) and 'repentance' (vv. 1392 and 1419), and Tristran can only repeat 'faire ne le puis' (v. 1408). So it does not seem that on this occasion the lovers are disposed to recognise their guilt.

But we must also observe that the two arguments, besides being opposed, are coloured in completely different manners. The lovers' position is seen and judged by Ogrin from a rigorously moral viewpoint.[15] He speaks of sin, repentance and pardon, says the sinner is as a dead man,[16] quotes and illustrates the Bible, advises the two to separate, suggests deeper meditation, and expresses the hope that they will accept the solace of penitence. In all this we find nothing that is not in accordance with a coherent moral, and exclusively moral, outlook. For the two lovers Tristran asserts:

> Mex aim o li estre mendis
> Et vivre d'erbes et de glan
> Q'avoir le reigne au roi Otran. [vv. 1404-6]

Nothing could be more eloquent. When the lovers define their own position, and the dramatic side of it, what emerges is not moral disorder but, above all, the social aspects—their status as exiles and beggars, their physical discomforts, the strain of everyday life. The great nobility of these words lies not in the excess of their sin but in the overwhelming devotion of their love.

When the three years have ended and the effect of the potion has worn off, a flood of fresh nostalgia assails the ill-starred couple and they become conscious of their guilt. But once again the two conflicting forces are love and the rich, refined life of their century, the very forces with which we are already familiar from the first visit to the hermit. Now, however, the nature of the conflict is different because the effect of the potion has worn off, so that the attractions of social life come to the fore again. And, without thinking in terms of anything so grand as 'le reigne au roi Otran', the lovers would like to regain the most modest comforts of Marc's dominion. But now they speak openly of 'pechiez' (v. 2264) and 'repentir' (v. 2271) and immediately the memory of Ogrin reappears, with his Biblical teachings ('la loi escrite', v. 2266, as compared with 'les profecies le l'escrit' of v. 1396). All the same, it should be noted that the wish to return to Ogrin is based primarily on practical considerations rather than on religious ones.[17] In fact Tristran says:

> Encor enuit ou le matin,
> O le consel de maistre Ogrin,
> Manderon a nostre talent
> Par briés sanz autre mandement.   [vv. 2281-4]

And Yseut adds:

> Au riche roi celestïen
> Puison andui crïer merci,
> Q'il ait de nos, Tristran, ami!   [vv. 2286-8]

It is this mixture of ethical and practical motives which dominates the second encounter with Ogrin, but it seems that critics have exaggerated a good deal in judging the episode as totally lacking in significance and seriousness from the religious point of view. Here again the hermit speaks first, still censuring the couple's 'folie' (v. 2297), although not without a touch of human compassion,[18] and exhorting them to repent: 'Et, queles, quar vos repentez!' (v. 2299). In Tristran's reply we can see, despite the lacuna, that there is no explicit reference to repentance nor to any kind of religious view of their own situation. He simply asks if there is any way 'de la roïne racorder' (v. 2306) and says he is willing to leave Marc and go 'en Bretaigne ou en Loenois' (v. 2310) unless Marc should wish him to do otherwise; at all events, he is prepared to submit to Ogrin's advice (v. 2318). But even in this speech, which is concerned with purely practical considerations, it can be seen that the barrier between the irreconcilable positions of the first meeting has disappeared; on that occasion Tristran had said he was unable to give up the queen according to the hermit's advice, while now he is in a position to accept that advice. Further on, Yseut earnestly promises that she will never again have 'corage de folie' (v. 2323), even if she does specify that she will preserve an honest affection for Tristran, hastening to add that there will be no further carnal relations between them. It could be objected that there is no explicit mention of repentance and that all this refers only to the future, without condemning the past; but the negative use of the verb *repentir*, which is so designed as to let her continue her *bone amor* for Tristran, surely means that Yseut repents of everything else.[19] Certainly the hermit sees a very close connection between repentance and the request for advice, since he immediately thanks God that the couple 'de lor pechiez A moi en vindrent consel prendre' (vv. 2336-7) and soon after says:

> Qant home et feme font pechié,
> S'anz se sont pris et sont quitié
> Et s'aus vienent a penitance
> Et aient bone repentance,
> Dex lor pardone lor mesfait,
> Tant ne seroit orible et lait. [vv. 2345-50]

This is quite proper and perfectly orthodox; and it is clear that he regards his duties as completely discharged without there being any question of laxity. One should simply admire Beroul's flair for narrative synthesis—one of his consistently strong points—and not argue that he ought to have described a full-blown confession, as other poets did, although it was not strictly necessary.[20]

So far, then, we find nothing strange, still less questionable, in Ogrin's behaviour. If at all it is now that the real problem begins, with the assertion that 'por honte oster et mal covrir Doit on un poi par bel mentir' (vv. 2353-4) and the subsequent reasoning. But it must be borne in mind that at this precise moment the terms of the problem are radically altered. The lovers have purged themselves of their sin, which Ogrin metaphorically buries in vv. 2345-50. They have become pure again, but adultery is a sin which consists of more than the adulterers' guilt in the eyes of God; it also involves a third party, the deceived husband, and the injury done to him is irreparable on the moral plane. All that can be done is to reunite the divided couple as best one can. This is about to be effected, and since the two sinners' offence against God has been erased by His infinite mercy the religious problem is closed and, let us repeat, in a completely proper and orthodox manner.

There remain several other considerations: the social effects of the sin on the community at large, the dishonour of both king and queen, the irregular and scandalous situation which has arisen through their separation, Tristran's social position, and the apparent triumph of the sinners. None of this has anything to do with the destiny of their souls or with their consciences; it is no longer a matter of *pechié* but of *honte*. At this level it is not that Ogrin's attitude is flexible; it is his specific duty, imposed on him by the whole ecclesiastical tradition, not to aggravate with misplaced rigidity the social disorder created by the sin, but now that the sin is a thing of the past to put things right at all cost, even at the cost of stating that a sin has not been committed when it would be more accurate to say that, from the religious point of view, it has been annulled and is in a sense non-existent. In this way the *mentir* not only acquires smaller proportions and slighter significance but is also authorised by tradition, and indeed by morality, as a reliable means of preventing the sin from having any further repercussions on society.[21]

This examination of the two Ogrin scenes shows that, contrary to the most widely held view, they really include nothing that clashes with the appropriate ethical standards; it also shows that the moral problems raised by sin and guilt make little impression on Beroul's imagination and therefore have little significance in the actions and sufferings of his characters. This is because their moral sensitivity is slow to awaken and in any case is never of more than secondary importance. The Ogrin episodes are thus an essential turning point in the romance, not because they represent the culmination of an intense torment in the characters' consciences, but because they are the starting point for scenes the first of which is intensely dramatic and the second functionally necessary. Besides this they are contrapuntally linked to each other by a subtle, effective interplay of echoes and antitheses.

Furthermore, our conclusion seems to be confirmed by different but parallel considerations if we turn our attention to other moments in which the poet's insight into his heroes' hearts is clearly revealed.

If they had been uneasy about the sin, this could have shown through as a sense of guilt or at least a tangle of conflicting feelings in the lovers' relations with Marc, the innocent victim of their actions. But we find nothing of this, because it is another problem of which the poet seems to be barely aware. At times he does mention Tristran's position *vis-à-vis* the king, but only in passing. When the hero is caught red-handed and seized he decides not to resist:

> Ne fust por vos acorocier,
> Cist plez fust ja venduz molt chier;
> Ja, por lor eulz, ne le pensasent
> Que ja de lor mains m'atochasent;
> Mais envers vos n'en ai je rien.   [vv. 789-93]

This is merely a tactical move based on the assumption that he will be granted an *escondit*, as is explained shortly afterwards:

> Bien se quidoit par chanp defendre.
> Por ce ne vout il vers le roi
> Mesfaire soi por nul desroi;
> Qar, s'il seüst ce que en fut
> Et ce qui avenir lor dut,
> Il les eüst tüez toz trois,
> Ja ne les en gardast li rois.   [vv. 818-24]

The evidence, then, would suggest an objective respect for Marc as king rather than as a blood relation, were it not for Dinas's words, which indicate another dimension:

> Vos estes oncle et il tes niés;
> A vos ne mesferoit il mie.
> Mais vos barons, en sa ballie
> S'il les trovout, nes vilonast,
> Encor en ert ta terre en gast.   [vv. 1104-8]

Even so, we cannot help but see the formal nature of Tristran's respect, which has nothing to do with his inner feelings or still less with any sense of guilt or any other form of moral complication.[22] Here again, then, the poet passes over an opportunity for moral and psychological analysis. There is nothing to suggest that he regards the complex relationship into which the adultery throws the three protagonists as anything more than a purely external situation.

3
Marc

This conclusion is certainly correct as regards Tristran and Yseut, but not as regards Marc. If the lovers can remain oblivious to everything in their passion and suffering, if they possess an autonomy of interests which can detach them from the world and thus from the king, Marc on the other hand has no *raison d'être* other than his position *vis-à-vis* the lovers. And sure enough, while any search for verses attesting concern in the lovers for Marc's feelings will be fruitless, we are considerably better informed of the king's reactions, since it is only in this light that he can have a human, individual personality of his own.

Beroul gives us a brief portrait of Marc in Perinis' words to Artu:

> Li rois n'a pas coraige entier,
> Senpres est ci et senpres la. [vv. 3432-3]

Certainly the king is forced into these vacillations by the traditional structure of the romance, but we must observe their nature and significance in Beroul's treatment. Even his feelings towards his nephew and his wife do not really seem to be very fully analysed, since Beroul's psychology, as will by now be clear, is expressed in situations and actions rather than analyses or lucid, rational presentations.[23] We no longer possess the initial sections in which the relationship between uncle and nephew was developed and consolidated before the appearance of Yseut, but we have no reason not to suppose that like other writers Beroul emphasised the tone of almost father-and-son affection. Even in our fragment Marc's affection still seems deeply felt, and never disappears for more than a short while. His anger flares up instantly at the discovery of the blood on the flour and in the bed, and again at the proof of the lovers' guilt, but immediately afterwards he begins slowly to calm down until his mood becomes one of sorrow. When Tristran is caught, his uncle's words are incisive, sarcastic and irrevocable:

> 'Trop par a ci veraie enseigne;
> Provez estes,' ce dist li rois,
> 'Vostre escondit n'i vaut un pois.
> Certes, Tristran, demain, ce quit,
> Soiez certains d'estre destruit.' [vv. 778-82]

His silence at Tristran's entreaties is even more expressive, and when another character begs him to show mercy his refusal is still expressed 'par ire' (vv. 888 and 1126). But only a short time later, when Husdent is continually howling because he has lost his master, the king is drawn towards his absent nephew by a deep but unexpressed longing:

> Li rois a dit, a son corage—
> Por son seignor croit qu'il enrage—
> 'Certes, molt a li chiens grant sens:
> Je ne quit mais q'en nostre tens,
> En la terre de Cornoualle,
> Ait chevalier qui Tristran valle.' [vv. 1467–72]

Later, when a forester runs to tell him that the lovers are sleeping together in the wood, and their guilt is proved beyond any shadow of doubt:

> Li rois l'entent, boufe et sospire,
> Esfreez est, forment s'aïre. [vv. 1895–6]

And in the secrecy of his own mind he prepares to take the couple by surprise:

> Li rois a fait sa sele metre,
> S'espee çaint, sovent regrete
> A lui tot sol la cuvertise
> Que Tristran fist, quant il l'ot prisse
> Yseut la bele o le cler vis,
> O qui s'en est alé fuitis.
> S'il les trove, molt les menace,
> Ne laira pas ne lor mesface.
> Molt est li rois acoragiez
> De destruire; c'est granz pechiez. [vv. 1943–52]

His judgement is again harsh ('la cuvertise Que Tristran fist') and his intentions sanguinary ('molt est li rois acoragiez De destruire'), but his inner nature does not share these resolute attitudes and veils his anger with its customary melancholy affection ('sovent regrete'); later his raised sword does not fall on the sleeping lovers. When Tristran is bold enough to carry in person the letter written by Ogrin to the window of the king's chamber, Marc springs to his feet while his nephew is retreating and

> Par trois foiz l'apela en haut:
> 'Por Deu, beaus niés, ton oncle atent!' [vv. 2472–3]

With this endearing allusion to their blood relationship Beroul again expresses, in his economical narrative style, an undercurrent of affection, still almost involuntary and lacking the strength to proclaim its existence as an antidote to the bitterness of thwarted love and wounded honour. But eventually the relationships become settled with Yseut's return to court, implying recognition of the innocence claimed by the lovers, Tristran is banished on the barons' advice, and the wicked barons return to office; then Marc's regret for his nephew's absence explodes violently:

> Cent dehez ait par mié la cane
> Qui me rova de lui partir! [vv. 3068–9]

It also hovers over the recurrent motif:

> Par vos est il hors du païs. [v. 3065]
> Lui ai chacié. [v. 3067]
> G'en ai por vos chacié Tristran. [v. 3136][24]

The king's feelings for Yseut are still more delicate and tender. His *mautalent* towards her is mentioned at the very moment in which he renounces it (v. 2660). After hearing the barons' counsel he orders his chaplain to waste no time in writing the letter of pardon:

> Hastez le brief; molt sui destroiz,
> Molt a ne vi Yseut la gente;
> Trop a mal trait en sa jovente. [vv. 2642–4]

The last time he saw her was in the wood, sleeping beside Tristran, when he used his gloves to exclude the ray of light falling on her and exchanged rings with her.

Thus the poet seems to have interpreted the figure of Marc in a consistent, successful manner, neither as the *cocu* of the *fabliau*, cheated and content,[25] nor as the cruel tyrant typified in the lord of Fayel or En Ramon de Castel Roussillon. From an emotional point of view his personality is clearly defined, quick to anger when anger is almost demanded by the situation but ready to heed the counsel of his heart, which rises above logic and proof.[26] Even in his characterisation of Marc Beroul chose not to emphasise the reaction to the lovers' conduct in terms of sin or even of an offence to the marriage, despite the fact that Marc is the injured husband, and to the blood bond: Marc's only view of the sin is the one we have seen, of *cuvertise*, a strictly feudal term and the opposite of another equally typical concept, *franchise*.[27]

We should therefore turn from the moral to the social plane, or at least from the plane of transcendental morality to that of the ethics of social life, close to, and almost coinciding with, legal considerations. On this level another decisive factor influences Marc's actions, the intervention of the three barons. Here we are concerned only with its effect on the king's character, and it is in this context that we can understand his lack of *coraige entier* mentioned by Perinis. But we must be careful not to confuse two different points of view: the three wicked barons with the pressure they bring to bear determine Marc's actions but not his feelings. They oppose the promptings of his heart by a series of arguments and proofs which, as we shall see, are juridically unassailable, but which cannot modify the king's inner being. Marc's inconsistency exists only in practice, because his brief and violent fits of anger are not enough to suggest inconsistency in his feelings. And in practice it is inevitable; it is an unwilling submission to the duties which feudal law imposes even on a king. In Marc's violent reaction to the barons' renewed demand for an *escondit* by Yseut, when Beroul feels the need to give a clearer picture of Marc's character, he adds these verses to those already quoted, and thus clarifies his inner attitude:

Vos me sorquerez, ce me poise;
Quel mervelle que l'en si toise! [vv. 3071–2]

N'avez cure de mon deport;
O vos ne puis plus avoir pes. [vv. 3074–5]

With these sentences, which are, as usual, fairly calm and deliberate, the poet clarifies from within what Perinis judges from without as inconsistency, that poetic nucleus in the figure of Marc which has so often escaped the reader's notice. For him as well as for the lovers, life means suffering, tribulations and lost peace of mind. The experience of being a suffering human being, which Beroul denies to the antipathetic characters but grants to the hero and the heroine, whom he surrounds with poignant sympathy, is also granted to Marc, and despite the difficulties involved it redeems the characterisation of him both on the level of imaginative interpretation and on that of richness in human qualities.

With this not unimportant critical conclusion we can stop, but not without noting that once again we have found Beroul pushing into the background the purely ethical aspect of the lovers' drama, an aspect which does not seem to appeal to his imagination or to have much weight in his view of the world. Nevertheless, the virile, impassioned tone of his narrative style implies an involvement which is not in the least irresponsible; thus in the next chapter we must try and track down the mental attitude so vigorously implied in his poetry.

Notes

1 On this problem see in particular Le Gentil ('La Légende de Tristan' and 'L'Episode du Morois'), with whom, as will be seen, I am in only partial agreement, and who moreover formulates the problem in a different manner.
2 Cf. vv. 2133 *et seq.*
3 In Thomas (cf. Bédier's edition, vol. 2, p. 226, and Fourrier's *Le Courant Réaliste*, p. 67, but, in opposition to their views, Pauphilet's *Le Legs du moyen âge*, p. 129). Marx (in *Nouvelles Recherches*, pp. 281–8), maintains that this version is the earlier, and is supported by Le Gentil in 'L'Episode du Morois', p. 271; the latter, however, somewhat arbitrarily attributes to Beroul the idea that if the potion did not create their love it did at least transform it into unbridled passion. As can be seen from the passages quoted, there is no suggestion in Beroul that any form of love emerged before the taking of the potion.
4 Nor are Yseut's reasons any different later, when she is assailed by a flood of regret: 'Je sui roïne, mais le non En ai perdu par ma poison Que nos beümes en la mer.' These are her words in vv. 2205-7, but cf. again vv. 2217-20 and above all Tristran's words in vv. 2257-60.
5 'Mais si, en fin de compte, la roue de Fortune est le symbole de la fatalité qui détruit les puissances de chair sans qu'intervienne la notion de mérite ou de démérite, les âmes n'appartiennent qu'à Dieu: avec l'aide de la grâce, elles peuvent travailler à leur salut' (Frappier, *La Mort le Roi Artu*, p. xx).
6 Gilson (*The Spirit of Medieval Philosophy*, pp. 339 *et seq.*) contrasts the Greek and Christian notions of sin, which are differentiated by precisely this awareness or unawareness in the sinner; while the Christian sinner knows what good is and therefore knows he is sinning, in the Socratic and Aristotelian view the sinner is not conscious of what he is doing. It should also be noted that, in another sphere, Aristotle considered it much better for the tragic hero to be unaware of the terrible nature of his actions (*Poetics*, XIV, 1453b–1454a).
7 Marc could have accepted the inevitable and left Yseut to Tristran.
8 V. 960; and cf. vv. 2380 *et seq.*
9 One could also add a passage which is not directly relevant to the problem of the adultery but has considerable significance in its tone

of invocation, which almost seems addressed to a pagan god. When Tristran sees Godoïne's face at the window of Yseut's chamber:

> Ha! Dex, vrai roi, tant riche trait
> Ai d'arc et de seete fait;
> Consentez moi que cest ne falle!
> Un des trois feus de Cornoualle
> Voi, a grant tort, par la defors.
> Dex, qui le tuen saintisme cors
> Por le pueple meïs a mort,
> Lai moi venjance avoir du tort
> Que cil felon muevent vers moi! [vv. 4463–71]

10 Nor is it ever said that divine aid is justified by the potion or the lovers' freedom from responsibility which could be derived from it.

11 A quick glance at the dictionary of Tobler and Lommatzsch, vol. 4, coll. 105–6, will demonstrate the distinctly juridical use of *garantir* in *Roland*, v. 1864, *Lanval*, v. 466, and above all *Fergus*, v. 32, from which it emerges that *garantir une contree* is one of a lord's duties. There are also countless passages in which the verb is referred, as it is here, to God.

12 Quoted in Gilson, *op. cit.*, pp. 346–7 and n. 4. For the relationship between the will and the intention, its essential component, cf. *ibid.*, pp. 347 *et seq.*

13 Cf. Gilson, *op. cit.*, pp. 348 *et seq.*; and Bréhier, *La philosophie du moyen âge*, p. 161.

14 This passage could be interpreted differently. In his first edition, Muret printed: 'Se ele m'aime (en bone foi, Vos n'entendez pas la raison), S'el m'aime, c'est par la poison.' But Muret and Defourques have the same text and punctuation as Ewert and it does seem rather forced to relate 'en bone foi' to 'vos n'entendez pas', since it would thus be superfluous. So I accept Ewert's interpretation as the right one but it seems only fair to point out the debatable nature of a point which is so important for the interpretation of the whole episode.

15 The opening passage in which Ogrin warns Tristran of the proclamation should be regarded as due to narrative necessities; there is nothing which would permit us to attribute to Ogrin the wish to put the lovers on their guard in order to help them evade punishment, though even this would be quite legitimate.

16 Cf. Jonin's *Les Personnages Féminins*, pp. 348 *et seq.*

17 So that this second meeting fits in better with the traditional motif of the visit to the hermit for advice, which has its prototype in St Brendan's visit to Barintus (cf. Waters's edition, p. lxxxiv n., where various other examples are mentioned) and later recurs in *Girart de Roussillon*, giving rise to Murrel's excessively hypothetical arguments in *Girart de Roussillon and the Tristran Poems*.

18 Which was not absent even in the first encounter, since he broke his own rules and sheltered the couple for a night in his hermitage.
19 'Ge ne di pas, a vostre entente, Que de Tristran jor me repente Que je ne l'aim de bone amor Et com amis, sanz desanor' [vv. 2325–8].
20 Jonin, *op. cit.*, pp. 352 *et seq.*, in particular insists on this. But 'un poète n'est pas obligé de tout dire et de tout expliquer' (Frappier, *Les Chansons de Geste* . . ., p. 168), and this is why we have no right to accuse him of convenient ethical simplification of the kind cynically propounded in the *Lai du conseil*, vv. 504 *et seq*.
21 The popular conscience seems to be quite convinced of the legitimacy of Ogrin's action, as can be seen in the proverbs 'Bon fait mentir pour paix avoir' and 'Bons mentirs a la fois aiue' (Morawski's collection, Nos. 280 and 292). In the case of Guinevere's love for Lancelot, Arthur reproaches Gawain for not bringing the insult to his notice; even though the adultery is still continuing, Gawain, the perfect knight, replies, 'Certes . . . onques ma traïson ne vos fist mal' (*Mort le Roi Artu*, section 87, 59–61). So even he deceives *par bel* and, unlike Ogrin, while the adultery is still continuing. Ogrin finds a stalwart supporter in Le Gentil ('L'Episode du Morois', pp. 273–4), who appropriately cites the Pope's intervention, again in the *Mort Artu*, to persuade the king to take Guinevere back; but Le Gentil himself feels that the hermit goes beyond the bounds of orthodoxy, even though it may be for the purpose of restoring order and of satisfying himself that Tristran and Yseut have fully renounced their indulgence in the sin and the fatalistic view of their passion. But there seems to be no specific evidence to suggest that the two lovers' reason for not wishing to expiate their sin is that they do not consider themselves guilty; the religious consequences of the sin are of no interest to the poet or, therefore, to his characters. The text provides no confirmation for the idea that Ogrin regards the restitution of Yseut to Marc as the first in a series of steps along the road towards the lovers' renunciation of each other.
22 The only time Tristran seems to have a clear notion of the offence against Marc is immediately after the three years have ended: cf. vv. 2195–8 (and cf. v. 2774). Pauphilet, in *Le Legs du moyen âge*, p. 128, gives a penetrating justification for this fact; among other things he writes, 'Conception assez simpliste, mais d'un dur réalisme: si l'histoire de Tristran et d'Iseut est celle de la toute-puissance de l'amour, il est juste et beau que cette toute-puissance ne rencontre, dans l'âme des héros, aucun obstacle.' It should be noted that Lancelot in the *Mort Artu* is similarly superficial in his declarations of innocence and his lack of remorse; but of course he is not even a blood relation of the king.
23 Guerrieri Crocetti, in *La leggenda di Tristano*, p. 111, wrote that Beroul's characters 'never summon enough concentration, even in solitary meditation, to read into the lowest depths of their own hearts'.

24 Cf. also vv. 3085-6, 3134-5, 3195 and 3197 *et seq*.
25 For the opening scenes, which are slightly out of keeping with this characterisation, cf. chapter 5.
26 Pauphilet, *op. cit.*, pp. 131-3, makes some very fine observations on the figure of Marc.
27 Compare too Thomas, Sneyd fragment 1, vv. 137 *et seq*. It must be added that Marc is a striking exception to the rule that Beroul's characters fall into two groups, friends and enemies of the lovers; therefore for him characterisation simply through his reactions to the *aventure*. which we mentioned on p. 60, is invalid. This enables us to see how difficult it must have been to characterise this complex figure, and makes the result more considerable. As a matter of fact Marc's feelings and actions depend more than those of any other character on ignorance of the potion and its inexorable power. 'La beauté de ce rôle de Marc, et je dirai son indispensable vérité, c'est justement cette région douteuse où il erre, si humainement, de l'aveuglement à la fureur et de la tendresse à la cruauté' (Pauphilet, *op. cit.*, p. 133).

4
Feudal forms and human suffering

Religious and moral considerations are almost totally foreign to Beroul's outlook on life, which tends towards evaluations in completely human, material and social terms. This does not mean that he slips into mediocrity, into plain common sense, into colourless, non-literary preoccupations; on the contrary, Beroul's personality comes over extremely clearly in this sphere. We should therefore look into it more closely.

I
The theme of the escondit

One theme which colours our fragment from beginning to end is that of the *escondit* by the guilty lovers. It appears as early as v. 131, in which Tristran complains about the king and says:

Il ne me lait sol escondire;

straight after this he makes a specific suggestion:

Dame, ore li dites errant
Qu'il face faire un feu ardant,
Et je m'en entrerai el ré;
Se ja un poil en ai bruslé
De la haire qu'avrai vestu,
Si me laist tot ardoir u feu;
Qar je sai bien n'a de sa cort
Qui a batalle o moi s'en tort.   [vv. 149–56]

From this point onwards the continual recurrence of the words *escondit* and *escondire*, *deraisne* and *deraisnier*, *soi alegier* and *esligier* shows how important and fundamental the theme is. As soon as the problem of the lovers' guilt arises again from the ruse of the flour on the floor, the theme of juridical self-defence reappears negatively in Marc's mouth in the verse 'Votre escondit n'i vaut un pois', which Tristran immediately echoes by begging compassion for the queen:

Qar il n'a home en ta meson,
Se disoit ceste traïson

> Que pris eüse drüerie
> O la roïne par folie,
> Ne m'en trovast en chanp, armé.[1]   [vv. 799–803]

It is for the same reason that Tristran allows himself to be bound by the three wicked barons: he is sure that once he gets as far as the *escondit* no one will dare fight against him.[2] After the long parenthesis of the flight to the wood, the weakening of the effect of the potion results in the renewed wish for a settlement; this is how Tristran presents to Yseut the probable terms of an agreement:

> Bele amie, se je peüse,
> Par consel que je en eüse,
> Faire au roi Marc acordement,
> Qu'il pardonnast son mautalent[3]
> Et qu'il preïst nostre escondit,
> C'onques nul jor, n'en fait n'en dit,
> N'oi o vos point de drüerie
> Qui li tornast a vilanie,
> N'a chevalier en son roiaume,
> Ne de Lidan tresque en Dureaume,
> S'il voloit dire que amor
> Eüse o vos por deshonor,
> Ne m'en trovast en chanp, armé.[4]   [vv. 2223–35]

Ogrin's *conseil*[5] is identical with this, and later in the letter written in Tristran's name by the hermit we find:

> Ge sui tot prest que gage en donge,
> Qui li voudroit blasme lever,[6]
> Lié alegier contre mon per,
> Beau sire, a pié ou a cheval—
> Chascuns ait armes et cheval—
> Qu'onques amor nen out vers moi,
> Ne je vers lui, par nul desroi.
> Se je ne l'en puis alegier
> Et en ta cort moi deraisnier,
> Adonc me fai devant ton ost;
> N'i a baron que je t'en ost.   [vv. 2568–78]

Neither in the barons' counsel to Marc nor in his reply is there any suggestion of an *escondit*,[7] but when Tristran gives Yseut back to Marc he says,

> Ci voi les homes de ta terre
> Et, oiant cus, te vuel requerre

Feudal forms and human suffering

> Que me sueffres a esligier
> Et en ta cort moi deraisnier
> C'onques o lié n'oi drüerie,
> Ne ele o moi, jor de ma vie.
> Acroire t'a l'en fait mençonge;
> Mais, se Dex joie et bien me donge,
> Onques ne firent jugement,
> Conbatre a pié ou autrement,
> Dedenz ta cort, se ge t'en sueffre;
> Se sui dannez, si m'art en soffre.
> Et, se je m'en pus faire saus,
> Qu'il n'i ait chevelu ne chaus . . . [*lacuna*]   [vv. 2853-66]

It might be wondered whether this is in fact an *escondit* or yet another, unanswered, request for one. Tristran's use of 'requerre' and the fact that it is not mentioned again in the negotiations make the latter hypothesis the more likely, but we should bear in mind that the only reason why all the knights of Cornwall have been assembled at the Gué Aventuros is to witness this declaration, the one requirement for a reconciliation.[8] The convocation formula should not be overlooked:

> Devant le Gué Aventuros
> *Iert* pris acordement de nos.   [vv. 2747-8]

So the reconciliation is not established by the exchange of letters, but must be completed by Tristran's declaration, which brings the previously agreed conditions into effect. This interpretation is confirmed by Marc himself when he objects to the wicked barons' coming to ask for a further *escondit* by Yseut:

> Chascun de vos que li demande?
> N'offri Tristran li a defendre?
> Ainz n'en osastes armes prendre.   [vv. 3062-4]

And still more clearly:

> Seignors, molt a encor petit
> Que vos oïstes *l'escondit*
> Que mes niés fist de ma mollier;
> Ne vosistes escu ballier.   [vv. 3125-8]

Perinis tells Artu how

> La roïne s'est acordee
> O son seignor, n'i a celee;

> Sire, la ou il s'acorderent,
> Tuit li baron du reigne i erent.
> Tristran s'offri a esligier
> Et la roïne a deraisnier,
> Devant le roi, de loiauté;
> Ainz nus de tele loiauté
> Ne vout armes saisir ne prendre.[9] [vv. 3415-23]

 This is the last we see of the theme of Tristran's *escondit*, but it is already intertwined with that of an *escondit* or *deraisne* by Yseut,[10] which in its turn extends over more than 1200 verses. We shall examine the two related themes separately. The first and most important conclusion is obvious: whereas we found very little consideration given to the theme of sin, we find that the theme of legal justification is given strikingly full treatment and the sort of prominence we might have expected for the former theme. We descend from the divine to the human plane. The poet is not interested in resolving the conflict of conscience, to which he pays little attention, whereas he thinks it essential to reconcile the conflict between the lovers and society. The two problems are undeniably connected, in the first place because they have a common root in the passion of Tristran and Yseut, but also because the particular juridical forms in question presuppose a relationship between the law and God. Tristran follows a procedure which can be summarised thus: he solemnly and publicly declares 'C'onques o lié n'oi drüerie, Ne ele o moi, jor de ma vie,' a formula which, although more general, is equivalent to that in vv. 2228-30, where he adds 'n'en fait n'en dit' and 'drüerie qui li tornast a vilanie', and is practically identical with that found in the letter (vv. 2573-4). This declaration can be contested by the witnesses, but they must be prepared to fight the consequent judicial duel.[11] We should note at the outset that, unlike Yseut, Tristran lies openly but does not directly submit to God's judgement; invocation of God remains the responsibility of any opponent who may come forward. This certainly does not happen by chance: it is true that the hero bases his declaration on the knowledge that no one will dare challenge him to a duel, but this means precisely that he approaches the lie on a verbal, formalistic level, in the knowledge that he will not be called upon to defend it in a duel.[12] It is obviously an extremely sophistical distinction, but one which is formally valid—we know how formalistic medieval juridical practice was. That this is not an over-subtle distinction of our own can be proved from the *rendez-vous épié*, during which

Tristran suggests an *escondit* for the first time (as far as we can tell), but as a direct judgement of God through the ordeal of fire, since he says no one would dare fight against him. The purpose of this speech is to convince the king by the use of hyperbole and is empty verbiage rather than a serious proposal. It is intended to convince Marc by an immediate and powerful emotional impact, but is not meant to lead to action. In spite of the barons' continuing hostility, Tristran does not dare to renew this proposal later in the story since it commits him to undergoing a specific and decisive test in which he may fail.[13]

Thus the religious issue is once again evaded, though not ignored, and the struggle is played out on the juridical plane, which is *par excellence* the social plane. The key to everything is no longer the guilty conscience but the proof of guilt. This proof seems to be furnished by the ruse of the flour on the floor. Only the dwarf sees the lovers together ('a la lune Bien vit josté erent ensenble Li dui amant'), not the king, who is also the judge; but the blood from Tristran's wound stains the sheets and the flour:

> Ha! Dex, qel duel que la roïne
> N'avot les dras du lit ostez!
> Ne fust la nuit nus d'eus provez;
> Se ele s'en fust apensee,
> Molt eüst bien s'anor tensee.   [vv. 750–4]

Here the poet clearly feels that the lovers are confronted by overwhelming evidence against them and will be unable to *tenser* their honour; this is why he hastens to assure the reader that they will come to no harm. Since the lovers have been caught red-handed, Marc has the right to condemn them summarily, without permitting any *escondit*.[14] None the less Tristran writes to Marc that he has condemned them 'a gran tort' (v. 2587), 'a tort' (v. 2596); by making this claim long after they have been caught *in flagrante delicto* he can argue the need for an *escondit*. Moreover, God's intervention in their favour, which is here specifically mentioned,[15] seems to confirm that the lovers were wrongly condemned by Marc.

2
Yseut's deraisne

The action is once more set in motion by the three barons, who ask for an *escondit* on the part of Yseut;[16] this demand not only determines the course of events but also sets their tone, because it is completely illegal and thus gives final proof of the villainy of the barons, who will very shortly be killed. Their proposal is as follows:

> Rois, or entent nostre parole:
> Se la roïne a esté fole,
> El n'en fist onques escondit.
> S'a vilanie vos est dit;
> Et li baron de ton païs
> T'en ont par mainte foiz requis,
> Qu'il vuelent bien s'en escondie
> Qu'on Tristran n'ot sa drüerie;
> Escondire se doit c'on ment.
> Si l'en fai faire jugement
> Et enevoies l'en requier,
> Priveement, a ton couchier;
> S'ele ne s'en veut escondire,
> Lai l'en aler de ton enpire. [vv. 3041–54]

Marc's reaction, which we have frequently had cause to mention, is one of violent disapproval, and by insisting on the complete adequacy of Tristran's *escondit*, whatever its formal defects, he makes it clear that the barons' demand has no legal foundation.[17] Indeed, when the three barons return to withdraw their demand the poet says of the king,

> S'il eüst or la force o soi,
> La fusent pris, ce dit, tuit troi. [vv. 3107–8]

And what is more, the three barons offer no other legal justification for their interference than their right to tender advice to the king, which they share with all the king's barons, and which is hardly relevant here:

> L'en devroit par droit son seignor
> Consellier; tu nos sez mal gré. [vv. 3112–13]

They admit that the king is entitled to act as he chooses and even ask him for pardon:

> Quant ne nos croiz, fai ton plaisir;
> Assez nos en orras taisir.
> Icest maltalent nos pardonne. [vv. 3119–21]

But the king has chosen to regard the illegal request as an offence and decides to punish the three barons:

Or gerpisiez tote ma terre.[18]   [v. 3131]

Having rejected any other settlement ('Mais n'i porent plai encontrer', v. 3141), the king becomes angry and goes away:

> Cil s'en partent du roi par mal;
> Forz chasteaus ont, bien clos de pal,
> Soiant sor roche, sor haut pui;
> A lor seignor feront ennui,
> Se la chose n'est amendee.[19]   [vv. 3143-7]

As we can see, the new demand is made and treated from the purely juridical angle and as a result brings the situation to the brink of feudal war. It is obvious that the barons are in the wrong and the king fully in the right. In fact this time it is Yseut who spontaneously offers to submit to an *escondit*, which, being voluntary, will be of her own formulation;[20] and it is she who asks that Artu and his court shall be present so that they can act as witnesses and guarantors in case of further dispute.[21] So Yseut's declaration, too, is worked out on a precise legal basis, which is more than scrupulously observed.[22] When the appointed day finally arrives Artu expresses himself severely to Marc:

> 'Rois Marc,' fait il, 'qui te conselle
> Tel outrage si fait mervelle;
> Certes,' fait il, 'sil se desloie.
> Tu es legier a metre en voie.'   [vv. 4141-4]

Against the wicked barons' *desloier*[23] Artu sets the queen's spontaneous desire to justify herself:

> La franche Yseut, la debonere,
> Ne veut respit ne terme avoir.   [vv. 4150-1]

Having thus clearly interpreted the facts of the situation and having reaffirmed that he will guarantee observance of the outcome of the trial, Artu concludes by setting out the procedure to be followed and its legal consequences:

> Or oiez, roi: qui ara tort,
> La roïne vendra avant,
> Si qel verront petit et grant,
> Et si jurra o sa main destre,
> Sor les corsainz, au roi celestre

> Qu'el onques n'ot amor conmune
> A ton nevo, ne deus ne une,
> Que l'en tornast a vilanie,[24]
> N'amor ne prist par puterie.
> Dan Marc, trop a ice duré;
> Qant ele avra eisi juré,
> Di tes barons qu'il aient pes.' [vv. 4158–69]

Marc agrees that in allowing the *deraisne* to take place he has gone beyond the legal requirement[25] and when all is ready Artu again repeats to the queen 'de qoi on vos apele':

> Que Tristran n'ot vers vos amor
> De puteé ne de folor
> Fors cele que devoit porter
> Envers son oncle et vers sa per. [vv. 4193–6]

As we know, Yseut in fact uses a different formula which permits her to tell the truth, though of course in a misleading form. She has Tristran disguise himself as a leper and carry her through the mire of the Mal Pas so that she can honestly say,

> Si m'aït Dex et saint Ylaire,
> Ces reliques, cest saintuaire,
> Totes celes qui ci ne sont
> Et tuit icil de par le mont,
> Q'entre mes cuises n'entra home,
> Fors le ladre qui fist soi some,
> Qui me porta outre les guez,
> Et li rois Marc mes esposez;
> Ces deus ost de mon soirement.
> Ge n'en ost plus de tote gent;
> De deus ne me pus escondire:
> Du ladre, du roi Marc, mon sire.
> Li ladres fu entre mes janbes
> [*lacuna*]
> Qui voudra que je plus en face,
> Tote en sui preste en ceste place. [vv. 4201–16]

To us it seems that an oath of this nature must immediately appear ambiguous, at least to the three barons, if only because it departs from the formula prescribed by Artu. But in fact right from the start Yseut reserves the right to choose the form of her oath ('Escondit mais ne lor ferai, Fors un que je deviserai', vv. 3233–4).

Feudal forms and human suffering

Nor does Artu lay down a precise formula: he simply sets out 'de qoi on vos apele'. Yseut's oath is not vaguer but more specific than Artu's words, and this is also the opinion of the spectators:

> Tant en a fait aprés droiture!
> Plus i a mis que ne disoient
> Ne que li fel ne requeroient. [vv. 4220-2][26]

To the listeners the mention of the *ladre* seems to refer to a detail which is in itself insignificant and only serves to emphasise Yseut's scrupulous precision, while the exclusion of Tristran seems to be clearly contained in 'Ge n'en ost plus de tote gent'. The fairness and completeness of the oath are recognised by all those present, including the three barons, who leave the court the objects of everyone's hatred.[27]

Once again we cannot deny that the situation is built up around what is basically a moral issue, but what we can say is that the narrator is not interested in the moral aspect and does not make the slightest mention of it, even in a comment on the oath itself. Here too the claims of conscience seem to be replaced by those of the law, which are again fully respected as a whole and meticulously observed in their detail, with a true lawyer's scrupulousness. Jonin[28] attempts to explain away the mention of St Ylaire in the oath by some theory he has on marriage, but in view of what we have said this seems pointless: the taste for such pregnant allusions seems completely foreign to our author.[29] What matters to the narrator is apparently not Yseut's moral position when she has to make a false oath to save herself; for one thing, she is not forced into the oath at all, but voluntarily submits to a test she could easily avoid, and conducts herself with greater dignity than Marc himself. The episode has entirely different functions in the overall structure of the romance and has been misinterpreted precisely because critics have attempted to find in it problems which it could, and possibly should, contain but does not, and have not given due consideration to its significance in its proper context.

3
The wicked barons

The functional aspect of the Blanche Lande episode can be studied from two different points of view, and from both points of view the part it plays in the story is clear. We shall first examine it as a moment in the broader theme of the three barons and later return to consider it in the context of the lovers' situation.

We have already noted several times the importance in the whole romance[30] of the theme of the lovers' enemies, and it is worth while examining it as a whole. It appears as early as v. 26 of our text, in Yseut's words to Tristran:

> Se li felon de cest'enor,[31]
> Por qui jadis vos conbatistes
> O le Morhout, quant l'oceïstes
> Li font acroire, ce me senble,
> Que nos amors jostent ensemble,
> Sire, vos n'en avez talent;
> Ne je, par Deu omnipotent,
> N'ai corage de drüerie
> Qui tort a nule vilanie.[32]   [vv. 26-34]

We shall not here examine every passage in which the theme comes to the surface; and we shall not repeat our earlier observations on the maledictions of the lovers, the 'chorus' and the poet himself which generally punctuate the theme, making it abundantly clear what is the narrator's, and therefore the audience's, emotional attitude towards the lovers' enemies, and in what light they are presented. What concerns us here is the objective angle.

How many of the barons are hostile to Tristran? We return here to the problem of the anonymous enemy killed in the wood by Governal, and later apparently still alive. At first no individuals stand out from the body of Cornish barons, who all seem to be opposed to Tristran. Thus the hero makes no distinctions when he says to Yseut,

> Por ses felons vers moi s'aïre,
> Trop par fait mal qu'il les en croit;
> Deceü l'ont, gote ne voit.
> Molt les vi ja taisant et muz,
> Qant li Morhot fu ça venuz,
> Ou nen i out uns d'eus tot sous
> Qui osast prendre ses adous.   [vv. 132-8]

Marc, too, convinced of the lovers' innocence, realises that he indiscriminately 'mescroit les barons du reigne' (v. 288) and resolves that he 'N'en crerra mais Corneualan' (v. 468). It seems to be the dwarf who is responsible for the king's hiding in the pine tree

(vv. 265 *et seq.*), but Tristran has already been banned from the royal palace and although we are not explicitly told who is responsible for this it must still be 'les barons du reigne'. Only in v. 581 does the theme crystallise in specific characters:

> A la cort avoit trois barons,
> Ainz ne veïstes plus felons;
> Par soirement s'estoient pris
> Que, se li rois de son païs
> N'en faisot son nevo partir,
> Il nu voudroient mais soufrir,
> A lor chasteaus sus s'en trairoient
> Et au roi Marc gerre feroient. [vv. 581-8]

However, the three barons remain anonymous until their request for Yseut's *deraisne*:

> Devant lui vienent li felon,
> Godoïnë et Guenelon
> Et Danalain qui fu molt feus. [vv. 3137-9]

It has been argued that these proper names are an innovation which is the sign of a new 'hand'. But in fact we are bound to accept that this habit of suddenly naming characters as if their names were already familiar to us is typical of the immediacy of Beroul's narrative,[33] and once this is realised we can see that the purpose of the device is to bring the personalities of the traitor barons into ever sharper focus as the tale unfolds. There are at least three phases in this focusing process, in the first of which there is no discrimination at all between the wicked barons and all the other barons. In the intermediate stage the traitor barons are characterised as a group and distinguished from their fellows, as their activity becomes more complex and individualised, moving on from vague insinuation to the preparation of a specific trap. At the same time, as the narrative draws towards the lovers' capture, the narrator feels the need to balance the emergence of the wicked barons with a 'chorus', as well as certain characters such as Dinas, who will echo his own feelings of sympathy for the lovers. The focusing process culminates in the naming of the three barons, which finally establishes their individuality, when they are approaching their deaths, that is to say, when each of them is about to find himself face to face with his own personal destiny. It is worth emphasising the fact that their deaths occur not collectively but individually and on different occasions.

And what of the traitor who is already dead? We have already sought a justification for this episode in the context of the imaginative development of the romance.[34] We shall now add that, while the episode must have seemed necessary to Beroul to summarise figuratively the dangers of the life in the forest, there seems to be another reason which prevented him from reducing the number of traitor barons to two, which would have been the logical consequence: he seems to have some mysterious obsession, which must have a meaning, although we cannot say what it is, with the fact that the barons form a trinity. I am inclined to regard this as an obsession because it comes to the surface even where it seems superfluous. When Frocin is deciding to whom he will indirectly reveal the secret of Marc's ears, he chooses 'les trois de vos' (v. 1319);[35] when Husdent is chained up and howls ceaselessly, 'De Cornoualle baron troi En ont araisoné li roi' (vv. 1473–4). There is nothing to identify the three barons who on these occasions stand out from the crowd with the three traitor barons; this makes it all the more interesting that when narrative requirements demand that he single out a small group from the indistinct mass of the Cornish court he always fastens onto the number three.[36]

But let us re-examine vv. 581 *et seq.* The first notable element is that the three barons are called 'felon' without any apparent justification for this derogatory appellation. Later their wickedness will be explained in terms of their refusal to defend king and country against the Morholt, to which Tristran has already alluded in vv. 136 *et seq.*, quoted above. But the three barons' wickedness is not determined by any specific action or actions: it is inherent in their very nature, an immutable characteristic which renders them odious even leaving out of consideration each particular instance of their behaviour. Moreover, their behaviour is always conditioned by this unchangeable quality, to which they seem desperately and inexorably condemned by the poet right up to their deaths. But we shall be saying more of this later. What emerges from these verses is, once again, the juridical formulation of their activity, which is certainly not enough to redeem their nature but which is always seen lucidly and used by the poet to set their activity in the context of a definite established social pattern, though it does not run counter to the primary tendency of Beroul's ideal world.

The three wicked barons join forces 'par soirement' in order to get Tristran banished, and to take common action if he is not. Action directed to such a precise goal must have a legal justification and

Feudal forms and human suffering

must follow legal forms. In fact we are told that they have seen Tristran and Yseut in a garden 'en tel endroit Que nus hon consentir ne doit' (vv. 591–2) and then lying naked in the king's bed; but the generic *nus hon* implies not Marc, as could be thought, but themselves, for they tell the king immediately afterwards, 'Tes niés s'entraiment et Yseut, Savoir le puet qui c'onques veut' (vv. 607–8), which does not lead to the conclusion 'Avenge this grave offence against your honour' but 'Et *nos* nu volon mais sofrir' (v. 609) and 'Par foi, mais nu *consentiron*' (v. 614). They threaten that if Tristran is not banished for good

> Ne nos tenron a vos jamez,
> Si ne vos tendron nule pez;
> De nos voisins feron partir
> De cort, que nel poon soufrir.
> Or t'aron tost cest geu parti;
> Tote ta volenté nos di. [vv. 621–6]

To our way of thinking this is strange behaviour, in that the barons are evidently not common slanderers or informers but, as it were, depositaries of a right which has been infringed, and infringed (stranger still) by Marc, against whom they propose to wage war.

Marc's behaviour is equally foreign to our modern way of looking at things: we would expect either a stiff reaction to the informers or the wish to avenge himself on the culprits, beside which the existence and importance of the informers would fall into second place. On the contrary Marc sighs, bows his head, hesitates, and then speaks in unequivocally feudal terms ('Seignor, vos estes mi fael', v. 627) and although he refuses to believe Tristran's guilt without question ('molt me mervelle', v. 628), he says,

> Conseliez m'en, gel vos requier;
> Vos me devez bien consellier,
> Que servise perdre ne vuel.
> Vos savez bien, n'ai son d'orguel. [vv. 631–4]

These are revealing words which, by referring explicitly to the duty of vassals to advise their lord[37] and to their *servise* in times of danger,[38] confirm that the key to this episode is in feudal law. Even so, we should still be unable to understand what was the juridical basis for the barons' action if we ignored the motivation already given:

> Par foi, mais nu consentiron;
> Qar bien savon de verité

> Que tu consenz lor cruauté,
> Et tu sez bien ceste mervelle. [vv. 614-17]

These verses can be compared with the forester's words to the king:

> En une loge de Morroi
> Dorment estroit et enbrachiez.
> Vien tost, ja *seron* d'eus *vengiez*.
> Rois, s'or n'en prens aspre venjance,
> N'as droit en terre, sanz doutance. [vv. 1900-4]

Like the barons, the forester feels directly offended by the lovers' guilt, he too presents the king with a choice between vengeance and unworthiness, and to him as to the barons Marc is unable to reply.

It does not seem sufficient to reiterate the excellent observation that for a medieval poet honour is always a matter of public reputation rather than private integrity.[39] The fact is that the sovereign, in that he seems to be tacitly consenting to the lovers' sinful relationship,[40] is neglecting his duty of moral integrity and justice, and since he is morally unworthy he no longer has '*droit* en terre', as the forester says. In fact this situation is identical with that of Louis the Pious (though the latter is differently motivated) in the *Couronnement de Louis*:

> Reis qui de France porte corone d'or
> Prodom deit estre et vaillanz de son cors;
> Et s'il est om qui li face nul tort,
> Ne deit guarir ne a plain ne a bos
> De ci qu'il l'ait o recreant o mort:
> S'ensi nel fait, donc pert France son los;
> Ce dit l'estoire coronez est a tort.[41] [vv. 20-6]

Thus the situation is perfectly clear. The lovers' adultery certainly offends only Marc's honour but if he fails to avenge it he neglects his legal duty and therefore sullies himself in his turn with a very serious failing in that he mars his regal perfection and holds up his unworthiness for all to see. It is this and not directly Yseut's adultery which infringes the rights of both vassals and humble plebeians, and in fact what the barons directly demand is not punishment of the lovers' crime but only that Tristran's banishment shall render the crime impossible, removing any suspicion that Marc knows of it without punishing the offender, thus making himself unworthy.

It thus emerges clearly that Tristran's enemies act in a perfectly legitimate manner, exploiting rights which no one dreams of contesting. But this does not mean that they can evade the charge of wickedness. On the one hand their evil nature condemns them *a priori*,[42] on the other it is they themselves who bring the nature of the lovers' relationship to Marc's notice and inevitably impose on him the duty of intervening: it is they who upset the social harmony. This they do legally but none the less evilly. In the *Mort Artu* it is Agravain and Mordret who reveal Guinevere's adultery to the king, while the perfect knights Gauvain and Gaheriet consistently refuse to breathe a word about it.

French literature was already familiar with equally complex characters and situations. Up to Yseut's return to court the three barons' position is similar to that of Ganelon at the council of barons in the *Chanson de Roland*.[43] Condemned by their nature to an activity which is evil but unassailable from the legal standpoint, such figures seem, from the earliest examples onwards, to be the objects of poets' contempt and hatred. In our text Beroul violently refuses to tolerate the slightest hostility to the lovers, but the action of the barons, because it is legally correct, does not draw down immediate retribution on themselves.[44] The situation changes after Tristran's *escondit*, which is not contested because of the barons' cowardly nature;[45] the wind is temporarily taken out of their sails, and it is only now that Perinis, Artu and his knights accuse Marc of weakness, ignoring his refusal. But the three barons' evil nature[46] cannot be curbed for long and they must needs return to the attack. This time Marc can and does resist, and their wish is fulfilled only by the queen's compliance. As is repeatedly emphasised, there are now no legal grounds for further action on the part of the barons, so that they can no longer play a useful role in the narrative. The poet can therefore obey his emotional promptings and condemn them to their long-awaited punishment. Immediately after Yseut's *deraisne* they acquire fresh evidence to support their case[47] but Tristran's vengeance strikes them down in quick succession (and this must surely include Guenelon) before they can take action. Tristran's oath is finally fulfilled:

Ja n'avrai mais bain d'eve chaude
Tant qu'a m'espee aie venjance
De ceus qui li ont fait pesance [to Yseut];
Il sont traïtre fel prové.[48]   [vv. 3336-9]

4
The element of feudal law

We have found that the central theme of the *felon*, like the other themes so far examined, takes on forms which reveal a mentality accustomed to feudal law, and the way in which this theme is developed shows us the fundamental importance of the episode of Yseut's *deraisne*. But, as we have already said, it can and must also be examined in the context of the lovers' adventures. By this I mean that it must be studied in relation to the earlier motif of Tristran's *escondit* because the two themes are inseparable, although this has often not been realised by critics, who have been dazzled by the striking novelties of subject matter and style which are certainly to be found in the oath scene,[49] and have confined their attention exclusively to these.

What links the *deraisne* to the *escondit*[50] is that the one is substantially a repetition of the other; the problem of how the lovers shall protect themselves when confronted with a demand that they shall prove their legal innocence is explored in two separate situations which differ not only in circumstances but also from the legal point of view, and which lead to different solutions. But in both tests the lovers come out on top, safeguarding their love as well as their social respectability, and inexorably smashing all the wicked barons' plots.

There is a sharp contrast between the protagonist on each occasion: in the first case it is Tristran who is put to the test, conscious of his strength and confident that it will always bring him victory over his enemies; in the second case the central figure is Yseut, a defenceless woman without support from her family.[51]

There is an equally sharp contrast in the legal position: Tristran's task is to disprove something the truth of which seems established and on which judgement was given when he was condemned to the stake; Yseut, on the other hand, has simply to confirm the declaration already made by Tristran. Her accusers are formally in the wrong while in Tristran's case they were in the right.

There is a further contrast between the ways in which the two situations are resolved: the accusation against Tristran is juridically in order, and he justifies himself by making an untruthful declaration which he formulates in such a way that it is up to others to attack its veracity, and which, in default of such attack, is accepted as true; the accusation against Yseut is irregular, and since she is unable to save herself, like Tristran, by availing herself of the forms of legal procedure, she has to fall back on a trick. But the contrast is still more complete in that Tristran tells a lie which is formally correct, while Yseut swears the truth with an intent to deceive.[52]

Beroul does not make the relationship between these episodes too obtrusive: he is too spontaneous a narrator and too concerned with immediate effects for this. On the other hand, there is no reason to suppose that he was incapable of planning ahead and deliberately designing this pattern of contrasts. However this may be, they are there and they enrich the significance and the echoes of the oath scene, thereby helping to cement it firmly into the structure of the romance.

We must not overlook the fact that this subtle interweaving of contrasts certainly corresponds to a search for narrative effect and has the purpose of making it seem obvious that the lovers will overcome every obstacle, but once again it is worked out over a framework of motifs which involve (in the broadest sense) the position of the individual in society. As Jonin has carefully demonstrated, even after the bloodstains on the beds and the flour have made the lovers' guilt manifest, their sentence is pronounced with conscientious respect for legal forms. This extreme case serves to show that all the vicissitudes of the lovers' fate in Beroul occur not according to exclusively narrative patterns, or unforeseeable human reactions, or the psychology of courtly love, or the eternal business of crime and punishment, but according to the canons of feudal practice, which are felt to provide an equally valid scheme. Only once does something foreign to them intrude, when Tristran leaps desperately from the chapel window and escapes. And even this miraculous episode is in a sense brought back onto a human plane when we are made to see it as a divine guarantee of the lovers' innocence.

Before we draw any conclusions from these features of the romance in our search for a clearer picture of the author, we should note that contemporary literature was often meticulous in its attention to legal forms; this applies to works of the most varied nature, from the *Roland* to Chrestien or *Lanval*, from *Garin le Loheren* to *Guillaume de Dole* or the *Renart*. Moreover, in order not to over-estimate the importance of feudal law and the juridical way of thinking in the context of either the ideals or the artistic results of the romance, it should be clearly understood that, at least as far as this text is concerned, the law is not the centre of interest but the form of human existence against which the author's passion and imagination must struggle. Beroul's understanding and intuition of life are never rational but emotional.

5
The exchange of swords

The distance between the social situation, calculable in legal terms, and the human situation, which can be defined only in terms of the heart, is exemplified in the episode of the exchange of swords. In the hut of leaves the outlawed lovers have lain down to rest because of the great heat, and because Tristran is weary as a result of a deer hunt.

> Yseut fu premire couchie;
> Tristran se couche et trait s'espee,
> Entre les deus chars l'a posee.
> Sa chemise out Yseut vestue—
> Se ele fust icel jor nue,
> Mervelles lor fust meschoiet—
> Et Tristran ses braies ravoit.
> La roïne avoit en son doi
> L'anel d'or des noces le roi,
> O esmeraudes planteïz. [vv. 1804-13]

When Marc is told of this by the forester, he comes to the hut with his sword unsheathed:

> Li rois en haut le cop leva
> —Ire le fait, si se tresva.
> Ja decendist li cop sor eus
> —Ses oceïst, ce fust grant deus—
> Qant vit qu'ele avoit sa chemise
> Et q'entre eus deus avoit devise,
> La bouche o l'autre n'ert jostee
> Et quant il vit la nue espee
> Qui entre eus deus les desevrot,
> Vit les braies que Tristran out . . .[53]
> 'Dex!' dist li rois, 'ce que puet estre?
> Or ai veü tant de lor estre,
> Dex! je ne sai que doie faire,
> Ou de l'ocire ou du retraire.' [vv. 1991-2004]

Feudal forms and human suffering

The presence of the sword and the fact that they are clothed combine to convince him that Tristran and Yseut do not love each other *folement*:

> N'en ferrai nul; endormi sont:
> Se par moi eirent atouchié,
> Trop par feroie grant pechié;
> Et se g'esvel cest endormi
> Et il m'ocit ou j'oci lui,
> Ce sera laide reparlance.[54]
> Je lor ferai tel demostrance
>Ançois que il s'esvelleront,
> Certainement savoir porront
> Qu'il furent endormi trové
> Et q'en a eü d'eus pité. [vv. 2014-24]

On his wife's finger Marc sees the ring which he himself gave her and decides to exchange it for the one which she gave him. He also has with him the gloves which Yseut brought him from Ireland:

> Le rai qui sor la face brande—
> Qui, li fait chaut—en vuel covrir;
> Et quant vendra au departir,
> Prendrai l'espee d'entre eus deus
> Dont au Morhot fu le chief blos. [vv. 2034-8]

This he does, after first shutting out the glare of the sun and taking off the ring:

> Souef le traist, qu'il ne se mut.
> Primes i entra il enviz;
> Or avoit tant les doiz gresliz
> Qu'il s'en issi sanz force fere. [vv. 2044-7]

Having finally put down his sword in place of Tristran's, the king dismisses the forester and rides away. Meanwhile the queen dreams she is in an ornate tent in a wood, and attacked by two hungry lions, each of which takes one of her hands:

> De l'esfroi que Iseut en a
> Geta un cri, si s'esvella.
> Li gant paré du blanc hermine
> Li sont choiet sor la poitrine. [vv. 2073-6]

Tristran is also awakened by her cry, his face 'vermelle' with shock; he jumps to his feet and seizes the sword:

> Regarde el brant, l'osche ne voit;
> Vit le pont d'or qui sus estoit,
> Connut que c'est l'espee au roi.
> La roïne vit en son doi
> L'anel que li avoit doné,
> Le suen revit du dei osté.
> Ele cria: 'Sire, merci!
> Li rois nos a trovez ici.'
> Il li respont: 'Dame, c'est voirs.
> Or nos covient gerpir Morrois,
> Qar molt li par somes mesfait.
> M'espee a, la soue me lait;
> Bien nos peüst avoir ocis.'
> 'Sire, voire, ce m'est avis.'
> 'Bele, or n'i a fors du fuïr.
> Il nos laissa por nos traïr;
> Seus ert, si est alé por gent,
> Prendre nos quide, voirement.
> Dame, fuion nos en vers Gales.
> Li sanc me fuit.' Tot devient pales. [vv. 2081–100]

Governal joins them and Tristran repeats to him that the exchange is a clear sign of trickery and they must flee; they all travel towards Wales as fast as they can.

This episode is common to all the versions and is substantially modified only in the prose romance. In Thomas the lovers sleep in their cave with the sword separating them and are discovered by Mark's chief huntsman. We are not told what the king's feelings are, but there is no reason why they should be particularly malicious, since it was he himself who exiled them; the lovers' sleeping position convinces him of their innocence, but he does no more than cover Yseult's cheek with his glove to keep the sun off. When they wake up the lovers realise what has happened from the presence of the glove and do not know what to do, but on the whole they are quite pleased that the king found them in an innocent posture and soon after they are recalled to court.[55] The *Roman de la Poire* also has a naked sword, but this is a ruse of the two lovers who, having been surprised by Mark, place the sword between them and pretend to be asleep; Mark believes the evidence of the sword, covers the hole in the hut with his glove to keep out the sun and goes away.[56] The

Berne *Folie* is similar here,[57] though only Tristram feigns sleep and the sword does not seem to be used deliberately. The *Escoufle* is also similar, though there the lovers really are asleep.[58] Thus the only version close to Beroul's is that of Eilhart, who also has the exchange of swords but expresses surprise that Tristram should place the sword between them as—so he tells us—is his custom; not even Eilhart has the exchange of rings. His episode seems somewhat thin, with its seventy-two verses[59] as compared with Beroul's 340.

Marc's reaction to the naked sword lying between the lovers is not surprising, since there are other cases in medieval narrative where it appears as a symbol of chastity.[60] It would be more interesting to know how it ever comes to be there; as far as we can make out, its presence and position in Beroul are fortuitous, which is all the more surprising since the lovers are embracing each other (vv. 1816–25). And what is the meaning of Marc's actions? In all the texts he leaves his glove; in Beroul, Eilhart and therefore in their common source he exchanges his sword for Tristram's, in Beroul only he exchanges his ring for Yseut's, and yet in Beroul and Eilhart the lovers take fright and flee. What seems more surprising than anything else is the lovers' reaction to what is intended to be, and certainly ought to be, a clear sign of the king's affection, and is interpreted as such by Thomas.

Marx's suggestion[61] seems interesting: he observes that Marc's three actions are three forms of investiture, *per guantum, per anulum* and *per ensem*. So while, by taking Tristran's sword and Yseut's ring, the king could be taking pledges, by making the exchanges and leaving his glove he would be re-affirming his rights as sovereign, and restoring the fugitive lovers to the feudal bond.[62]

We should certainly not discount the possibility that writers of the Tristram legend tended to see a juridical significance in Mark's actions,[63] but any such significance does not seem to be essential to Beroul's text. Marx observes that when the effects of the potion wear off it is above all their loss of standing which troubles the lovers; this is true, but has no apparent connection with the scene under discussion. There is nothing to confirm that 'la reine, à son réveil, se sentira reprise' (p. 295). It should also be added that both the ring and the glove when used for investitures were not *Gegenstandssymbole* but *Handlungssymbole* and were thus taken back by the lord after the ceremony.[64] It seems clear that the exchange of rings is an addition by Beroul[65] and there seems to be no reason why it should not have its normal significance as a token of affection, as indeed it has in this same text, at v. 2729.[66] And it is quite obvious that by leaving his glove to keep the sun off Yseut's face Marc is giving a sign of his tender feelings towards his wife. Thus we are left with the exchange of swords, in which connection we should mention the early Germanic custom, mentioned by Cassiodorus, of adoption *per armas*, which was not extinct in Beroul's time and leaves traces in literary texts: for instance the Cid exchanges swords with the *infantes* of el Carrión as a sign of friendship, and in the *Roland* a Saracen offers his sword to Ganelon, again as a token of friendship.[67] Marc's action is thus both in intention and in form a friendly gesture.

So even if the version which Beroul found in his sources did contain one of those situations wrapped in juridical significance which, we have seen, he found so attractive, it here becomes obvious that the juridical element takes a subordinate place in his poetic treatment and that the human and affective aspects of the tale are for him considerably more important than the social aspects. It might well be true that in the minds of the narrator and his audience, attuned to the customs of their time, the sword, the glove and the rings did have some feudal significance. But first and foremost they are emblems of a human relationship. Marc carries away the sword which killed the Morholt and the ring which he himself gave to his wife. There is nothing to suggest that they are taken as tokens of a *saisine*, and a significance of this nature, which could not be apprehended immediately, as an interpretation based on feudal allegiance could, would have had to be made explicit. But it is clear that by their very nature they have a sentimental value for him, in that they will serve to remind him still more strongly of Tristran, his champion against the dreaded monster, and of Yseut, his dearly loved wife. The sword and the ring are thus in reality signs of his constant attachment to the two fugitives, of his indissoluble link with the past. Although Marc explicitly says he wishes to show compassion for the lovers, the effect is the opposite, because the sword, the ring and the gloves have the same meaning for the lovers as the head of the enemy killed by Governal in the preceding episode, namely that of ever-present and ever-imminent danger; this is in addition to the associations the objects have for them too, with a past which cannot be erased, a suspended human relationship which can never be regarded as finally terminated. For all three the objects which are exchanged are a reminder of the constant sorrow of their state. We should look again at the beginning of the episode:

> Seignor, ce fu un jor d'esté,
> En icel tens que l'en aoste,
> Un poi aprés la Pentecoste.
> Par un matin, a la rousee,
> Li oisel chantent l'ainzjornee. [vv. 1774–8]

The lovers fall asleep:

> Vent ne cort ne fuelle ne trenble;
> Uns rais decent desor la face
> Yseut, que plus reluist que glace. [vv. 1826–8]

This conventionally charming scene-setting underlines the illusion of peace, and its illusory nature is already shown by the narrator's references to the *paine* to come (v. 1783). The second passage is characterised by a tense immobility which contrasts with the delicate, graceful touch concerning Yseut's face. The next descriptive passage concerns Yseut's dream, and is the description of a nightmare.[68] The contrast between the initial tranquillity and the final whirlwind of emotion which cancels the effect of the idyllic setting in the lovers' breathless flight ('Grans jornees par poor font', v. 2128) is carefully contrived; and in the same way the dream (for Yseut) and the active, terrible and oppressive fear of the enemy and of death (for Tristran) become emblems of the dramatic return, which is thus clearly marked, to a situation of inescapable suffering. This is thus an obvious illustration of how the author uses, and even emphasises, juridical motifs and social customs, though they remain secondary beside the dominant emotional elements. It should be sufficient to consider the poet's delicacy in his description of Yseut and Marc's gentle feelings towards her, as it emerges insistently and tenderly even in the passages we have quoted. The act of exchanging rings and swords is a symbol in Beroul, but not (or not only) of a feudal relationship: it is chiefly the sad and moving symbol of an indissolubility of bonds, of a tragic and unresolvable emotional situation.[69] This is what makes it moving and imprints it in the memory as an exemplary motif.

6
The Morrois

It will now be profitable to extend our enquiry to the whole of the Morrois episode. When Yseut is rescued from the lepers,

> Tristran s'en voit a la roïne;
> Lasent le plain, et la gaudine
> S'en vet Tristran et Governal.
> Yseut s'esjot, or ne sent mal.
> En la forest de Morrois sont,
> La nuit jurent desor un mont;
> Or est Tristran si a seür
> Con s'il fust en chastel o mur. [vv. 1271-8]

Tristran goes hunting and builds a *loge* of branches and leaves, while Yseut strews more leaves on the floor of the hut; Governal lights a fire and cooks, though they have neither milk nor salt; the queen leans on her lover and falls asleep. Thus the episode opens with an atmosphere of bustling activity and their solitude finally seems to provide all they need for unlimited happiness. But gradually the insistence on this same solitude becomes oppressive and begins to represent a shadow over the life of the three outlaws:

> Seignors, eisi font longuement
> En la forest parfondement,
> Longuement sont en cel desert. [vv. 1303-5]
>
> Longuement sont en cel boschage;
> La ou la nuit ont herberjage,
> Si s'en trestornent au matin. [vv. 1359-61]
>
> Aspre vie meinent et dure;
> Tant s'entraiment de bone amor,
> L'un por l'autre ne sent dolor. [vv. 1364-6]

When Ogrin tells them of the proclamation against them and of the barons' oath to bring them to justice, the circle seems to close in on them still further, and it is a fearsome circle. There is no escape, not even in spiritual terms: the hermit shelters them for one night but does not absolve them. The oppressive fear becomes constant: even the arrival of Husdent represents a danger, at first because they fear that the king may be following the dog, and then because the dog's barking might give them away:

> El bois somes, du roi haï;
> Par plain, par bois, par tote terre,
> Dame, nos fait li rois Marc quere;
> S'il nos trovout ne pooit prendre,
> Il nos feroit ardoir ou pendre. [vv. 1554-8]

Husdent is trained but the lovers' life is still hard, completely dominated by fears and difficulties:

> Seignors, molt fu el bois Tristrans,
> Molt i out paines et ahans.
> En un leu n'ose remanoir;
> Dont lieve au main ne gist au soir:
> Bien set que li rois le fait querre
> Et que li banz est en sa terre
> Por lui prendre, quil troveroit.
> Molt sont el bois del pain destroit,
> De char vivent, el ne mengüent.
> Que püent il, se color müent?
> Lor dras ronpent, rains les decirent;
> Longuement par Morrois fuïrent.
> Chascun d'eus soffre paine elgal,
> Qar l'un por l'autre ne sent mal:
> Grant poor a Yseut la gente
> Tristran por lié ne se repente;
> Et a Tristran repoise fort
> Que Yseut a por lui descort,
> Qu'el repente de la folie. [vv. 1637–55]

As if to incarnate the nightmare, one of the traitors appears while the lovers are asleep; Governal kills him and cuts his head off, but when Tristran wakes up and sees the head dangling by its hair from the branch to which Governal has tied it, his impression is one of present danger ('Tristran s'esvelle, vit la teste, Saut esfreez, sor piez s'areste', vv. 1739–40). The terror spread by the news of this killing gives the lovers a moment of security, but is not sufficient to alleviate their wretched condition, in which they lack even bread (vv. 1769–70). However, the worst moment has yet to come, when Marc arrives and raises his sword over their heads. The king spares them but the lovers wake up terrified, firstly because of Yseut's dream ('De l'esfroi que Iseut en a Gieta un cri, si s'esvella', vv. 2073–4), secondly because of the effect of Yseut's cry on Tristran ('Tristran, du cri qu'il ot, s'esvelle, Tote la face avoit vermelle; Esfreez s'est, saut sus ses piez, L'espee prent com home iriez', vv. 2077–80), and finally because they realise that the king has been there. The themes of flight[70] and death[71] reappear, and the lovers begin their wanderings all over again:

> Molt les avra amors pené:
> Trois anz plainiers sofrirent peine,
> Lor char pali et devint vaine. [vv. 2130–2]

When the three years are over the effect of the potion wears off and their evaluation of the situation changes. Tristran stops in the wood while he is hunting and, as well as repentance, feels more strongly than ever the weight of his sufferings and the loss of his knightly dignity:

> Oublïé ai chevalerie,
> A seure cort et baronie;
> Ge sui essillié du païs,
> Tot m'est falli et vair et gris,
> Ne sui a cort a chevaliers. [vv. 2165–9]

> Or deüse estre a cort a roi,
> Et cent danzeaus avoques moi,
> Qui servisent por armes prendre
> Et a moi lor servise rendre.
> Aler deüse en autre terre
> Soudoier et soudees querre. [vv. 2173–8]

His regret extends to Yseut's wretched condition:

> Et poise moi de la roïne,
> Qui je doins loge por cortine;
> En bois est, et si peüst estre
> En beles chanbres, o son estre,
> Portendues de dras de soie;
> Por moi a prise male voie.[72] [vv. 2179–84]

The same themes appear in Yseut's monologue, which is parallel to this and which is also tinged with nostalgia for the gay life of former times (vv. 2201 *et seq.*). The two monologues merge into a dialogue, where the same themes are taken up yet again ('Roïne gente, En mal uson nostre jovente', vv. 2221–2). But although the effect of the potion has worn off, the past leaves a residuum of memories which cannot be erased; it leaves love, no longer a fatal love, but one reduced to human proportions:[73]

> Roïne franche, ou que je soie,
> Vostre toz jorz me clameroie. [vv. 2249–50]

This reawakening of awareness culminates in the return to Ogrin, who will reconcile Tristran with the king, but with the thought of impending separation a fresh note of grief creeps in:

> 'Dex!' dist Tristran, 'quel departie!
> Molt est dolenz qui pert s'amie!

Feudal forms and human suffering

> Faire l'estuet por la soufrete
> Que vos avez por moi fort trete;
> N'avez mestier de plus soufrir.' [vv. 2681–5]

A conscious effort is made to stifle the grief of their separation with positive reasoning in its favour, both here and in Yseut's words when she thanks her lover for the gift of Husdent (vv. 2700 *et seq.*). Then the outlaw has a further doubt:

> Tristran chevauche et voit le merc.
> Souz son bliaut ot son hauberc;
> Quar grant poor avoit de soi,
> Por ce qu'il out mesfait au roi. [vv. 2771–4]

But the hero too says regretfully that

> Nos ne porron mais longuement
> Aler nos deus a parlement. [vv. 2783–4]

The experience of solitary life in the forest ends for good:

> Vers la mer vet Tristran sa voie.
> Yseut o les euz le convoie;
> Tant con de lui ot la veüe,
> De la place ne se remue.
> Tristran s'en vet . . . [vv. 2929–33]

The most felicitous interpretation of this episode would seem to be that which inclines towards symbolism: the anti-social life in the forest appears to be an emblem of the anti-social nature of the love itself and of the impossibility of loving to the point of total dedication and total happiness within society; the end of the effect of the potion seems to represent the disintegration of the oblivious rapture of love, so that their anti-social existence no longer seems bearable because it has become pointless, and the lovers return, in different ways and indeed in different places, to social normality. Whitehead is one of those who have seen the episode in this light: 'The episode is in fact constructed round the idea that they can only enjoy their love in its full perfection while they are isolated from the rest of society';[74] and he adds that their isolation seems to be such as to render them safe from moral penalties.[75]

But it should be noted that it is generally difficult to say whether or not judgements such as this refer to a particular text, because critics very often write of *Tristram* without troubling to specify, and probably considering the poem in its supposed original form. It is clear that this interpretation is due in particular to the influence of Gottfried, for whom it is perfectly valid; but Beroul is not Gottfried. None the less, Stauffer wrote specifically of Beroul, 'The forest is the province of this free, unhindered love, of private, individual happiness';[76] she identified the forest with love and individualism, and the non-forest with collectivity, concluding that 'there is no private happiness within the community'.[77]

This interpretation, besides giving a very rigid picture of the thematic structure in terms too abstract to be plausible in a context like Beroul's, leaves out of account, or at least under-estimates, the suffering constant throughout this episode, which is barely forgotten even in the initial illusion of well-being. If we make a schematic distinction between happiness outside society and a return to society as soon as the love which is the basis of that happiness has ceased to be, we lose not only the nuances but the poetry and the very meaning of the romance, according to which there is no such thing as total 'private happiness' either without or within human society.

Bernheimer more correctly observes that although medieval tapestries preach the doctrine that the fullest enjoyment of love is attained by abandoning everything and going off to the woods, severing all bonds with the human community in order to safeguard the values of absolute loyalty and fidelity which are imperilled by the multitude,[78] in romances ranging from *Tristram* to *Aucassin* and *Guillaume de Palerne* the lovers take refuge in the forest only because their loves are illegal or hampered in some other way, so that even for these cases his initial definition of the term 'wildness' is appropriate: 'The word implied everything that eluded Christian norms and the established framework of Christian society, referring to what was uncanny, unruly, raw, unpredictable, foreign, uncultured, and uncultivated.'[79] This seems to be the sense of the wild wood of the Morrois in Beroul.

In Beroul the social problems are overcome during a brief initial period, then recur suddenly and insistently, no longer in the lovers' relations with other people but as an impending danger to themselves. Thus they do not disappear but shift to more extreme issues, and it is the whole relationship between the individual and society which, instead of ceasing to exist in the fullness of love, develops into antagonism and mortal struggle. All men have become their enemy, not by the desire of the lovers but as a result of the king's ban of outlawry. Isolation does not mean indifference towards the outside world but complete and involuntary opposition to it, a situation of crisis and not of serenity. At the same time the stakes of the struggle become very high: it is a matter of life and death.

It is in this intensification of their relationship to society to the point where only extreme solutions are possible, in this shift to the ultimate values of man's life in the world, in the reduction of life to the most essential needs (a hut and food), that love celebrates its triumph, itself attaining a supreme, exemplary value. Tristran and Yseut forget everything in their love:

> Mex aim o li estre mendis
> Et vivre d'erbes et de glan
> Q'avoir le reigne au roi Otran. [vv. 1404-6]

But this oblivion cannot be equated with that presented by Thomas, nor still less with Gottfried's *Minnegrotte*. Beroul's lovers always retain full awareness of their position: they never think of their difficulties and privations, but they are unable to quell the most spontaneous and therefore the clearest sign of their humanity, namely their fear, the sense of the fragility of this happiness which has already caused so much sadness. Beroul's lovers may not suffer from their hardships, they may be unaware of their guilt, but they constantly feel that they are only one step away from death, a destiny which no intensity of love can avoid. In this way the Morrois, if it is not a symbol of the lovers' anti-social happiness, nor ultimately a symbol of anything else, serves in Beroul as a vigorous depiction of the desperate situation of those who are forced out of society and can be induced to accept all this only because they have been rendered blind by a supernatural power. 'It forms the only possible surroundings for the existence of two mortals placed beyond human laws and social conventions by a violent passion',[80] but it is not enough, it cannot be enough for them. For Beroul, man lives in a world which permits no evasion, not even if it is paid for in terms of hardship.

7
Adversity and death

Up to now Beroul has not shown much interest in moral or religious questions, and even after the effect of the potion has worn off, what interest he shows is not very considerable and is pushed into the background by themes of a different kind; neither has he so far shown any sensitivity to sophisticated love problems, and this is a further reason why it would have been strange if his presentation of the life in the Morrois had proved compatible with the myth of love realised fully in isolation from society; he has, on the other hand, shown a lively interest in legal forms, and when the magical effect of the potion disappears he reveals the significance of this to the full. The lovers now return to complete awareness of their condition, which they are no longer prepared to accept unconditionally, sacrificing everything in order to remain together. This fresh consideration of their position is barely tinged with any sense of guilt; the dominant theme is a purely worldly one, the contrast between an existence befitting their social status and the life in the forest, a contrast which is constantly expressed through effective antitheses. In this way even the social situation becomes a material situation: just as the *cortine* is set against the *loge,* so too the extremely human theme of *travail,* of *paine,* of youth wasted in suffering, frequently comes to the fore. With the slackening of tension the alternative solutions become less drastically opposed: before, it was a matter of life and death, whereas it is now the humble life against the life of a queen. These are worldly terms for a spiritual problem. For such is Beroul's most intimate nature that his feeling for social life is the expression of the totality of human existence, and every social situation becomes the symbol of a problem which is not external (which *would* mean it was purely material) but involves the individual in his entirety. The lovers' adversity is the total of three forms of suffering: the suffering of acute danger to their lives, that of wasting their youth in tribulation and that of losing their status and comforts. Life within society is the whole of life. Thus even the law is nothing other than the mould which gives form to social life, and as such the necessary mould for an existence which can be played out only in society; this means that it is the form and not the substance of the narrative (the substance is always human life), or even, as it were, the individual's shield against peril and death. In Beroul only the unjust perish.

Beroul's insistence on social relations, which form the necessary backcloth for the life in the forest to be resolved in the wish to return, gives an added meaning, a meaning which is anything but cold and external, to the theme of the wicked barons, who are, as it were, the obstacle which society puts before the individual; the wicked barons, however, are not the symbol of the obstacle, but the concrete, living example of it—they represent the inevitable antagonists of every human being. They too are characters who act according to the logic of the law, not because this is their *raison d'être* but because it is their mental structure, the necessary form of any typically social action such as theirs. Their *raison d'être* lies elsewhere, in the perennial antagonism of individuals in society, in the interplay of passions, and still more in the inevitable conflict between personalities.

But in Beroul the individual, though so integrally and dramatically a social animal, has his solitude and in it suffers for his misdeeds. It could be significant that the wave of remorse and melancholy comes over the lovers individually and that it is only later that their monologues merge in dialogue. But there is more to it than this. Their existence may be reducible to social relations, but not completely; here too there is an element which cannot be eliminated, something to which Beroul's characters are desperately tied as isolated individuals and which saves them from that lack of depth which could be argued from the absence of religious and ethical interests: it is their sense of the presence of death.

We have seen how this weighs on the fugitive lovers, how it becomes the constant feature of their continual trials. But even here their situation is nothing more than an extreme and emblematic form of a situation which is common to everyone and unavoidable. In fact they carry it with them right from the opening verses, when Yseut exclaims under the pine tree,

> Mex voudroie que je fuse arse,
> Aval le vent la poudre esparse,[81]
> Jor que je vive que amor
> Aie o home qu'o mon seignor. [vv. 35-8]

Like other parts of this conversation, these words look like an attempt to mystify the reader, or at least a sort of calculated prophecy of the death by fire to which she is later sentenced, but she adds,

> Il me feroit ardoir en ré;
> Ne seret pas mervelle grant. [vv. 192-3]

Tristran proposes an *escondit en ré* (v. 151) and every time an *escondit* is mentioned it is linked with the idea of death, up to v. 2864: 'Se sui dannez, si m'art en soffre.'

This feeling for death never leaves the lovers but it is not confined to them. The three wicked barons are also affected by it, and not only through the promises of vengeance contained in the poet's or the characters' comments on their actions. When the king threatens to summon Tristan back to court the three of them 'entre eus dient',

> S'il ça revient, de nos est fin;
> Ja en forest ne en chemin
> Ne trovera nul de nos trois
> Le sanc n'en traie du cors, frois. [vv. 3095–8]

Death always presents itself to the minds of Beroul's characters with this terrifying, barbaric grandiosity, as a violent end to existence, having a tragic character which is almost tangible in the ghastly features with which it is accompanied. And it is clear why it should be so. When it strikes it does so with terrible, cruel violence, it is a torment of the body and brings savage triumph to the killer:

> Governal saut de sen agait;
> Du mal que cil ot fait li menbre,
> A s'espee tot le desmenbre,
> Li chief en prent, atot s'en vet. [vv. 1708–11]

> Tristran li preuz fu desfublez.
> Denoalen est tost alez;
> Ainz n'en sout mot, quant Tristran saut.
> Fuïr s'en veut, mais il i faut;
> Tristran li fu devant trop pres,
> Morir le fist. Q'en pout il mes?
> Sa mort queroit; cil s'en garda,
> Que le chief du bu li sevra.
> Ne li lut dire: 'Tu me bleces.'
> O l'espee trencha les treces. [vv. 4381–90][82]

> La seete si tost s'en vait
> Riens ne peüst de lui gandir;
> Par mié l'uel la li fait brandir,
> Trencha le test et la cervele;
> Esmerillons ne arondele
> De la moitié si tost ne vole;
> Se ce fust une pome mole,
> N'issist la seete plus tost.
> Cil chiet, si se hurte a un post,
> Onques ne piez ne braz ne mut;
> Seulement dire ne li lut:
> 'Bleciez sui! Dex! confession . . .' [vv. 4474–85]

Death always strikes unexpectedly, without giving time for an exclamation, for repentance, or for the comforts of religion. Not only is it the end: it is a tragic end, which approaches with the inexorable blind fatality which the Middle Ages identified in the figure of Fortune. In fact this name itself appears before the killing of the anonymous baron:

> Nus retorner ne puet fortune. [v. 1697][83]

The presence of death in Beroul's poem is of fundamental importance. It prevents his outlook on human life from seeming exclusively bound up with temporal patterns in society, and restores an absolute dimension to it, a horizon which, if not transcendent, does at least remain fixed and is therefore above the circumstances of the individual episode. The lovers' destiny rises above the pain of the single event to become the perennial suffering of the human condition. Their action is no longer simply an effort to overcome an obstacle or to escape a snare, but emerges on a broader plane as an emblem of the agony of existence. In this way the affairs of Tristran and Yseut are an example not in the didactic sense but because they are a superlative projection of human experience:

> Fu ainz mais gent tant eüst paine? [v. 1784]
> Nule gent tant ne s'entramerent
> Ne si griment nu conpererent. [vv. 1791-2]

Notes

1 This verse is identical with v. 2235.
2 Cf. vv. 809-26.
3 This verse is almost identical with v. 2363.
4 This verse is identical with v. 803.
5 Cf. vv. 2361-70 and 2397-403.
6 *Lever blasme* is a judicial technical term meaning 'to bring a charge'. For the meaning of *lever* cf. Niermeyer's *Lexicon minus*, s.v. *levare*, section 12.
7 Except in the verses immediately following the reading of the letter: 'Li baron oient la demande, Qe por la fille au roi d'Irlande Offre Tristran vers eus batalle' (vv. 2621-3).
8 Cf. v. 2398 with v. 2853, quoted above, and with v. 3418, which we shall quote shortly; from these verses we can see that the presence of all the barons of the kingdom is a necessary formality for Tristran's declaration to be valid. The barons are indeed all present. Cf. also v. 2678, 'li plez'.
9 The reason for Tristran's exile is not that he does not make his

escondit, or at any rate *escondit* and exile are not mutually exclusive. Tristran has already suggested that a decision on his future be made *after* the *escondit* and therefore independently of it and not as an alternative. The barons advise Marc to send Tristran to Gavoie (vv. 2629 *et seq.*), but this is obviously a precautionary measure, to calm the troubled waters. In fact they suggest later (v. 2635) that he be recalled, without adding that he will then have to *soi escondire*. 'Ne savon el qel voie tienge' (v. 2636). Cf. also the way in which the problem is formulated in vv. 2669 *et seq.*, and by the three wicked barons in vv. 2897 *et seq.*

10 Lejeune, in 'Les "Influences Contemporaines" ', p. 148, maintains that *deraisne* and related forms are used only by Beroul II, whereas Beroul I uses *escondit*, etc, for the same thing. From an examination based on an unpublished paper by L. Caulier she concludes that the division between Beroul I and Beroul II should be placed before v. 2227, with the appearance of remorse after the three years have ended. If we reject such an early division (cf. my Introduction) and work for the sake of argument with the traditional turning point at v. 2750 approximately, we are left with occurrences of *deraisnier* at vv. 2237 and 2576. Furthermore, in Beroul I *escondire* appears only twice while occurring seven times in Beroul II, and *escondit* twice as against nine times in Beroul II. Thus all we can say is that these terms are more frequent in the second part of the romance than in the first, and this is not surprising, since it is there that we find the scenes narrating Yseut's return to court and her oath. There is no concrete difference between the two groups of terms, even though *escondire* generally seems to be used for the oath rather than the duel, for which *deraisnier* seems to be more frequent; but, as Esmein wrote (quoted in Jonin's *Les Personnages Féminins*, p. 80, n. 2), 'chacun de ces mots recouvrait des procédés divers qui se réunissaient dans cette idée: faire tomber l'offre de preuve ou la preuve de l'adversaire'.

11 'Le principe qui domine, c'est que le fardeau de la preuve incombe au demandeur et que cette preuve doit se faire par des témoins d'une espèce particulière, qui viennent affirmer en pleine cour, sous la foi du serment, une formule arrêtée d'avance par un jugement; l'adversaire peut essayer de faire tomber le témoignage en *faussant* ou en *levant* le témoin, c'est-à-dire en le provoquant en duel judiciaire' (Esmein, *Cours Elémentaire d'histoire du droit français*, p. 261). Thus the text of Beroul quoted above is perfectly orthodox.

12 It seems, too, that in the medieval preference for the judicial duel questions of dignity are involved as well as confidence in a character's strength. This is particularly clear in the case of Horn, who is accused of corrupting the king's daughter and called upon to *soi escondire* by

an oath; but Horn, who is innocent, refuses and says that a strong young man of such noble birth does not make oaths but fights duels:

> Ainz me larraie traire e le quoer e le feie
> Ke serement face: franc qu'il fait, se desleie . . .
> Le parage de mei, s'il vus plest, ne 'l otreie;   [vv. 1975–9]

he does not even give in to the entreaties of Rigmel, and the king, refusing the duel ('Asez savom de vus k'estes pruz e vaillant; Pur çoe ne truverai ki en seit cumbatant', vv. 2089 and 2091), finally sends him into exile. Conversely, a solution through a judicial duel is always preferred, even in cases which to us would seem more suited to settlement by other means. When Fromont is besieged in St Quentin by King Pepin and the Lorrainers and can hold out no longer, although he is completely in the wrong, he asks the king for permission to *s'amender* by the judgement of the barons (*Garin le Loheren*, vv. 5416–18) and his opponent Begon, instead of advising Pepin to finish off the offenders by taking advantage of their desperate plight, says,

> S'uns de vos prinches ou .j. de vos marcis
> A ci vers vos de nule rien mespris
> Et il le vient amender devant ti
> Au jugement des parons del païs,
> Vos nel devés eschiver ne guencir.   [vv. 5421–5]

13 Also because at the beginning, when he is suspected but not charged, he would be able directly to choose a judicial duel; a defendant, on the other hand, was allowed a judicial duel only with the consent of the plaintiff (Esmein, *op. cit.*, p. 89), which is excluded in the present case, or by *faussement* of either witnesses or judge (cf. *infra*).

14 Cf. Jonin's *Les Personnages Féminins*, pp. 61 *et seq.*

15 Cf. vv. 2581 *et seq.* Tristran is now using a device which gives him the right to a judicial duel but not to an exculpating oath (Esmein, *op. cit.*, pp. 260–1). This however is refused because he is an outlaw, whom the king can pardon but who has no rights (Jonin, *op. cit.*, pp. 77 *et seq.*). But as a matter of fact (vv. 2621 *et seq.*) it seems that the barons' only reason for turning down his request for an *escondit* is their fear (cf. also vv. 3063–4), though they expressly deny the validity of the previous judgement. The arguments of Jonin (*op. cit.*, p. 66) are thus not entirely based on the text, especially since it is not the king but the council which rejects the proposal for a duel.

16 But Tristran already seems to be alluding to this in v. 2237.

17 Jonin (*op. cit.*, pp. 79–80), on the other hand, maintains that the demand is legal, since 'la justification après toute plainte est un usage constant et qui ne souffre guère d'exception', but he does not so much

as mention Tristran's words when he handed over the queen (vv. 2853 et seq.). However this may be, we are not naively thinking as Yseut thinks or pretends to think; Marc, Artu's courtiers and all the characters share our opinion, viz. that everything is due to the 'haine implacable de l'entourage royal', or more precisely of the three wicked barons. Nor does Yseut 'se résigne à l'escondit', which Marc has resolutely refused: on the contrary, it is she who suggests it.

18 Later he says to Yseut, 'Mais se encor nes en desment, Que nes enchaz fors de ma terre, Li fel ne criement mais ma gerre' (vv. 3188–90).

19 The barons seem to have some form of right to feudal war in the principle that 'the dispute is legally valid only on condition that the lord refuses to open his court to the vassals' (Kienast, *Untertaneneid und Treuvorbehalt*, p. 137) and above all because they have been expelled by the king: one needs only to think of the case of the Cid, magnificently studied by Menéndez Pidal in *La España del Cid*. We should note what is probably an intentional contrast between this scene and the earlier one where the three barons succeed in obtaining Marc's compliance with their demand for the punishment of the lovers by threatening to renounce their allegiance and wage private war; the contrast neatly underlines the legal difference between the two situations. On the earlier scene cf. *infra*, pp. 106 *et seq*.

20 Jonin, *op. cit.*, pp. 81 *et seq.*, shows that the defendant was clearly not entitled to formulate her own exculpatory oath, but we must not forget that Yseut is making a voluntary oath and is not compelled to do as a defendant, as Jonin insists (*ibid.*, p. 82). Cf. vv. 3221 *et seq.* and particularly vv. 3232 *et seq.* (the term *deviser* is technically correct: cf. *ibid.*, p. 84).

21 On the guarantee cf. Jonin, *op. cit.*, pp. 86 *et seq.*

22 The 'chorus' at Artu's court also regards Tristran's exile and Yseut's *deraisne* as legally unnecessary: 'Li rois fait ce que il conmandent, Tristran s'en vet fors du païs' (vv. 3452–3).

23 *Se desloier* is translated by Tobler and Lommatzsch, vol. 2, col. 1640, as 'to violate the law; to act disloyally or outrageously', two meanings which coincide completely in feudal jurisprudence.

24 Cf. v. 34, which is almost identical.

25 He says to Artu, 'Tu me blasmes, et si as droit, Quar fous est qui envieus croit; Ges ai creüz outre mon gré [in fact it is Yseut who has agreed to the *escondit* against the king's will] ... Ce saciez vos, Artus, frans rois, C'a esté fait, c'est sor mon pois' (vv. 4171 *et seq.*).

26 See also the following verses. It is legitimate to suppose that the lost v. 4214 was similar to v. 4229.

27 Cf. Jonin, *op. cit.*, p. 98. Even after the oath Artu still reproaches Marc for yielding to the *felon* (vv. 4257 *et seq.*), to which Marc replies, 'Se gel faisoie D'or en avant, si me blasmez.' These passages, while

filling out the characterisation of the hesitant, tormented Marc already outlined by Perinis during his embassy to Artu's court, also emphasise once again that the barons' request was beyond the bounds of legality.

28 *Op. cit.*, pp. 343–8.
29 If anything, Legge's observation in her review of Jonin's book is more interesting: she notes the existence of a parish of St Hilary near St Michael's Mount in Cornwall, to the west of our location of the Mal Pas. In fact it would be perfectly natural for Yseut to swear by the local saint, or perhaps even the same saint on whose relics the oath is made.
30 'The whole romance' as far as we know it. It is difficult to estimate the importance of the theme in the complete romance. From what we possess today Mergell's reconstruction (*Tristran und Isolde*, pp. 77–90) is not unconvincing but remains completely hypothetical and gratuitous. So while I accept his extremely valuable observation on the importance of the theme of the wicked barons (pp. 83–4), which I shall develop here and in chapter 5, I do not see it as a criterion for reconstructing the romance or interpreting the text in its complete form; I regard it simply as a line of approach in our quest for a better understanding of the fragment in our possession.
31 V. 26 recurs in identical form at v. 44, again on Yseut's lips, where it is followed by four verses which are illegible.
32 This verse is almost identical with v. 4165.
33 Cf. the case of Ogrin, mentioned on p. 81.
34 Cf. pp. 30 *et seq*.
35 Cf. p. 26.
36 In *Lanval*, when the protagonist is accused of trying to seduce Arthur's wife, 'Fors de la chambre eissi li reis, De ses baruns apela treis; Il les enveie pur Lanval, Ki asez a dolur e mal' (vv. 329–32). In his commentary Rychner mentions 'la coutume de l'ajournement par les pairs, qui voulait qu'un noble ne pût être ajourné sinon par le truchement de ses pairs, au nombre de trois, précisément, dans certaines coutumes' (p. 78). It would not be surprising if Beroul was influenced by this juridical custom, applying the number three to the accusers instead of those summoning the defendant to trial. Del Monte, in his *Tristano*, p. 20, thinks the number three has a symbolic value in Beroul (the potion lasts three years, three characters know the secret concerning it, three flee to the wood).
37 'Consilium et auxilium domino suo fideliter praestet, si beneficio dignus videri velit, et salvus esse de fidelitate quam iuravit', wrote Fulbert of Chartres in 1020 (quoted by Ganshof in his book *Feudalism*, p. 84; on the *consilium* cf. *ibid*., pp. 92–3).
38 Even Charlemagne has to yield to the demands of barons, who are

threatening to abandon him: cf. the *Quatre Fils Aymon*, vv. 15105 *et seq*.
39 Cf. Whitehead's edition of *La Chastelaine de Vergi*, introduction, p. xix.
40 'Tu consenz lor cruauté', v. 616; similarly in v. 2899, 'en consent lor felonie'.
41 A far more significant parallel was to be found in the lost Spanish poem on the *Condesa traidora*. While her husband, the count of Castille, Garci Fernández, was ill, the countess was seduced and taken away by a French count. Garci Fernández left his county, found the lovers in France, killed them, returned to Castille, assembled the vassals at Burgos, showed them the heads of the two lovers and said, 'Ahora soy digno de ser vuestro señor, que estoy vengado, y no antes, que vivía en deshonra' ('Now that I am avenged, I am worthy of being your lord, and not before, when I lived in dishonour') (cf. Menéndez Pidal's *Historia y epopeya*, pp. 1–27; the sentence quoted is on p. 7). Turning from narrative to theory, cf. Carlyle and Carlyle, *A History of Mediaeval Political Theory in the West*, vol. 3, pp. 125 *et seq*.
42 And leads them into exaggeration. Cf. v. 616, quoted above, which is untrue and unfair.
43 Cf. Pellegrini's *Studi rolandiani*, pp. 122–35, and Burger's 'Le Rire de Roland'.
44 Why are the three barons given the specific epithet 'felon'? Although felony was originally a crime against feudal bonds (and therefore not imputable to these barons), the meaning of the word was gradually extended, especially in the twelfth century (cf. most recently Dessau's 'L'Idée de la trahison'). In the *Aspremont* there is explicit mention of 'le felon ome qui enjure son per' (v. 7174), so that *fel* and *losengier* eventually become synonymous; of Naimon, the perfect courtier, we read, 'Savez de Namle quels fu li sien mestier. Il ne servi onques de losengier Ne volt franc ome a la cort empirier' (vv. 20–2). The same equivalence is explicit in *Horn*: 'Taunt i ad de feluns e sunt si mal parler; Bien e mal lur est tut a dire communer, Quant sunt devant le rei e voelent losenger, E ainz creit hom le mal ke le bien al premier' (vv. 894–7). The *felon* of *Horn* are particularly close to Beroul's because they too reveal to the king the love affair of his daughter Rigmel and Horn, but they are said to be part of a whole race of *felon*, an idea not found in Beroul. Cf. also Hollyman's *Le Développement du vocabulaire féodal*, pp. 152–5.
45 The *felon* are often cowards; cf. *Horn*, v. 1836.
46 We have no specific justification for the wicked barons' hatred for Tristran, though it is probably due to jealousy. In any case, medieval narrators tended to treat this kind of maliciousness as an innate

quality needing no rational or psychological explanation; as a result the traitors were all absorbed into a single family, that of Ganelon, so that it was enough for a poet to say, 'Bien le vient de lignage qu'il ait cuer de felon' (*Gui de Nanteuil*, v. 200, and cf. the characteristic, though for us psychologically improbable, speech of Anmanguins in *Paris la Duchesse* quoted by Hofer in 'Das Verratsmotiv in den Chansons de Geste', pp. 596 and 601; an enumeration of the members of the family of traitors was made by Sauerland in his *Ganelon und seines Geschlecht*). Beroul does not feel the need for the hereditary factor (although he does in a sense make his traitors emblematic by naming one of them Guenelon) but neither does he feel obliged to introduce alternative motivation (for cases of non-hereditary and equally superficially motivated treachery cf. Hofer, *art cit.*, p. 596 n.). However, he is not completely unaffected by the tendency when he has Marc say, 'J'ai trois felons, d'ancessorie' (v. 3186) and he finds it necessary to define the malicious forester as 'le forestier des tres' (cf. vv. 4045–6), which is quite illogical because the forester reveals his discovery only to Marc and has no actual connection with the wicked barons. Beroul does not appear to use the normal motif of the traitors' descent to hell, but with him as with other writers their deaths show no sign of Christian repentance (cf. *infra*).

47 This time, however, they do not intend to state their case until they are entirely sure of their facts.

48 The traitors' downfall is a certainty to the feudal way of thinking, in which treason is a crime of exceptional gravity. When the Pope absolves Guillaume of his sins in advance in return for defending Rome, he explicitly excludes treason ('Se tant puez faire de traïson te guardes', *Couronnement de Louis*, v. 393). In the same poem Guillaume says of the Last Judgement, 'Nuls om traïtre n'i avra guarison' (v. 1012).

49 Cf. pp. 176 *et seq*.

50 For the sake of simplicity we shall refer to Tristran's self-defence as the *escondit* and Yseut's as the *deraisne*, though no differentiation of any kind is intended between the terms (cf. p. 128, n. 10).

51 'Rois, n'ai en cest païs parent Qui por le mien destraignement En feïst gerre ne revel' (vv. 3239–41). This is important in view of contemporary customs, which led Marie to write even of such a valiant knight as Lanval, 'Huem estranges, descunseilliez, Mult est dolenz en altre terre, Quant il ne set u sucurs querre' (vv. 36–8). On the motif of the defenceless woman maliciously attacked by traitors cf. Hofer, 'Das Verratsmotiv in den Chansons de Geste', p. 601.

52 It could be added that the *escondit* is several times offered and turned down, while the *deraisne* is demanded and at first refused. On Yseut's

iuramentum dolosum cf. the comments and parallels of Jonin, *op. cit.*, pp. 99–105.

53 For these verses we have adopted the punctuation of Henry, given in his *Etudes de syntaxe expressive*, pp. 62 *et seq.*
54 Is this an echo of the 'male chançun' in the *Roland* (v. 1466; cf. also *Aspremont*, vv. 8644, 9488, 10138, 10462, *Moniage Guillaume II*, v. 5468)? Cf., more generally, Wilmotte's 'Corrections', p. 124.
55 Bédier's edition, vol. 1, pp. 240–3.
56 *Ibid.*, vol. 2, p. 257.
57 Vv. 196 *et seq.*
58 Bédier's edition of Thomas, vol. 2, p. 257.
59 Vv. 1617–88.
60 Cf. Heller's 'L'Epée symbole et gardienne de chasteté'. This use of the sword occurs particularly in *Amis et Amile*, in certain redactions of the *Sept Sages* and in *Bueve d'Hamtone*, all extremely well known texts.
61 *Nouvelles Recherches*, pp. 289–97.
62 However, the idea that the threefold investiture is a particularly early practice (p. 273) seems to be unsupported by evidence. There is a case of investiture *per guantum* in the *Charroi de Nîmes*, v. 585.
63 As is perhaps confirmed by a passage from a very well known Spanish romance, which here seems to be clearly derived from the Tristram tradition. The king discovers the *infante* Gerineldo sleeping beside the *infanta* after a night as lovers; his first impulse is to kill the two of them but he then changes his mind: 'Pondré mi espada por medio Que me sirva de testigo' ('I will put my sword between them: may it serve as my witness'). When he has gone away the *infanta* wakes and cries to her lover, 'Levántate, Gerineldo, Levántate, dueño mío, La espada del rey mi padre Entre los dos ha dormido' ('Arise, Gerineldo, arise, my lord; the sword of the king my father has slumbered between the two of us'). Cf. Menéndez Pidal's *Flor Nueva de romances viejos*, pp. 56–9.
64 Cf. Ganshof's *Feudalism*, p. 126.
65 There seems to be no reason why Eilhart should have eliminated it if he found it in his source.
66 Or, for example, in *Horn*, laisse 100 (and cf. laisse 200) or in the *Renart*, ed. Roques, vol. 1, vv. 1507 *et seq.*
67 *Cantar de mio Cid*, vv. 2093, 2577 and 3158; *Roland*, v. 1448. See also the commentary of Menéndez Pidal, *Cantar de mio Cid*, vol. 3, pp. 661–2, as usual invaluable for its wealth of material.
68 On this passage see Jonin's 'Le Songe d'Iseut'; but one wonders what useful purpose is served by introducing modern psychological theories into the study of a twelfth-century literary dream, especially when the attempt is so unfruitful as here, and we have the obvious and indubitable interpretation suggested by the text itself to fall back on.

69 On the significance of the objects and gestures in this episode we could echo Eberwein's words when she refers to a use of language 'which cannot be broken down into rational and irrational elements, but in which communication is by means of the image and at the same time the meaning of the communication, for both the speaker and the listener, is also expressed through the image' (*Zur Deutung mittelalterlicher Existenz*, pp. 37–8).
70 'Gerpir' (v. 2090), 'fuïr' (v. 2095), 'fuion' (vv. 2099 and 2121).
71 'Voiant le pueple, nos veut prendre, Faire ardoir et venter la cendre' (vv. 2119–20).
72 Note that Tristran does not know why these thoughts have come to him: in fact in the following verses he asks God for the strength to give the queen back to Marc, as if they were still under the influence of the potion.
73 The new element of recollection is obvious in Yseut's words in vv. 2819–21, and, broadly speaking, it would seem to justify the continuation of the love after the effect of the potion has worn off, which is a striking incongruity in Beroul's romance.
74 'Tristran and Isolt in the forest of the Morrois', p. 393.
75 *Ibid.*
76 *Der Wald*, p. 56.
77 *Ibid.*, p. 57.
78 It seems legitimate to add that ideas of this kind are obviously influenced by theories on the value of the eremetic existence for members of religious orders.
79 *Wild Men in the Middle Ages*, pp. 162 *et seq.*, and, for the sentence quoted, pp. 19–20.
80 Guerrieri Crocetti, *La leggenda di Tristano*, p. 55.
81 'Ardoir me faites et en polre venter' (*Aspremont*, v. 6468); 'A grant martire sera vo cors livrez, Penduz ou ars, et la poudre venté' (*Charroi de Nîmes*, ed. Perrier, vv. 1383–4); 'Tuit seroiz mort a grant destruction, L'os et la poldre venterons par le mont' (*Prise d'Orenge*, vv. 795–6). Cf. also Thomas's *Tristan*, ed. Wind, Cambridge fragment, v. 23; *Cligés*, vv. 6451–2; *Lai du Cor*, vv. 393–4. This is thus a commonplace but not therefore meaningless.
82 Guerrieri Crocetti (pp. 53–4) wrongly believed that he could show that the first of these scenes was not Celtic by drawing a parallel with the quite different scene where Enide is struck in the face. But it should be observed that the savage cruelty of these scenes is not an isolated phenomenon in Old French literature. In *Garin le Loheren* Begon kills the Bordelais Isoré in a duel:

> Ausi le fent con li lex fait brebis;
> Le cuer du ventre entre ses mains en prit,
> Puis est venus en la cit de Paris,

> Fiert en Guilliaume de Monclin enz o vis,
> Puis li escrie con ja porrez oïr:
> 'Tenez, vassal, le cuer de vostre ami,
> Or le poez et saler et rostir!
> Onques Garins vers le roi ne mesprist.'   [vv. 6527–34]

This is a judicial duel to decide the accusation against Garin of having tried to poison Pepin.

83 I have, of course, taken into consideration the fact that all these scenes concern the deaths of traitors, but they do not differ in any way from the inherent tragicality of the lovers' frequent forebodings, so that my generalisation is justified. Moreover, unlike Beroul, the poet of *Garin le Loheren*, for instance, was able to lament even the slaughter of the traitors: 'Dieus! quel damaje et quel dolor a ci, Car il estoient baptisié, Diu merci!' (vv. 14172–3).

5
Narrative technique and figurative patterns

What we have seen up to now may at times have given the impression that Beroul's narrative art can be described as realistic. Such a description would not, however, be very meaningful, since the term 'realism' cannot be used in relation to twelfth-century writers in the sense in which it is used in connection with nineteenth-century novelists. The only meaning it would retain would be the broad sense of 'attitude towards reality' or 'mimetic disposition', and in this sense there is no artist who is not in some way or other a 'realist'—that is, who does not have some manner of placing himself in relation to reality. What is important to establish is the perspective, the significance and the nature of this attitude, which is different in every case and therefore cannot be treated under a single heading.

There has been a recent attempt to single out a 'realistic trend', or the beginnings of one, in the twelfth-century romance,[1] but I am of the opinion that an investigation which starts by separating imagination from rational thought, and judges the degree of realism of individual works by the extent to which rational thought is more prominent than imagination, must inevitably result in fallacious conclusions. Psychological verisimilitude, careful linking of cause and effect, contemporary events or characters reflected in disguised form in the narrative—these matters are peripheral and not central to the concept of realism; they bear witness to the control and deliberation of a certain style of narrative rather than to anything fundamentally new in the approach to the problem of reality in art. To measure the realism of the twelfth century with the yardstick of the poetic canons of the age of Louis XIV must unavoidably lead to questionable conclusions, especially since it begs the question of what importance Chrestien's contemporaries might have attributed to what we call reality.[2]

But in any case we cannot speak of realism or the degree of realism in a work without establishing from the living texture of the style the precise form and tone of the narrator's favourite formal schemes. We have seen how much of contemporary moral and social reality is reflected in Beroul's romance and contributes to its structure, but in order to characterise the romance as poetry we should now complete our examination of it from the point of view of form. Nor, in order to arrive at the conclusions we are seeking, will it be necessary to undertake a complete examination of the stylistic devices used by the narrator: on the contrary, we shall restrict ourselves to the study of one feature only, but one which is particularly expressive and has already been noted frequently: repetition.

I
Repetition as a rhetorical device

It has often been observed that Beroul has a habit of repeating a whole word group or verse. But scholars have contented themselves with pointing the fact out and treating it as a mere reflection of a particular stylistic tradition.[3] A particular study of how and why Beroul uses this device has not yet been undertaken. But as soon as it is realised that this stylistic feature is not an exclusively epic one (for example, Wace uses and abuses it[4]) then one needs to see what use Beroul made of it.

There is no doubt that the practice of repetition is in origin connected with the rhetorical devices of the schools; but its striking frequency in early vernacular literature cannot be accounted for simply by Cicero's words 'Commoratio una in re permultum movet'.[5] Repetition comes into its own above all when it reflects a taste for variation without much quick movement forward: while keeping the narrative at a standstill it can, on the one hand, throw the situation into high relief and, on the other, either bring about a gradual modification of it, or, without changing it, explore it from various angles. The technique of repetition, in its best, classic applications, expresses the static and emotional vision of the Middle Ages and at the same time transcends it. Without harming the narrative, it offers several refinements: it affords subtler ways of expressing pathos; it can make up for lack of psychological introspection; it enables the poet to put in perspective individual events which he regards as objective, real and absolute facts; it solves the problem of harmonising the fixed and variable elements in a situation; it permits fluidity of detail within the static framework. This important function, in a sense contradictory in its double tendency, was admirably demonstrated in the epic *laisse*, where the problem of continuity between individual metrical sections was felt more acutely; in the continuous flow of the romance, however, the repetitive *reprise* loses much of its importance and is better suited to more limited tasks, promoting immobility rather than continuity, dwelling on a situation, or a figure, or a feeling. Thus, although originally a stylistic device with a double function, it developed a tendency to specialise in a single direction, unless it degenerated into part of a rhetorical system applied mechanically, virtually devoid of expressive power.

We shall begin by going right back to those repetitive devices which are most clearly rhetorical, because from them we shall discover in Beroul evidence of a considerable formal education and at the same time an ability to use it in an interesting manner.

A case in point is anaphora.[6] It is not always intended, as it should be, to create an intensive effect. In the case of

> Li ros li çoine qu'il retort.
> Li rois en haut le cop leva, [vv. 1990–1]

it is clearly used to establish continuity between two scenes which are in themselves separate. In the first verse Marc restrains the forester's eagerness to enter the hut in which the lovers are sleeping; the second is concerned with the king, the guilty lovers and the sword raised for the kill. Here the expressive value of the device is more concealed and more persuasive, but in other passages the tone is clearly one of pathos. When the lovers are riding to meet Marc to restore Yseut,

> Tristran chevauchë o s'amie,
> Tristran chevauche et voit le merc. [vv. 2770–1]

It can be seen how the anaphora covers both an extended period of time and a long distance, and stops abruptly at the sight of the *merc*, the boundary stone, which is a sign of danger because it is a sign of Marc's sovereignty:

> Souz son bliaut [Tristran] ot son hauberc;
> Quar grant poor avoit de soi,
> Por ce qu'il out mesfait au roi.[7] [vv. 2772–4]

Anaphora can serve to attenuate a shift of narrative perspective, as in the first of the examples quoted; but whereas in vv. 1990–1 the 'pivot' employed is a character and the shift is one of place, in other instances a complete inversion of narrative perspective occurs because the repeated element is used in a different grammatical function:

> Au roi a dit le mandement.
> Li rois l'escoute bonement. [vv. 2517–18]

If we now turn to instances which are purely and formally rhetorical, the only two we shall find which consist of nothing more than simple duplication are the repetitions of two vocatives in direct speech (*Rois*, vv. 655 and 667; *Dame*, vv. 157 and 159). Direct speech is in fact the most suitable context for repetition in a purely oratorical function and a number of other cases may be mentioned here. As early as Yseut's first speech to Tristran beneath the pine tree we have two repetitions (of which one is identical), arranged in an elegant chiasmus:

Ne me mandez nule foiz mais.	[v. 17]
Se li felon de cest'enor . . .	[v. 26]
Se li felon de cest'enor . . .	[v. 44]
Ne me mandez por nule chose.[8]	[v. 61]

Again, in Ogrin's speech to the lovers when they have come to wish for an honourable solution we find

Tristran, entent moi un petit— Ci es venuz a mon habit— Et vos, roïne, a ma parole Entendez, ne soiez pas fole.	[vv. 2341-4]
Tristran, roïne, or escoutez Un petitet, si m'entendez.	[vv. 2351-2]

At the moment of their separation, Yseut says to her lover,

Manderai toi par Perinis Les noveles de la roi cort.	[vv. 2830-1]
Manderai toi de ci mon estre Par mon vaslet.	[vv. 2835-6]

And immediately before this, with the two elements of the repetition even closer together:

Beau chiers amis, et g'en ai dote; Enfer ovre, que les tranglote! Ges dot, quar il sont molt felon.	[vv. 2825-7]

Repetitions such as these clearly have a rhetorical function, and it is precisely as rhetorical ornament that they are introduced into direct speech, in all three cases with a certain insistence which betrays calculation. However, it can be said that Beroul handles sophisticated stylistic devices with some skill and fluency. To prove the point we shall quote a similar echo in different but parallel speeches, spiced with subtle irony. When two mysterious knights, who later turn out to be Tristran and Governal, appear at the tournament at the Blanche Lande, Girflet ostentatiously explains to Gauvain,

>Il sont faé, gel sai sanz dote. [v. 4019]

And in his turn Gauvain says to the others,

>Saciez que cil dui sont faé. [v. 4062]

To return to rhetorical figures which can be precisely categorised, Biller[9] points out three cases of anadiplosis in the first part of Beroul plus two others in the dialogues, which are the following:

>'Et je sace soit vostre gré.'
>'Dame,' fait il, 'Dex gré te sace!' [vv. 2802-3]
>   'Cil son ami.'
>'Ami? Et qui?' [vv. 4298-9][10]

The paronomasia of vv. 62-3,

>Je ne seroie pas tant ose
>Que je i osase venir,[11]

is also close to the forms of school rhetoric: to this can be added the uses of *escondit* and *escondire* in vv. 3043-53 and the complicated etymological play of vv. 4441 *et seq.*, which we shall quote below. But to evaluate Beroul's rhetorical tendencies as a whole it is as well to add straight away that he does not favour the coupling of synonyms[12] and is generally sparing in his use of adjectives. What counts most in the way he handles rhetorical stylistic devices is his agility and variety, as well as his moderation. Cases in point are two further examples of repetition in chiasmus, each with a quite different effect. Marc, undecided and perplexed, appeals to the barons:

>Conseilliez m'en, jel vos requier;
>Vos m'en devez bien consellier. [vv. 2529-30]

And Yseut, on whom is focused the attention of all the knights at the Mal Pas, meticulously prepares to cross the ford:

>Le poitral oste Yseut la bele,
>Au palefroi oste son frain. [vv. 3892-3]

2
Remote repetition

We shall now pass on to a number of repetitions made a long way after the initial phrase, sometimes over a thousand verses later. One such repetition is:

Li nains Frocins, plains de voisdie.	[v. 328]
Molt fu li nain de grant voidie.	[v. 673]

The traitor barons present the king with a choice:

Or t'aron tost cest geu parti,	[v. 625]

but later it is Marc who offers a choice to the barons:

Ge vos ferai un geu parti.	[v. 3077]

The lepers describe to the king what Yseut's life will be like with them:

Avra de pieces, de quartiers,	[v. 1208]

and Yseut tells that she has felt a good supply of victuals about the person of the leper on whose back she has ridden (Tristran):

Les pains demiés et les entiers	
Et les pieces et les quartiers	
Ai bien parmié le sac sentu.	[vv. 3967-9]

The difference between these cases and the epic formula is obvious. The first of the three repeated phrases quoted can be regarded as a personal cliché, which, unlike the epic formula, does not change with the rhyme, and is closer to the decorative formula, not unknown to Beroul.[13] The second may be considered an example of a single metaphor used in two situations which are parallel but reversed, and therefore with a touch of irony. The third case, too, is a sort of retaliation by Yseut, who sarcastically says she has observed in someone else what had been predicted for her. In each of these repetitions, then, there is a new, individual undertone which is deliberate and does not have the gratuitous nature of a formula.

Nevertheless this technique of infusing individual expressiveness into a standard stylistic device remains at a fairly elementary level, and the same must be said of repetitions which close episodes treating similar themes. In fact, remote repetition sometimes serves simply to pick up the interrupted thread of the narrative. After the *rendez-vous épié,* Marc wishes to take revenge on the dwarf, who has prudently left the court:

> Li rois vait molt le nain querant;
> Nu puet trover, s'en a duel grant. [vv. 337-8]

The narrative focus then shifts to Yseut and Brengain, and later to Tristran and Governal, after which the narrator returns to Marc with v. 385:

> Ne pout son nain trover li rois.

But even uses of this kind can attain a high degree of expressiveness. The following verses are almost identical:

> Tristran gesoit en sa fullie. [v. 1673]
> Tristran se jut a la fullie. [v. 1729]

In the meantime one of the enemies has come dangerously near but has been ambushed and decapitated by Governal. The verbal repetition underlines the continuity of Tristran's sleep and thus serves both to end the episode and to heighten its dramatic effect.

3
Parallel scenes and variations of perspective

There are passages where Beroul definitely seems to come close to the conventional technique of *laisses similaires*. The best and most obvious example occurs in vv. 3101 *et seq.*:

> Enmié l'essart li rois s'estot;
> La sont [the three barons] venu; tost les destot,
> De lor parole n'a mes cure . . .
> 'Sire,' font il, 'entendez nos . . .'

The wicked barons are seeking to propitiate the king after irritating him with their request for an *escondit* by Yseut, but Marc is not mollified and orders them to leave his kingdom. After the two direct speeches (vv. 3109-36) the poet continues

> Devant lui vienent li felon,
> Godoïnë et Guenelon
> Et Danalain que fu molt feus;
> Li troi l'ont aresnié entr'eus,
> Mais n'i porent plai encontrer;
> Vet s'en li rois sanz plus ester.
> Cil s'en partent du roi par mal . . . [vv. 3137-43]

These verses return to the point in the narrative reached by v. 3101 and summarise what has happened since, this time in indirect speech, before moving forwards from v. 3142.

The reading of Ogrin's letter first to Marc and then to the council of barons is related along similar lines. When Marc receives the letter

> Li rois esvelle son barnage.
> Primes manda le chapelain,
> Le brief li tent qu'a en la main.
> Cil fraint la cire et lut le brief;
> Li roi choisi el premier chief,
> A qui Tristran mandoit saluz.
> Les moz a tost toz conneüz,
> Au roi a dit le mandement.
> Li rois l'escoute bonement;
> A grant mervelle s'en esjot,
> Qar sa feme forment amot.
>
> Li rois esvelle ses barons,
> Les plus proisiez mande par nons;
> Et qant il furent tuit venu,
> Li rois parla, il sont teü.
> 'Seignors, un brief m'est ci tramis . . .'   [vv. 2510–25]

Strictly speaking, these two scenes (vv. 2511–20 and vv. 2522 *et seq.*) have no *motif* in common: in the first the king has the letter read to him by his chaplain, in the second he holds a council of his barons, during which the letter is read out in full, so that, if anything, it is the first episode which summarises a part of the second. But the two scenes are introduced by two verses which are identical except for a change in the rhyme word; as a result, both scenes fall into a single category: they are both scenes in which the king awakens the barons. This is another typically epic process.[14] The scenes depicting Tristran's encounter with the lepers have likewise a parallel structure. The first centres on the hero:

> Fiert le destrier, du buison saut,
> A qant qu'il puet *s'escrie en haut*:
> 'Ivain, asez l'avez menee;
> Laisiez la tost, qu'a cest'espee
> Ne vos face le chief voler.'   [vv. 1245–9]

The second has a similar opening but centres on Ivain, the leader of the lepers, and as if to make the reversal of perspective more obvious the words which remain unchanged in the repetition are also reversed:

> Ivain s'aqeut a desfubler,
> *En haut s'escrie*: 'Or as puioz!
> Or i parra qui ert des noz.' [vv. 1250-2]

This second traditional process, which is another epic feature, serves to create a static parallelism between two scenes, which may well be immediately consecutive in time but are presented as mutually related and built round a single theme ('Li rois esvelle son barnage / ses barons' and 's'escrie en haut / en haut s'escrie'). Thus in a sense it is a way of reducing to unity elements which, though interrelated, are diverse.

There are two other fairly frequent devices which are similar to the double presentation of a single scene from different points of view (the first technique exemplified above). The knights arriving at the Blanche Lande find difficulty in crossing the Mal Pas:

> Molt a grant noise en cel Mal Pas:
> Li passeor sollent lor dras;[15]
> De luien puet l'om oïr les huz
> De ceus qui solle la paluz. [vv. 3697-700]

The two couplets correspond in every detail except the perspective of place; the point of reference in the first is 'cel Mal Pas', in the second it is 'de luien'. The same aspects, the 'noise', 'les huz', are brought into focus in two different and immediately consecutive ways.

When the barons capture Tristran,

> Tant ploroit, mais rien ne li monte,
> Fors l'en ameinent *a grant honte*.
> Yseut plore, par poi n'enrage.
> 'Tristran,' fait ele, 'quel damage
> Qu'*a si grant honte* estes lïez!' [vv. 901-5]

The same event occurs first as part of the narrative and second in Yseut's despairing comment, but the action is in no way developed; the moment illuminated by the second perspective is the same as that narrated in the first. The most obvious case of this device occurs when the lovers realise they have been discovered while asleep and are overcome by panic. Tristran narrates the whole episode to Governal and concludes,

> 'Fuion, n'avon que demorer.' [v. 2121]

The narrator immediately repeats the idea in his own comment:

> N'avet en eus que demorer. [v. 2122]

4
Repetition as an element in the narrative rhythm

In these cases the *reprise* seems intended to create, with certain particular undertones, the effect which it has generally in the romance, that is to say, the effect of slowing down the narrative. However, the undeniable similarity of the repeated phrases must not induce us to overlook the undertones, because it is these which give the stylistic device its true significance. Instead of remaining gratuitous, Beroul's repetition permits him to dwell on and unobtrusively underline the deepest theme of the narrative moment; it is often a means of capturing an action or an object and retaining it for an instant in the flow of the narrative, filling it with particular echoes, charging it with the emblematic value of a figure significant in its own right, a figurative synthesis of an emotional reality.

Beroul has a direct, spontaneous and extremely personal rhetoric, which, throughout the romance, does not fail to become dramatic when the tension requires it to. When the forester discovers the lovers asleep he rushes to the court:

> Li forestier grant erre acort,
> Qar bien avoit oï le ban . . . [vv. 1856-7]
> [the content of the proclamation]
> Li forestier bien le savoit,
> Por ce acort a tel esploit [vv. 1861-2]
> [Marc is at the court]
> Li forestier du mont avale
> Et s'en est entré, molt vait tost. [vv. 1866-7]

Yseut sees Godoïne's face at her window and when she asks Tristran, who is unaware of what she has seen, to nock an arrow and stretch his bow,

> Tristran l'estent, si s'apensa,
> Oiez! en son penser tensa;
> Prent s'entente, si tendi l'arc. [vv. 4441-3]

Narrative technique and figurative patterns

When the king decides that the lovers shall be burnt at the stake,

> Li rois conmande espines querre
> Et une fosse faire en terre.
> Li rois, tranchanz de main tenant,
> Par tot fait querre les sarmenz,
> Et assenbler o les espines
> Aubes et noires o racines. [vv. 867-72]

When Tristran leaps onto the queen's bed,

> Sa plaie escrive, forment saine;
> Le sanc qui'n ist les dras ensaigne.
> La plaie saigne; ne la sent,
> Qar trop a son delit entent. [vv. 731-4]

In the wood Tristran has to teach his dog to hunt silently, and when, the first time it barks, he beats it,

> Li chien a son seignor s'areste,
> Lait le crïer, gerpist la beste;
> Haut l'esgarde, ne set qu'il face,
> N'ose crïer, gerpist la trace. [vv. 1613-16]

When Tristran's request for an *escondit* is put before the assembly of barons,

> Li baron oient la demande,
> Qe por la fille au roi d'Irlande
> Offre Tristran vers eus bataille.
> N'i a baron de Cornoualle
> Ne die: 'Rois, ta feme pren...' [vv. 2621-5]

The hunters find the corpse of the baron decapitated by Governal, and when the news of this spreads,

> Poor en ont tuit et esfroi. [v. 1722]

> Poor ont tuit par la contree. [v. 1747]

Despite their variety, all these uses of repetition, by virtue of their frequency and basic homogeneity, need to be considered under a single heading. Repetition thus emerges as the principal device, though not the only device, determining Beroul's characteristic narrative rhythm. At the beginning of this monograph we discussed the episodic pattern of the narrative; what we said there is not contradicted by our observations on repetition, since the few examples of distant repetition fit comfortably into the network of links and echoes which govern the tension between episode and romance. Most repetitions, however, occur within a single episode and give it an individual wholeness, by means of a highly effective interplay of formal and expressive echoes. Beroul's episode is thus not merely a chapter within the narrative: it is a moment which aspires towards independence, not in the sense of the *branche*, which has narrative unity because it recounts a complete *aventure*, but in as much as it attains completeness of significance within the framework of one overall story. For this precise reason the episode, by exploiting repetition, tends to create a broader situation which is as static and emblematic as possible.

5
Dynamic repetition

We must not disregard what we might call the 'active' repetitions. In certain cases there is a slight forward movement in time, again reminiscent of the epic *laisses similaires*. When Ogrin goes to St Michael's Mount to procure better clothing for the queen,

> Aprés *achate ver et gris*. [v. 2735]
>
> Ogrins l'ermite tant *achate*
> Et tant acroit et tant barate
> Pailes, *vairs et gris* et hermine
> Que richement vest la roïne. [vv. 2741-4]

This last verse adds something new, prepared for by the fact that the repetition is formulated in such a way as to demand a consecutive clause following it; thus the repeated phrase is not statically parallel to its preceding occurrence but paves the way for a step in the narrative not previously arrived at. At times, indeed, change of perspective is closely bound up with the time element, so that the function of the repetition is no longer that of a commentary but that of skipping over an 'empty' period of time. This can be achieved simply by presenting the first occurrence of the repeated phrase in direct speech as a command or statement demanding corroboration by the subsequent action. When Tristran proposes to carry Ogrin's letter to Lancïen himself, he says,

> 'Bien sai l'estre de Lancïen.' [v. 2438]

That night he sets out with Governal:

> Bien sot tot le païs et l'estre.
> A Lancïen, a la cité,
> En sont venu, tant ont erré. [vv. 2452-4]

The narration confirms the familiarity Tristran has claimed. Or again, when Marc orders the chaplain to take the letter of reply to the agreed place,

> 'A la Croiz Roge le pendez.' [v. 2646]
>
> Quant l'ot li chapelain escrit,
> A la Croiz Roge le pendit. [vv. 2649-50]

In other cases the perspectives of time and place vary together in a more subtle and complex manner. When Tristran learns from Brengain that the king has sanctioned his return to court,

> *A la chanbre* painte *s'en vont*
> La ou li rois et Yseut sont.
> Tristran *est en la chanbre entrez*. [vv. 549-51]

The action presented is the same but in two successive moments; in addition, although attention remains focused on the entrance to the chamber, the standpoint shifts from outside the chamber to inside. The first sentence is pronounced by the narrator as if he were outside the room behind the two characters, while the second comes from the interior, as is clear from the contrast between *aller* and *entrer*. In fact the viewpoint has changed from that of the narrator to that of the king, who speaks immediately after.

Further on, when Yseut returns to Lancïen, we read,

> Quar, ce saciez, ainz *n'i ot rue*
> *Ne fust de paile portendue*;
> Cil qui n'out paile mist cortine.
> Par la ou aloit la roïne
> *Est la rue molt bien jonchie*. [vv. 2967-71]

In the first three verses the time is that of the preparations and the perspective a purely narrative one; in the last two there is a shift to the moment in which the procession passes and the perspective seems to have become that of the queen and her attendant knights. Beroul has a particular liking for these double perspectives even where they are not accompanied by repetition, as may be seen in the following verses:

> S'il les trove, molt les menace,
> Ne laira pas ne lor mesface.
> Molt est li rois acoragiez
> De destruire; c'est granz pechiez. [vv. 1949–52]

Here we find in the first place the king's point of view, expressed in indirect form, and then the same ideas, though not the same terms, repeated from a more objective angle, as an observation no longer by the character but by the narrator.

In another passage a phrase of the same type as 'Li rois esvelle son barnage' is fused with the technique of shifting perspective. When Tristran is exiled and Yseut taken back to the court, Tristran and Dinas make their farewells:

> Dinas encor le convoiout,
> *Sovent le besse* et *li proiot*
> Seürement revienge a lui. [vv. 2935–7]

Then when Tristran has asked Dinas to do for him whatever he may ask through Governal,

> *Baisié se sont plus de set foiz.*
> Dinas *li prie* ja nel dot,
> Die son buen: il fera tot. [vv. 2944–6]

It should be noticed that there is a twofold inversion of time, from the present to the past for *baisier*, and from the imperfect to the present for *proier*, almost as if there were no difference between various tenses, so that what we have here is a parallel case to vv. 2967–71.

So besides repetitions which develop the tale only to a negligible extent from the point of view of time, there are others which cover a considerable stretch of narrative time, of the type exemplified by 'A la Croiz Roge le pendez / A la Croiz Roge le pendit.' To be sure, it could be pointed out immediately that these bold ellipses of narrative time are always centred on a single image, which thus serves as a sort of bridge. But it is more important to observe how Beroul's narrative contains another essential component besides the slowing-down technique, a component which preserves the dynamic balance of the episode and without which the episode would indeed be reduced to a static emblem, almost like an image in a bestiary, extraneous to time by its very nature. This component is narrative rapidity.

Although there are only a few of those repetitions which centre on a constant element but pass rapidly on to a later narrative moment, they do seem significant in that they consume in an instant a period of time which is useless because it is devoid of incident; they therefore correspond to the glossing over of time which we have already observed between separate episodes. Within a single episode they are in a sense less necessary, but the process is often identical; it provides a means of both smoothing an abrupt break and, more importantly, avoiding the banality which would be the inevitable effect if the whole period of time, already implicitly accounted for in what has gone before, were reported, justified and filled with a series of actions with no immediate narrative significance. Marc's chaplain does not reply to the king's order, does not procure the necessary materials for writing the letter, does not make the journey to the Croiz Roge: 'A la Croiz Roge le pendit.' A similar telescoping occurs when Marc agrees to send for the dwarf as requested by the barons, when their suspicions have been aroused again:

> 'Mandez le nain, puis soit asis.'
> Et il i est molt tost venuz. [vv. 638-9]

6
Narrative parataxis

Another problem similar to that of 'empty time' is the manner of co-ordinating narrative situations which are more or less contemporaneous but are not interrelated. At the end of the *rendez-vous épié* each of the three protagonists goes off on his own, Marc looking for the dwarf, Yseut confiding in Brengain and Tristran confiding in Governal (the dwarf has divined the king's anger and fled). In the end Marc goes to his wife.

> Molt tost s'en vet [li nains] fuiant vers Gales.
> Li rois vait molt le nain querant;
> Nu puet trover, s'en a duel grant.
> Yseut est en sa chanbre entree. [vv. 336-9]
>
> Tristran ravoit tot raconté
> A Governal com out ouvré. [vv. 381-2]
>
> Ne pout son nain trover li rois. [v. 385]

Here we have six actions. All are narrated in the present tense, except Tristran's words to Governal and the second mention of the king's failure to find the dwarf. Nowhere is there a link between the six actions, except that the difference of tense relates Tristran's action (which in any case is summarised very briefly), and Marc's search for the dwarf, to Marc's visit to the queen; but the link is of the weakest, most indeterminate kind imaginable. The first three actions, contemporaneous both in fact and in verbal expression, are simply juxtaposed and acquire meaning not from their place in a real time scale but purely from their narrative 'presence' at the moment in which they are narrated. Another case will confirm this interpretation. When Tristran has escaped by leaping from the chapel and has found Governal, his next impulse is to rush off and rescue Yseut:

> Ne laisast il qu'il n'i alast,
> Se son mestre ne li veiast.
> En la chanbrë un mes acort,
> Qui dist Yseut qu'ele ne plort. [vv. 1043–6]

Here again there is an instantaneous change of scene and the link between the two situations could not be more elliptical. Again there is absolutely no connection in time between the two scenes: they are linked only by the vague indication of place implied in the 'i' of v. 1043, which, in a totally unspecific manner, refers to Yseut. The following scene begins with nothing less than a particularising article ('*la* chanbre'), which is grammatically uncalled for because no mention has been made of either the chamber or any aspect of the place where Yseut is. Its presence thus confirms the quasi-autonomous nature of the individual scene, which is presented right from its opening words as unrelated to the rest. This does not mean the scene grows out of a haze of imprecision: on the contrary, it rests on the assumption that it has always been familiar. The first verse of each section of the romance is an opening *in medias res*.

The same happens even when one scene could have merged smoothly with another which is nothing more than the immediate development of it, with no change of place or characters. When Tristran brings Marc's reply back to the hermitage, Ogrin reads it and tells him what it says:

> 'Devant le Gué Aventuros
> Est le plez mis de vos et d'eus;
> La li rendroiz, iluec ert prise.
> Cist briés noient plus ne devise.' [vv. 2677–80]

Narrative technique and figurative patterns

With these verses the account of the exchange of letters between Marc and Tristran comes to an end; in view of the terms of the agreement, the lovers' separation is now imminent, and indeed this is the theme of the verses immediately following. The important point to note is that in this last scene, before the verses quoted, the spotlight is on Tristran as he goes to the Croiz Roge and brings back the king's letter, handing it over to Ogrin, who reads it and tells *Tristran* of its contents. Nowhere in this scene is there any mention of Yseut except in so far as she enters into the terms of the agreement. However, after the verses quoted we read,

> 'Dex!' dist Tristran, 'quel departie!
> Molt est dolenz qui pert s'amie!
> Faire l'estuet por la soufrete
> Que *vos* avez por moi fort trete;
> N'avez mestier de plus soufrir.
> Qant ce vendra au departir,
> Ge vos dorrai ma drüerie,
> Vos moi la vostre, bele amie.'   [vv. 2681–8]

Now that the previous theme has been tied up, the next one is immediately broached and its subject and tone are fixed right from the first verse, without the least indication of any change, without even anything intercalated between the two passages of direct speech, though they are completely without connection and between different pairs of interlocutors. Thus the reader's first impression could even be that Tristran is simply expressing to Ogrin or to himself a personal comment on Ogrin's words. But instead the figure of the hermit silently disappears, to return only later, in another fleeting appearance for narrative purposes, when the need arises to send him to St Michael's Mount; and equally silently, with the 'vos' of v. 2684, Yseut appears.

7
The narrative rhythm

The examples we have quoted are all concerned with breaking up the narrative and would be of only limited significance were it not for the fact that the whole narrative rhythm throughout the poem is constantly based on repetitions, even within narrative themes which are well defined and show no possibility of fragmentation. A case in point is the irruption of king and barons into the room where the adultery has just been committed. The scene begins with

L

a description of the positions of the three characters who were already in the room (the lovers and Perinis), and then the tempo quickens considerably:

> Sor la flor, chauz, li sanc parut.
> Li rois choisi el lit le sanc;
> Vermel en furent li drap blanc,
> Et sor la flor en pert la trace
> Du saut. Li rois Tristran menace.
> Li troi baron sont en la chanbre,
> Tristran par ire a son lit prenent.   [vv. 766–72]

The passage is particularly interesting because it contains several examples of repetition: 'sor la flor' in vv. 766 and 769, 'li/le sanc' in vv. 766 and 767, 'li rois' in vv. 767 and 770, 'lit' in vv. 767 and 772, 'Tristran' in vv. 770 and 772. But the passage, although short, does not acquire any greater cohesion because of this. On the contrary, three moments are clearly distinguishable, the appearance of the blood, Tristran confronted by the king, and Tristran faced with the barons. The repetitions actually contribute to the individual completeness of each of these moments; this would not have been achieved if, for example, despite the fact that we already know that Tristran is in bed, 'a son lit' had been omitted from v. 772 and replaced with a reference to what has already been said, or if the subject 'li rois' had not been repeated, which would almost have detached his *choisir* of the blood from his *menacer* of Tristran rather than unify them.

Another instance occurs soon after the hero's appeal to his uncle:

> Il li crie: 'Sire, merci!
> Por Deu, qui pasion soufri;
> Sire, de nos pitié vos prenge!'
> Li fel dïent: 'Sire, or te venge.'
> 'Beaus oncles, de moi ne me chaut;
> Bien sai, venuz sui a mon saut...'   [vv. 783–8]

Examples could be multiplied endlessly: Yseut passing through the lamenting crowd on her way to the stake:

> Amenee fu la roïne
> Jusquë au ré ardant d'espine.
> Dinas, li sire de Dinan,
> Qui a mervelle amoit Tristran,
> Se lait choier au pié le roi.
> 'Sire,' fait il . . . ;   [vv. 1083–8]

or the verses already mentioned:

> [the forester] Du bois s'en ist, cort a mervelle.
> Tristran avoc s'amie dort. [vv. 1850–1]
> Li forestier grant erre acort . . . [v. 1856]

The artistry is simple, but of consummate simplicity. This is shown by any rhetorical outburst, such as Tristran's exclamation when he has escaped from his guards:

> Eschapé sui! Yseut, l'en t'art! [v. 986]

Here juxtaposition turns into artifice, though the artifice is no less expressive and is so obvious that the effect is an ingenuous one. Elsewhere, on the other hand, when we turn our attention from affective colouring to narrative rhythm, the impression is never that the dominant feature is cold calculation or the use of prefabricated moulds. In fact Beroul's presentation in rapid, clashing juxtapositions really seems to be not art but nature, or at any rate it is a perfect fusion of intention and spontaneity. It is perhaps not so much the swift touch in itself, or the omissions, or certainly the fragmentary nature of the scenes, which is important: it is the way in which the scenes, unexpectedly juxtaposed as they are, are all depicted in the same shades, with strong light-and-shade effects, or perhaps even without any light and shade at all. As a result, not only does the narrative link remain implicit: the emotional link becomes elliptic, hinted at but not expressed, and yet never weak or vague. The artistic uniformity is maintained over the various scenes and does not falter; it is always used to a purpose and above all has an extraordinary expressiveness of its own.

Thus the sole effect of these rapid ellipses is that of emphasising the tone of the individual episodes and of the work as a whole: of the individual episodes by virtue of their sudden and extremely lively appearance, and of the whole because they maintain a constant, homogeneous level in every part.

It is clear by now that the two narrative modes, the static and the dynamic, do not contradict each other; and their alternating use does not cause them to interfere with each other as they would if they produced a series of fits and starts unskilfully interspersed with passages of tedium. Not only this, but it is also clear that they actually converge to form a style of composition in intensely illuminated situations, which follow each other in a pressing rhythm with no thought for periods of relaxation. In this way Beroul's narrative rhythm emerges as peculiarly unitary and effective, and even the pauses produced by the repetitions, when they are slowing-down repetitions, serve only to strengthen the single picture.

8
Figurative psychology and imaginative symbols

There is a further characteristic aspect which plays its part in forming this complex homogeneity and coherence in Beroul's narration. Many writers of Beroul's time, especially Thomas, have psychological interests leading to analyses of states of mind, which necessitate a different kind of narrative rhythm. One has only to think of the fundamental importance the courtly poet attaches to detailed investigation of his characters' behaviour, since it is this which characterises them more than the action, and one immediately understands the particular link between action and psychological analysis in texts of that kind. The narrative rhythm we have characterised in Beroul could hardly absorb such a heterogeneous, cumbersome element, and it is easy to imagine the lack of balance that would result. But, as we have repeatedly seen, it is scarcely possible to imagine a more unitary narrator than Beroul. His narrative rhythm is what it is not because it is not required to embrace psychological analyses, but because it is itself another product of his particular intuition of psychological reality, an intuition which is not analytic but synthetic and figurative, one which is immediately translated into images instead of being discussed, one which is seen, not investigated.

When Marc, perched in the tree, discovers to his relief that the lovers are not engaged in a sinful relationship,

> Souef m'en ris. [v. 492]

But when the dwarf, looking in through the window, sees them lying together,

> de joie en trenble. [v. 738]

The 'chorus' recalls the occasion when Tristran challenged the Morholt:

> Qant le Morhout prist ja ci port,
> Qui ça venoit por nos enfanz,
> Nos barons fist si tost taisanz. [vv. 848–50]

When Dinas's appeal for mercy towards Yseut is rejected,

> En piez se live o chiere encline. [v. 1132]
> Chiere encline, marriz et morne. [v. 1140]

When Ivain asks the king to give the queen to the lepers,

> Li rois l'entent, en piez estut,
> Ne de grant pice ne se mut.
> Bien entendi que dit Ivain,
> Cort a Yseut, prist l'a la main. [vv. 1217–20]

Marc's long uncertainty and his decision, which calls for immediate implementation before fresh uncertainties arise—all this is presented in a purely visual idiom. Yseut pleads for mercy but

> Li rois li done, et cil la prent. [v. 1223]

The end of the effect of the potion is presented in monologues which clarify the new psychological situation. But even before these it is portrayed, with captivating charm, in a single figurative contrast:

> Fuit s'en li cerf, Tristran l'aqeut;
> Que soirs fu plains tant le porseut.
> La ou *il cort* aprés la beste,
> L'ore revient, et *il s'areste*,
> Qu'il ot beü le lovendrant. [vv. 2155–9]

The monologue ends on another image equally charged with significance:

> Tristran s'apuie sor son arc,
> Sovent regrete le roi Marc,
> Son oncle, qui a fait tel tort,
> Sa feme mise a tel descort. [vv. 2195–8]

When the lovers return to Ogrin, who at an earlier stage has observed with disappointment their stubbornness in sin,

> L'ermites l'ot parler, si plore,
> De ce qu'il ot Deu en aoure. [vv. 2331–2]

When the lovers must separate before Marc's court, Tristran

> De la roïne congié prent;
> L'un l'autre esgarde bonement.
> La roïne fu coloree,
> Vergoigne avoit por l'asenblee. [vv. 2913–16]

It should be noted that the visual touch precedes its analysis, on the occasions when it is analysed. Still in the same scene, while Tristran is making his way towards the sea,

> Yseut o les euz le convoie;
> Tant con de lui ot la veüe,
> De la place ne se remue. [vv. 2930-2]

We have already looked at Marc's reaction when the barons demand an *escondit* on the part of the queen:

> Li rois escoute, mot ne sone,
> Sor son arçon s'est acoutez,
> Ne s'est vers eus noient tornez. [vv. 3122-4]

And there is an echo of Marc's laugh in the tree in Yseut's laugh when she sees Andret and the forester killed by Tristran and Governal:

> S'en rist doucement soz sa ginple. [v. 4056]

The poet's imaginative vision is always so clear that it can render every feeling and every emotional situation with compelling immediacy. We shall look at just one further example, which is not exactly a figurative translation of an inward state but still a piece of narration entirely resolved in visual terms, in images. It is a hunting scene:

> Tristran prist l'arc, par le bois vait,
> Vit un chevrel, ancoche et trait,
> El costé destre fiert forment;
> Brait, saut en haut et jus decent;
> Tristran l'a pris, atot s'en vient. [vv. 1285-9]

The death of the roe deer is described in considerable detail, but not because Beroul is striving for *vraisemblance* or logical motivation: it is translated completely in the cry of the wounded animal and its dying leap and fall.

We should also examine the dialogues and monologues, the context *par excellence* for any courtly psychological introspection, as can be seen simply by reading Thomas. In Beroul, though, there is hardly any trace either of the conventional stock of themes or of the customary dialectical patterns. Even the dialogues and monologues are made up of interwoven images, as is amply illustrated by the words of Tristran and Yseut at the *rendez-vous épié* or the lovers' monologues when they finally escape the effect of the potion;

these speeches are wholly built out of images of their happiness in the past.

Thus it can be clearly seen how far removed Beroul is from any form of naturalistic realism. His totally externalised, figurative psychology bears no relation to any programme of analytic observation of reality or 'non-intervention' on the part of the narrator. We have seen repeatedly how he does not think twice about intervening in his work, and in fact does it in such a way that it is a decisive factor in the tone of the romance. And, as we have now also seen, the organisation of the scenes is diametrically opposed to the demands of realistic *vraisemblance*, in that no account is taken of the apparatus necessary to justify the moments of dramatic intensity; it is such moments alone that are isolated and brought into focus in this isolation. Figurative psychology and elliptical structure do not merely correspond by not disturbing each other, but positively converge towards a single level of narrative presentation, thus eliminating the suggestion of any veristic aspirations in Beroul and making the romance much more what we might call (if we could strip the word of its modern connotations) an expressionistic work.

We should now go back to what we took as our starting point, the narrative rhythm of the work as a whole. This rhythm undoubtedly sets the tone of the whole tale, allowing room for its vigour, and creating its fascination. And since its function is to give maximum significance to individual scenes, in which the tale is not fragmented but welded together and brought alive, it is legitimate to look once again at these scenes. They are not slices of life but significant moments which contribute towards a coherent unity precisely because they are such. Reality is chopped up and put into perspective with no other guiding principle than the tendency to harmonise it in images—not figures which are arbitrary or which have significance only as links in a chain, but figures which are valid in themselves. This can be seen in vv. 766–70:

> Sor la flor, chauz, li sanc parut.
> Li rois choisi el lit le sanc;
> Vermel en furent li drap blanc,
> Et sor le flor en pert la trace
> Du saut.

These verses take up a theme which has already been formulated:

> Sa plaie escrive, forment saine;
> Le sanc qui'n ist les dras ensaigne.

> La plaie saigne; ne la sent,
> Qar trop a son delit entent.
> En plusors leus li sanc aüne. [vv. 731–5]
> Au tresallir que Tristran fait,
> Li sans decent—malement vait—
> De la plaie sor la farine. [vv. 747–9]

But now the blood seems to be the only thing there is in the room: its dramatic presence pervades everything.

It will now be clearer why we have occasionally used the word 'symbol'. But we are now in a position to be more precise and correct. Beroul's images are not 'symbols' in the everyday sense because they are not 'symbols of something', that is, they do not refer to some transcendent reality, nor to some other level of truth outside themselves, nor to some esoteric meaning. They are rather 'symbols of themselves' in that they have the expressive power of a symbol without its mediating function; in fact, the meaning is contained within them—is both their imaginative vitality and their passionate human background. So, rather than symbols, these are figurative emblems of a human situation which is created and brought to life by the imagination and therefore transformed into an absolute experience, an image with significance for everyone. It is this that leads us to see in these emblems, and in the rhythm which binds them together, the nucleus, the essence, of Beroul's poetry, because it is here that all the elements separated out by critical analysis flow together again and fuse with each other: the human passion, born of the moral and social problems, the tone of fantasy to which the most varied cultural experiences contribute, and the 'utilitarian' end of the tale. All these components are certainly fused into unity in Beroul's romance, even in the larger narrative elements; but there is no doubt that the power and cohesion of the poem are due to this very coexistence of the various components even in the smallest element, whether structural or imaginative.

Notes

1 Cf. Fourrier's *Le Courant Réaliste*, vol. 1.
2 What is suspect in Fourrier is not only the separation of imagination from rational thought, but also the identification of the former with the marvellous. One of the inevitable contradictory conclusions is that courtly literature is on the one hand realistic in that it takes the greatest

of pains over psychological verisimilitude, but on the other hand unrealistic because it is this same literature which adopts the Breton narrative material. The two contradictory tendencies are in fact related at a deeper level. Since Fourrier does not seem to have enquired what 'reality' meant for the twelfth century, he does not enquire whether the supernatural is only a mythological screen which allows the writer to give dignified expression to problems and desires essentially those of the moment in which the work was written.

3 See, for example, Schürr's *Das altfranzösische Epos*, p. 405 and p. 407, n. 19, though this does admittedly make a slight attempt at documentation by giving a couple of references. On the other hand Heinzel, in his 'Gottfrieds von Strassburg *Tristan*', had shown some interest in it, but merely for the purpose of his vivisection.

4 It is enough to look at the introduction to Arnold's edition, p. xc. More generally cf. Warren's 'Some features of style' and Biller's *Etude sur le style des premiers romans français en vers*, pp. 43–51.

5 *De oratore*, book III, 53, section 202.

6 Cf. Biller, *op. cit.*, p. 19.

7 A comparable situation arises in vv. 2927–34, and once again there is an abundance of repetitions.

8 Cf. also v. 436: 'Nule foiz mais ne me mandast.'

9 *Op. cit.*, p. 24n.

10 On this split dialogue cf. Warren, *art. cit.*, pp. 529 *et seq*.

11 Cf. Biller, *op. cit.*, p. 37n.

12 Cf. *ibid.*, p. 42.

13 Cf. just the one case of 'la bele Yseut' (vv. 3208, 3400, 3434, 3775 and 3958), and 'Yseut la bele' (vv. 3375, 3892, 3939, 3961, 4191 and 4244, and cf. vv. 4250 and 4426).

14 As can be seen from Rychner's *La Chanson de Geste*, pp. 80 *et seq*. Needless to say, chapter 4 of Rychner's book has been extremely valuable in my study of Beroul.

15 I have modified Ewert's punctuation, which is as follows: 3697 Pas; 3698 dras.

6
Beroul and the literary problems of his period

Even if one were to accept that the question of realism is of fundamental importance in medieval French literature, it would be difficult to show that it exerted any systematic influence before 1200. In discussing a twelfth-century text, for even a provisional cultural systematisation it is rather the question of *courtoisie* which should be regarded as the necessary touchstone.

With regard to Beroul, critics' judgements on this matter have until recent times been unanimous, and it seems opportune to exemplify them by quoting an authoritative exponent of the main stream of opinion, Robert Bossuat: 'Moins cultivé que Thomas, moins pénétré de moeurs courtoises, Béroul est plus éloigné d'*Enéas* que des chansons de geste, dont il a gardé l'esprit clair et naïf, en respectant certains de leurs procédés techniques.'[1]

We should emphasise the way in which Bossuat feels it necessary to determine Beroul's literary position by means of two co-ordinates, the *Enéas* and the epic; his judgement would not be substantially changed if the *Enéas* were replaced by Chrestien.

But this view, which was until recently the standard interpretation, has found an energetic antagonist in Pierre Jonin. Jonin undertakes a quite detailed analysis in which he places on one side all the elements suggesting non-courtly presentation and on the other all the courtly elements, seeking to determine which way the balance swings. Since it seems to him that the courtly elements have the greater weight, he considers himself authorised to conclude that Beroul can justly be called courtly.[2]

Jonin's study undoubtedly has the merit of being a meticulous, unbiased examination, but it does not seem that Beroul's literary position, or that of any writer, can be determined through an analysis which is quantitative rather than qualitative, particularly one which takes as its underlying terms of reference the two abstract concepts of courtliness and non-courtliness and seeks to discover which of the two better suits the text under discussion. What should carry much more weight is not the assignment of a label, which, as such, is bound to be unsatisfactory and skeletal, however numerous the arguments in its favour, but a concrete investigation of the precise shading resulting from the coexistence of heterogeneous elements, which is inevitable in any text, since no writer can help being affected in some way and to some extent by the influences and tendencies current in the cultural modes of his time. A study which sets out to isolate the most prominent tendency and to assign the whole text to it unreservedly, even if it is conducted with sufficient caution and impartiality to avoid obviously erroneous conclusions, does no more than impoverish a complex literary configuration by reducing it to a single denominator. On a wider scale, this kind of approach makes literary history into a series of pigeon-holes labelled by concepts which are identified by abstract means and become fundamental only secondarily and artificially, and transforms the critical process into the business of arranging works in these pigeon-holes despite the fact that none of those in a single compartment can really be identified either with its fellows or with the concept to which it has been reduced.

In fact the purpose of literary history is neither to produce a simplified classification of doubtful usefulness, nor to isolate critical forms such as courtliness and non-courtliness, but to examine the concrete, contradictory existence in a historical literary scene, and therefore in a field of active and passive influences, of individual works and individual authors. Abstract concepts should be continually related to the literature and treated in each individual case precisely as ideals of the past, or aspirations for the future, or programmes of a literary circle, or poetic theories of an author, or in any other appropriate manner, but always within, not above, the sphere of concrete reality and always as auxiliary concepts used for convenience towards the single primary purpose. That purpose can be nothing other than to characterise and investigate a work or an author or a relationship or a *milieu* in its totality rather than label it according to one of its aspects.

In Beroul's case the real problem is clearly the extent to which he adheres to, or is susceptible to the influence of, that series of related literary considerations which we call courtly, in other words, the distinguishing features of the *avant-garde* literature of the maturest and most informed literary circles of his time. But the object of our investigation cannot be to establish whether or not he may be regarded as courtly, but to determine the actual prominence and the actual tone in his work of courtly *motifs* and forms, and their relationship with *motifs* and forms of other origins. Thus, if we wish to identify Beroul's literary position in concrete terms, we shall have to examine his poem against the varied literary panorama of the late twelfth century, which, if our work is fruitful, we shall no doubt in our turn help to enrich and define.

I
The rendez-vous épié

In order to carry out this programme I do not believe the right approach is to isolate particular themes from the work as a whole. Since we wish to keep the object of our enquiry as concrete as possible, the greatest mistake would be precisely that of taking certain elements out of their various contexts and examining them under highly artificial circumstances. We shall therefore select complete episodes, beginning with the first, the *rendez-vous épié*.

The first part of the tale has been lost, but this creates no great difficulties, especially since the parallel with Eilhart here seems quite a close one. Tristran has been banished from the court, but has remained in contact with the queen by means of a trick. Through the garden of the royal palace runs a brook which flows through Yseut's chamber: Tristran comes at night to the spring which is the source of the brook and, by cutting wood chips in an agreed manner and putting them in the stream, makes his presence known to the queen, who comes to join him. But the dwarf Frocin has discovered their secret and arranges for Marc to hide in the pine tree beside the spring. The lovers then arrive but perceive that the king is there[3] and proclaim their innocence through misleading speeches. Tristran asks the queen to make representations to the king on his behalf, if nothing else to have his *hernois* released so that he can leave Marc's kingdom, but Yseut disdainfully refuses any kind of help. Marc listens with satisfaction and, while resolving to take his revenge on the dwarf, decides to authorise his nephew's return to court (vv. 1–319).[4]

We shall begin by examining the situation of Marc, which is quite out of keeping with his regal dignity even if we consider only the physical position he assumes by perching in a tree to eavesdrop; it would be difficult to find a parallel to this strange and uncomfortable position the monarch adopts. But what is more serious is that he is in the tree to play the role of the befooled husband: below him are his wife and her lover removing all doubt from his mind that their adultery is nothing more than base insinuation by a number of malevolent courtiers. From the top of the tree reality is turned upside-down in the eyes of the husband, and in fact this note is repeatedly struck in his monologue, right from the first words:

> 'Las!' fait li rois, 'or ai veü
> Que li nains m'a trop deceü ...   [vv. 265-6]
> Ge l'en crui et si fis que fous ...   [v. 273]
> Or puis je bien enfin savoir;
> Se [the adultery] feüst voir, ceste asenblee
> Ne feüst pas issi finee ...   [vv. 298-300]
> Au parlement ai tant apris
> Jamais jor n'en serai pensis.'   [vv. 313-14]

The theme is also expressed in the intermediate passage of indirect speech:

> Et mescroit les barons du reigne,
> Que li faisoient chose acroire
> Que il set bien que n'est pas voire
> Et qu'il a prové a mençonge ...   [vv. 288-91]
> Ne jamais jor ne mescroira
> Tristran d'Iseut.   [vv. 295-6]

In this conflict between differing versions of the truth ('En son cuer dit or croit sa feme Et mescroit les barons du reignc', vv. 287-8) the one Marc opts for is both the one more in line with his family affections and the one he seems to have discovered at first hand, while the other alternative is regarded by him as slanderous insinuation. He sets a very significant proverbial seal on his choice: 'Molt est fous qui croit tote gent' (v. 308), without realising the ironical tone which these words assume in his mouth since he has just been deceived. The 'mençonge' (v. 270) of dwarf and barons now appears to him as disgrace (v. 268), 'traïson' (v. 294), 'outrage' (v. 306), and the dwarf will have to pay the price for it:

> Se je le puis as poinz tenir,
> Par feu ferai son cors fenir.   [vv. 275-6]
> Or ne lairai q'au nain ne donge
> O s'espee si sa merite
> Par lui n'iert mais traïson dite.   [vv. 292-4]

The inversion of reality is thus complete and the penalty previously reserved for the lovers is now the threatened fate of the informer. This second transfer is underlined by the king's allusion to the vengeance of Constantine: he will punish Frocin in the same manner as the emperor dealt with the dwarf Segoçon for seducing his wife.[5] For Marc the parallel lies in the fact that in both cases the guilty party is a dwarf, but for poet and reader the allusion becomes a symbol of the lovers' deception and the king's transposition of truth and illusion.

It almost seems that the narrator, instead of making the king perch in a pine tree,[6] would have done better to put him in that pear tree made famous by Boccaccio and La Fontaine. The *motif* of the enchanted pear tree, characteristic of the *nouvelle*, was certainly widely known in the twelfth century and is found in a little work which is almost contemporary with Beroul and which later served as Boccaccio's direct source, the *Comedia Lidie*.[7] Lidia, after winning the love of Pyrrus through three difficult tests at the expense of her husband Decius, promises her lover something still more striking: she will make Decius a witness to the adultery without his believing the evidence of his own eyes. The three of them go into the garden and stop under a pear tree. Pyrrus is asked to climb the tree to pick some fruit, and while he is up there he accuses the couple of showing him an indecent spectacle. Decius takes Pyrrus's place to see the phenomenon for himself, and is stupefied when it is duly repeated with quite different realism between Lidia and Pyrrus. Decius is convinced of the enchanted nature of the tree, which is subsequently cut down. The tale is also found, without the pear tree, in a coarse *fabliau* by Garin,[8] in which it is a priest who tricks a peasant, and the hallucination takes place in a doorway.[9]

All these tales, and many similar ones which could also be mentioned, have in common the theme of confusion between truth and illusion:

> Miratur Decius et uix sibi credulus heret.
>   Plus stupet incertis certior illa uidens.
> 'Aut sic est, aut fallor,' ait, 'aut uisus inane
>   Ventilat, aut uigilans sompnia uisa puto.'
> 'Vt uidit, fateor, uidi, uerumque putaui;
>   Sed tamen hic uideo certius esse nichil.'[10]

The theme reaches the point of paradox in Marie de France's fable 44:[11] the *vilein*, watching the adulterous lovers from the door of his house, laments his misfortune and his wife replies, *curuciee*,

> 'Bien sai,' fet ele, 'n'en dut mie,
> que c'est vostre vieille folie:

> tu vuels tenir mençunge a veire.'
> 'Jel vi,' fet il, 'sil dei bien creire.'
> 'Fols iés,' fet ele, 'se tu creiz
> pur verité quan que tu veiz.'[12]

But these texts do not have that pathetic sense of the difficulty involved in arriving at the truth, such as we find in Marc's words. The other texts limit themselves rather to dull-witted amazement at the false appearance of truth and the convincing appearance of illusion; what is believed costs nothing in terms of trouble or suffering.

One element which distinguishes the Tristran story from the others is the fact that it does not make the deception so pronounced as to have the husband present at the consummation of the adultery. But it is not only this which saves us from mistaking the episode for a *fabliau*. We have seen how Marc is convinced that he has got to the truth and turns his wrath on the dwarf, who has talked him into the baseness of suspicion and eavesdropping; towards the lovers we hear him show only compassion:

> De la pitié q'au cor li prist,
> Qu'il ne plorast ne s'en tenist
> Por nul avoir; molt a grant duel,
> Molt het le nain de Tintaguel. [vv. 261–4]

Later he tells Yseut,

> Qant j'oï a Tristran retraire
> La bataille que li fis faire,
> Pitié en oi, petit falli
> Que de l'arbre jus ne chaï. [vv. 479–82]
>
> Pitié m'en prist a l'arbre sus,
> Souef m'en ris, si n'en fis plus. [vv. 491–2]

This feeling of compassion, which shrouds the lovers' present situation seen against the backcloth of their past, is quite different from the dull-witted credulity of the stock befooled husband, who is generally a purely passive character,[13] is tricked and convinced, and has no other reaction than, at most, inert credulity projected into the future to crown his stupidity.[14] Although Marc is subjected to a treatment which is basically the same, he has an infinitely richer human quality; it is this compassion for those who are deceiving him, which might be expected to be resolved in yet another comic *motif*, that redeems him, by pointing out his genuine sensitivity to other people's suffering and above all his emotional commitment. Such attributes are substantially alien to the traditional figure of the deceived husband, who is jealous rather than amorous and more concerned with his right of possession than wounded in his feelings. Marc's compassion is not comic because it is born of affection, and affection and compassion restore to the king, clownishly perched in the pine tree having the wool pulled over his eyes, a dimension quite foreign to the exceedingly slight figure typical of the comic tale; they give him a seriousness which none of his fellow victims ever had.

To qualify Beroul's personal mixture still more precisely, it should be said that those qualities which save Marc from being crudely comic also make him equally remote from the courtly world. In the courtly context the figure of the betrayed husband can be resolved in two ways. Sometimes his violent, brutal reaction alienates him from the ideal of refinement, which is incarnated rather in the lovers. Such is the case in *Laostic* or *Flamenca*, where the husband represents a kind of opposite extreme, an antithesis to the courtly ideal, living at a different cultural level from the other characters; his intervention is therefore bound to come from without, thus breaking the magic circle of courtliness. All these features serve to distinguish the traditional anti-courtly husband from the figure of Marc, as regards both his personality and above all his position with respect to the lovers. Alternatively, the husband can be on the courtly level and in that case the only course open to him is to keep out of the lovers' affairs, as if mysteriously absorbed in his own exercise of courtliness, like Arthur in the *Charrette*.[15] In no case does the husband of courtly literature embody that fusion of brutality, alienation, indulgent blindness and, arising out of this fusion, the grossly pathetic comic element characteristic of Marc, and in no case is he redeemed by his own human sensitivity, that is to say, his spiritual richness, which cannot be precisely qualified as courtly. Thus that same verse which at first seemed nothing more than a comment put ironically into his mouth now appears as an epigraph, as it were, on the difficulty of human knowledge: 'Molt est fous qui croit tote gent.'

The writers of the other Tristram romances also found it necessary to remould the figure of Marc in the tree, which becomes more problematic the more courtly the tone of the narration. The only significant descendant of Thomas at this point is Gottfried, who resolves the difficulty by reducing Mark's part to the minimum

and having him remain completely silent, in contrast with the
lengthy speeches of his lovers and the general richness of his
presentation:

> der trûrige Marke,
> der ûf dem boume dâ saz,
> der betrûret' aber daz
> und gieng im rehte an sînen lîp,
> daz er den neven und daz wîp
> z'arge haete bedâht,
> und die in dar an haeten brâht,
> die vervluochte er tûsent stunde
> mit herzen und mit munde.
> er verweiz ie genôte
> dem getwerge Melôte,
> daz ez in haete betrogen
> und ime sîn reine wîp belogen.
> si stigen von dem boume nider
> und riten an daz gejegede wider
> mit jâmer und mit leide.
> Mark' unde Melôt beide
> si haeten zweier hande leit:
> Melôt durch die trügeheit
> die er begangen solte hân;
> Marke durch den arcwân,
> daz er den neven und daz wîp
> und allermeist sîn selbes lîp
> sô haete beswaeret
> und z'übele vermaeret
> über hof und über lant.[16]

[Sorrowful Mark sitting in the tree was moved to sadness by it, and was deeply distressed for having suspected his wife and nephew of infamy. He called down a thousand curses on those who had led him into it—in his heart and also aloud. He roundly accused Melot the dwarf of deceiving him and of slandering his wife. They descended from their tree and rode back to the hunt in a state of great dejection. But Mark and Melot were aggrieved for very different reasons: Melot because of the deception that he was alleged to have practised; Mark because of the suspicion which had induced him to put his wife and his nephew, and most of all himself, to such annoyance and get them so ill spoken of, both at court and in the country][17]

Although, broadly speaking, the king's feelings cannot be very different, it is notable that there is no mention of the inversion of truth, emphasised by Beroul; Gottfried's remoteness from irony is indicated by the mention of the infamy perpetrated on the king himself, which in a less clearly profound and idealised context, such as Beroul's, would have made the humorous element too prominent, though in Gottfried it harmonises quite pleasingly with the general tone.

The scene of the *rendez-vous épié* is extended and reflected in the conversation between king and queen the following morning. To be quite accurate, Gottfried includes this conversation, but the king does not say he has eavesdropped on the lovers, simply,

> wan ich hân sîn unschuldekeit
> in kurzen zîten wol vernomen:
> ich bin es alles z'ende komen. [vv. 15008–10]
>
> [only a short while ago I learned of his [Tristan's] complete innocence and got to the bottom of it all!][18]

The *Tavola Ritonda*, however, has a preliminary dialogue between the king and the accusing counsellor, who is banished from the kingdom, and then another between the king and Tristram, though without any mention of the preceding episode. From this contradiction Bédier formulated only the generic sentence: 'Tous deux rentrent en grâce auprès de lui [Mark] et Tristan revient à la cour.'[19] In the prose romance, too, Mark banishes Audret and then speaks with Tristram before the whole court: 'J'ai vostre loiauté esprouvee en tel maniere que je sai tout vraiment que vos m'amez de bone amor . . .'[20] Only Eilhart (vv. 3652–4), together with Beroul, makes the king explicitly admit his presence at the *rendez-vous*.

So much for the other versions. In Beroul it is not the king but Yseut herself who first speaks of the assignation:

> Sire, le voir vos en desno . . .
> Gel vi et pus parlai a lui,
> O ton nevo soz cel pin fui;
> Or m'en oci, roi, se tu veus. [vv. 400–5]

This represents a particularly striking attitude, because instead of being cautiously content to reap the benefits of the first deception, she gambles with them with the boldest assurance, and in her calculated temerity, which is virtually without risk, she seems to be ruthlessly playing on her husband's good nature. But besides this aspect of her character there are others of a different kind, so that she emerges as a richer figure and the composite tone becomes more complex and conflicting. Yseut does not have the arrogant self-confidence of her fellows:[21] she returns from the spring 'descoloree' (v. 340), and when she concludes her account of the episode to Brengain by saying,

> Partie me sui du tripot, [v. 369]

these final words carry a tone of distaste, of a certain moral detachment.[22] Again, when the king comes, 'Iseut le voit, qui molt le crient' (v. 388).[23] In addition, the theme of truth returns like a nightmarish obsession. The king immediately says,

> Si ne me celez pas le voir,
> Qar la verté ne vuel savoir, [vv. 393–4]

and Yseut replies, as we have already seen,

> Sire, le voir vos en desno;
> Ne croiras pas que voir en die,
> Mais jel dirai sanz tricherie. [vv. 400–2]

After Yseut's account of her conversation with her lover, which she carries off with apparent shamelessness and with more sympathy for Tristran than she had shown at the spring, the comment is:

> Li rois sout bien qu'el ot voir dit,
> Les paroles totes oït. [vv. 459–60]

This *voir*, on which all are agreed, is a false, deceptive truth.

It is at this point that the king discloses Frocin's information and his own presence in the pine tree, with emphatic satisfaction:

> 'Sire, estïez vos donc el pin?'
> 'Oïl, dame, par saint Martin!
> Onques n'i ot parole dite
> Ge n'oïse, grant ne petite.' [vv. 475–8]

The figure of Marc would undoubtedly become a figure of fun were it not for the fact that what strikes him most in the lovers' dialogue seems to centre on the past and on his own emotions. The king does not say he has had proof of their chastity, nor even that he is convinced of their fidelity (it is Yseut who says it for him immediately afterwards); what he dwells on is Tristran's mention of his duel with the Morholt, his wife's allusion to her tending of the wounds inflicted on the hero by the dragon—both factors which conflict with the humble, and yet rejected, request for the 'quitance

De ses gages' (vv. 487–8)—and finally his own deep silent emotion. Whereas Marc is saved from being comic, Yseut seems to slip into a comic role instead when she brazenly pushes on to the logical consequences of the situation by the spring:

> Se il m'amast de fole amor,
> Asez en veïsiez senblant.[24]   [vv. 496–7]

But the most clearly comic tone is reserved for Brengain, who closes the episode with a clownish touch invented by Beroul: when Marc sends her to fetch Tristran she maintains that Tristran hates her *a tort* because he believes her to be guilty of the insinuations made to Marc:

> 'Sire, por Deu, acordez m'i,
> Quant il sera venu ici.'
> Oiez que dit la tricherresse!
> Molt fist que bone lecherresse:
> Lores gaboit a esscïent
> Et se plaignoit de maltalent.
> 'Rois, por li vois,' ce dist Brengain,
> 'Acordez m'i, si ferez bien.'
> Li rois respont: 'G'i metrai paine.
> Va tost poroc et ça l'amaine.'
> Yseut s'en rist, et li rois plus.   [vv. 517–27]

The gradation of the last verse is ironically unbalanced: the two characters both laugh, but for different reasons, and the one who has the better reasons to laugh *plus* is Yseut, not the king. Beroul is not afraid of emphasising his paradoxical innovation, which confuses the notion of truth still further. Brengain tells Tristran, 'Se li rois fait de moi proiere, Fai par senblant mauvese chiere' (vv. 545–6), and Marc goes as far as to make the two cases of 'mautalent' equal in weight when he says to Tristran,

> Ton mautalent quite a Brengain,
> Et je te pardorrai le mien.   [vv. 553–4]

But Beroul emphasises this *motif* only up to a certain point, and after v. 527 and the passage leading up to it there is no further mention of it; Tristran does not even return to it in his reply, which is full of hypocritically indignant reproaches and, in a different tone, completes the ironic texture of the episode:

> Legirement vos defendez
> Vers moi, qui ce m'avez mis sure,

> Dont li mien cor el ventre pleure,
> Si grant desroi, tel felonie! [vv. 556-9]

The concluding verse expresses the king's admission of his mistake and his humble promise:

> Non ferai je, beaus niés, par foi.[25] [v. 567]

    This example should serve to clarify what was said at the beginning of this chapter. Here the material supplied by tradition is so restrictive that it brings all the narrators of the legend face to face with a situation which does not square exactly with any analogous situation covered by the established *genres* of the time, whether the *fabliau*, the completely courtly tale or the *mal mariée*. And the less free the narrators the more significant the tiniest deviation. Gottfried tends to play down the king's part, thus diminishing the grotesque side of the episode, for since the lovers too have been betrayed and spied on and are therefore automatically in one sense in the right, it is unjust to regard their behaviour as completely unrefined when they lie and cover their words with ambiguities. The French and Italian prose romances do not abandon Gottfried's tendency, even if they have not the mastery of taste necessary to avoid all slips. Beroul does not shun the most comic aspects, in fact he adds new ones, but creates a mixture of tones which does not seem to be calculated or subtle; it is not an art of nuances and blended variations but, predictably, an art of juxtaposition, of blocks of colour deliberately clashing with each other, of veinings which are striking and robust but never completely prevalent. This multiplicity, or, as it might be called, this lack of selection of tones, has a striking effect and gives the poem a flavour which is at the same time figurative, imitative, emotional, the poet's own highly original creation (unlike other contemporary tastes), and has great richness and immediacy—a flavour which is both lively and thoughtful, ironic and pathetic, sceptical and resolute.

2
The lepers

However much in the case of the *rendez-vous épié* one must take into account the situation already formed by tradition before Beroul, there still seems to be a certain clear prevalence of tones which are enlivened by both their vigour and their wit. But it would be risky, if no worse, to decide on the basis of these qualities that Beroul

can be classified as plebeian. We shall take another passage and
consider it as an example, again quite a widespread episode,
Tristran's encounter with the lepers. The unfortunate band advances
straight towards the bush where Tristran is lying in wait, and
Tristran 'Fiert le destrier, du buison saut' (v. 1245), ordering Ivain,
the head of the unhappy colony, to free the queen, and threatening
to send his head flying with his sword:

> Ivain s'aqeut a desfubler,
> En haut s'escrie: 'Or as puioz!
> Or i parra qui ert des noz.'
> Qui ces meseaus veïst soffler,
> Oster chapes et desfubler!
> Chascun li crolle sa potence,
> Li uns menace et l'autre tence. [vv. 1250–6]

There is no doubt as to the intention of parody: on hearing the
challenge the lepers respond by accepting it and preparing for the
fight, but, since they are lepers, what they wave about threateningly
is not a sword but their paltry *potence*, their *puioz*, and in contrast with the silent confidence of the knights an animal-like rabble
is depicted, puffing, threatening and making defiant gestures. The
lepers are the only Cornishmen who dare engage in combat with
Tristran, but theirs is a pitiful parody of a combat, which cannot
help but recall similar grotesque pictures, such as that in *Garin le
Loheren*, when at the marriage of Pepin and Blancheflor one of the
many brawls breaks out between the two factions and Begon de
Belin, who is in the kitchen, calls the cooks to his aid:

> Dont veïsiez tant gros pestail saisir,
> Tante cuillier et tant crochet tenir,
> Et tant garçon de la cuisine issir,
> Qui ja vorrunt desor Fromont ferir,[26]

or such as a number of battle formations drawn up by the peasants in
the *Renart*:

> Qui lors veïst vilains venir
> et fremïer par mi la rue!
> Qui porte hache, qui maçue,
> qui flael, qui baston d'espine.[27]

In the *Tristran* the gulf separating the hero and his adversaries
has become enormous. Contrary to his threat,

> Tristran n'en vost rien atochier
> Ne entester ne laidengier. [vv. 1257–8]

It is Governal, running up with 'un vert jarri',[28] who overcomes Ivain and frees the queen. Beroul here departs from the vulgate (and in all probability from his own source) and considers it necessary to defend his version with all the weight of his authority, as we have seen before:

> Li contor dïent que Yvain
> Firent nïer, qui sont vilain;
> N'en sevent mie bien l'estoire,
> Berox l'a mex en sen memoire:
> Trop ert Tristran preuz et cortois
> A ocirre gent de tes lois.   [vv. 1265-70]

Here again we should look at parallels in other texts. Thomas and his imitators have nothing like this; in the prose romance Yseut is liberated by Governal and four of Tristram's companions, but no struggle is described;[29] Eilhart (vv. 4301 et seq.) has the same version as Beroul but there it is Tristram who kills the leader of the lepers, as well as some of his fellow outcasts; as regards the identity of the liberator, only the Berne *Folie* touches on the same version as Beroul.[30]

Thus the tone of the text can with some degree of certainty be attributed to Beroul, and despite the clear contrast between *vilain* and *cortois* (given that the adjective used to describe the *contor* can obviously be transferred to their narrations), it proves, as we suspected, to be irreducible to a simple definition. Certainly Tristran's conduct is in keeping with the sense of detachment which the courtly knight felt towards peasants, and it is in order to make this point that the poet has prepared the preceding anti-courtly picture of warriors who are not just servants or peasants but no less than lepers. Eilhart had not had these scruples, but the reason is simply that for him the head of the lepers is a duke and therefore noble too. This means that Beroul's source probably gave no suggestion on such questions of etiquette. But in order to give his audience and his rivals this lesson in *courtoisie*, Beroul had to insert into his text— and he did it willingly—together with the lepers, a tone of grotesque parody which is uncommon in contemporary texts by poets with courtly aspirations.[31] It is strange that in the one case where Beroul obviously wishes to raise the level of *Kultur* of his protagonist he is the first to break up the stylistic uniformity of the tale. This could seem to be a clear sign that he is incapable of maintaining a particular level which he has decided on in advance, and this may be true, but for a narrator with the power and ability of Beroul an observation of this kind would be merely pedantic and not critical. What it is important to emphasise is rather his indifference towards stylistic uniformity or, better still, his preference for a *pastiche* governed not by rules of rhetoric but by a vigorous taste for bringing things alive with great emotive expressiveness, paying more attention to the vivacity of the tale than to its complete homogeneity; the poem thus emerges as homogeneous not in its calculations based on poetic theory but in its intrinsic strength.

3
The Blanche Lande

The episode which most clearly shows Beroul's particular response to courtly precedents, and not only because of the presence of Artu, is that of the Blanche Lande. Right from the first verses concerning Artu the setting becomes characteristically and predictably literary: when Perinis is on the road to Isneldone, where he has been told the king is in residence, he asks for information 'a un pastor qui chalemele' (v. 3376), and the *pastor* hastens to tell him of the Round Table, 'qui tornoie conme le monde' (v. 3380).[32] The picture of the court is the usual one and the tone suddenly becomes tinged with refined gallantry:

> 'Dex saut,' fait il, 'le roi Artur,
> Lui et tote sa conpaignie,
> De par la bele Yseut *s'amie*!'[33]   [vv. 3398–4000]

Artu immediately conforms to this tone with these surprising words:

> 'Dex!' fait li rois, 'tant ai je quis
> De lié avoir un sol mesage!'   [vv. 3404–5]

hastening to guarantee the messenger fulfilment of his every request and promising to knight him 'Por le mesage a la plus bel Qui soit de ci jusq'en Tudele' (vv. 3409–10).[34] No less significant is the court's reaction to Perinis' message:

> Plorer en font o groses lermes;
> N'i a un sol qui de pitié
> N'en ait des euilz le vis mollié.   [vv. 3448–50]

Weeping as an expression of emotion, whether indignation, grief or even much more superficial feelings, is present throughout the text, but in general it does not seem incompatible with courtly self-control.[35] However this may be, the verses in question smooth the transition to the following scene, in which the sorrow collectively expressed by the 'chorus' in vv. 3451–6 crystallises in the challenges of Gauvain, Gerflet and Evain to Guenelon, Godoïne and Denoalan respectively.[36] This takes place in a manner vividly reminiscent of the challenges made before a battle by epic heroes, who advance one by one to make their request to the king,[37] recall their past victories and direct insults to their adversaries; but even here a courtly *motif* appears when one of the conditions which Gerflet imposes on himself until his vow is fulfilled is that

> Ja n'en enbraz soz le mantel
> Bele dame desoz cortine. [vv. 3480–1]

Moreover, Perinis regards the *menace* as one directed at Artu's court and does not doubt the effectiveness of the court's retaliation:

> Ainz a ta cort n'ot menacié
> Home de nul luintain reigné,
> Que n'en aiez bien trait a chief. [vv. 3499–501]

The king is pleased by the compliment and 'un poi rougi' (v. 3504). As far as he is concerned it goes without saying that the projected meeting will be courtly and therefore it is implicitly assumed that there will be jousting, the importance of which is heightened by the presence of Yseut (vv. 3513–14).[38] It is these plans, and not any wish to settle the case under judgement, that leads them all to wish the meeting could be the following day rather than a week hence. On his return journey Perinis is accompanied for a good part of the way by the king in person, needless to say 'Por la bele franche au chief bloi', who is the sole subject of their conversation, and whose 'demoine soudoier' Artu proclaims himself at their parting, willing to undertake any exploit because 'El me porra molt avancier' (v. 3545).

But now the scene changes and we are told how Tristran disguises himself as a leper, which is somewhat unbecoming for a courtly hero,[39] as is Governal's warning:

> Sire Tristran, ne soiez bric. [v. 3580]

But all this does not alter the fact that Tristran too seems to be affected by the courtly atmosphere when, as we have seen, he proposes to perform 'une esbaudie por l'amor Yseut m'amie'

(vv. 3601–2) and asks that the pennon 'Dont le bele me fist le don' (v. 3604) be put on his lance, which makes a striking contrast with the verse almost immediately following: 'Prist son henap et son puiot' (v. 3607). The description of Tristran squatting in the slime like a begging leper seems to be adumbrated, though nothing more than adumbrated, by the comic aspects of Guillaume d'Orange disguised as a monk:

> Ne senbla pas home contret,
> Qar il ert gros et corporuz,
> Il n'ert pas nains, contrez, boçuz. [vv. 3622–4]

More prominent, however, than the comedy of the contrast between reality and appearance is verbal comedy, that of the calculated trick: Tristran uses ambiguous phrases when asking for alms (vv. 3628–31) and obtains them because

> Tex a esté set anz mignon
> Ne set si bien traire guignon. [vv. 3635–6]

The scene takes on tones of low vulgarity when it describes the conduct of those passing in front of the leper, the insults of some of them and the blows Tristran inflicts with his *puiot*. There clearly emerges a crude taste which is almost picaresque, coloured in extremely rough hues and thrown into sharp relief by the preparations for the jousting ('Pavellons de maintes colors', v. 3666). In this contrast Tristran diabolically succeeds in vindicating his position by causing the knights to fall into the mud. He gives the wrong advice not only to his adversaries, who arrive later, but to all the knights, and enjoys the disastrous result, taking advantage of the situation by asking for alms.[40] The scene breaks every convention of courtly narrative: the protagonist becomes a rogue in both his clothing and his actions, and the traditional respect for knights who are not 'bad' disappears. The scene takes on an unusual perspective: Tristran's disguise and the mud soiling the knights are signs of a deliberate lowering of the tone of the tale towards an extremely elementary level of comedy.[41] And yet Beroul has no difficulty in finding motivation for bringing roguery and courtliness side by side, even verbally:

> Mais il le fait par lecherie,
> Qant or verra passer s'amie,
> Yseut, qui a la crine bloie,
> Que ele an ait en son cuer joie. [vv. 3693–6]

The importance of these verses lies in their function of eliminating the apparent duality of tones between courtly and comic scenes, which they perform by pointing out the participation, though it is a tacit participation, of Yseut; this is the justification and ultimate end of both the courtly atmosphere and the low comedy of Tristran's 'lecherie'. It is obviously not without significance that these developments were implicit in the narrative thread imposed by the traditional tale, even if it were to be maintained that this scene, missing in Eilhart, the prose romance and the *Folies*, and having its only parallel in Thomas,[42] were present in Beroul's source. It is thus these developments more than others that bear witness to Beroul's individual taste.

In the group of characters involved in the comic disguise *motif* no less a person than Artu is included, even if this is only to confirm his liberality with the gift of the scarlet *sorchauz*. The same is true of Marc, who gives Tristran the *aumuce*. Is this a depiction of manners? Is it a realistic picture? The situation must certainly not have been infrequent, but it should be noted that the dialogue with Marc is immediately resolved in a tangle of truth and illusion, of veiled allusions apparently without sense, as is in fact the case with the *Folies*.[43] Tristran says he has caught leprosy from the 'cortoise amie' he used to have, and the king asks him how this occurred:

'Dans rois, ses sires ert meseaus,
O lié faisoie mes joiaus,
Cist maus me prist de la comune;
Mais plus bele ne fu que une.'
'Qui est ele?' 'La bele Yseut;
Einsi se vest con cele seut.'
Li rois l'entent, riant s'en part.   [vv. 3771-7]

Here too, as in the Berne *Folie*, the yardstick of taste does not seem to be that provided by courtly rules, and admits the juxtaposition of the crudest obscenity with the mention of Yseut.[44] It is the same taste as that which, with orgiastic insistence, governs the scene where the *felon* cross the ford, which takes its rhythm alternately from Tristran's misleading counsels ('Oiez du ladre com il ment', v. 3812), which openly tends towards irony,[45] and from the wicked barons' floundering in the slime, which leads to the even greater disgrace of nudity.[46] The scene, demanded by the hatred for the traitors, is developed in a clearly unrealistic way, which confirms

what was said above. The attention of all those present is focused
on this spectacle:

> Cil qui bohordent sor le mont
> Sont acoru isnelement. [vv. 3810–11]
>
> Atant es vos Yseut la bele;
> El taier vit ses ainemis,
> Sor la mote sist ses amis;
> Joie en a grant, rit et envoise,
> A pié decent sor la faloise.
> De l'autre part furent li roi
> Et li baron qu'il ont o soi,
> Qui esgardent ceus du taier
> Torner sor coste et ventrellier. [vv. 3824–32]
> Poi en i a joie n'en ait. [v. 3837]
> Dinas estoit o la roïne,
> Aperçut soi, de l'uiel li cline,
> Bien sout Tristran ert soz la chape;
> Les trois felons vit en la trape;
> Molt li fu bel et molt li plot
> De ce qu'il sont en lait tripot. [vv. 3853–8]

But at the centre of the scene is Tristran in disguise, and in view of
the precarious *vraisemblance* of the situation it is obvious that the
attention with which everyone watches it decreases rather than
increases realism: as we have seen, the disguise is by its very nature
unsuited to the hero's physical build, and therefore if Beroul had
been concerned with realism he would have been wiser not to draw
attention to it and increase the likelihood of its failure. The meaning
and purpose of the scene are therefore to be sought elsewhere,
namely in the orgy of vengeance wrought on the traitor barons, in
the desire to make everyone taste and pay for Tristran's humiliation,
in the wish to present him as victorious and superior even in such a
dishonourable situation.[47] But Beroul can achieve this only because
he is indifferent to the distinctions between the various levels of style.
The barons, the two kings and above all Yseut are all involved in the
ironic humiliation of the three traitor barons and they all enjoy it
to an extent proportionate to their tendency to participate chorally
in the feelings of the protagonists, a participation which is here
pushed beyond the bounds of verisimilitude; but Yseut is made
openly to enjoy a situation which in itself is one of low clowning.
Here again there is a complete levelling of elements which differ
not only in origin but, more importantly, in quality.

An effect of this kind is significant not only in its own right, as a personal stylistic stamp: in this case it also performs a precise narrative function, since it continues without a break right up to the carrying of Yseut on the shoulders of the mock leper, which would otherwise have been very difficult to justify with the necessary plausibility. Yseut's personality features traits which are more pronounced and more clearly relieved than those of the model courtly heroine, and oscillates between extremes which are more varied and less controlled: it is this personality which gives a psychologically credible tone to her decision to climb on the leper's shoulders, a decision which is consistently backed up by her subsequent disdainful refusal to recompense him. It is not because the leper is Tristran, not because there is no difference of social status between them, that she has herself carried by him; the point is that she is carried by *any* leper, and in the many-faceted richness of her personality there are the margins of elasticity necessary to make such an incident possible, to render *vraisemblable* and even predictable a situation totally unthinkable for Guinevere or even Enide. The tone remains consistently unchanged; it, too, is sufficiently flexible to range without dissonance from touches such as

> Sor ses [Yseut's] espaules sont si crin,
> Bendé a ligne sor or fin;
> Un cercle d'or out sor son chief,
> Qui empare de chief en chief,
> Color rosine, fresche et blanche [vv. 3907-11]

to the other extreme:

> Ses cuises tient sor son puiot;
> L'un pié sorlieve et l'autre clot,
> Sovent fait senblant de choier,
> Grant chiere fait de soi doloir. [vv. 3935-8]

These two opposite tones, the one refined and the other violently realistic, are juxtaposed and summarised in two verses:

> Yseut la bele chevaucha,
> Janbe deça, janbe dela. [vv. 3939-40]

The element which links them here seems to be the grin:

> Yseut rist, qui n'ert pas coarde,
> De l'uel li guigne, si l'esgarde. [vv. 3873-4]
> Et lors s'en sorrist li deget; [v. 3932]

it is later unwittingly echoed by those who know and understand nothing:

> Grant joie en meinent li dui roi. [v. 3981]

Does this irony indicate realism? I do not think so, because the smile seems rather, with its ambiguous, elusive tones, to be just one aspect of the striking stylistic mixture rather than its key. This means that at no point does the author seem to depart from full participation in his tale, or appear ideally detached from it, or underline the changeability of his stylistic mixture by justifying it with secondary needs: this mixture turns out to be not a momentary exception but his normal style; what is more, he does not choose now one tone for one scene and now another for another, but co-ordinates both in an area where co-ordination is possible, namely, within the limits of a personal tone.

With the same ease of transition Tristran returns with Governal in courtly attire; the impression is that since the narration has been made to incline heavily in one direction it is now authorised to lay corresponding emphasis on the opposite tone. This can be seen in the whole description of the two knights' accoutrements. Tristran has never shown so much respect for heroic decorum, with his horse, which of course has a name of its own, Bel Joeor, and than which, needless to say, 'Ne puet on pas trover mellor', with the 'enseigne' 'Que la bele li ot tramise' (when, though?), and with the whole apparition dressed from top to toe in black:

> Coste, silie, destrier et targe
> Out covert d'une noire sarge;
> Son vis out covert d'un noir voil,
> Tot ot covert et chief et poil. [vv. 3999–4002]

Gauvain is amazed and does not seem to remember the identical appearance of Cligés;[48] Girflet, who seems pretty well informed in heraldic matters, has a ready answer:

> Noir cheval a et noire enseigne,
> Ce est li Noirs de la Montaigne.[49] [vv. 4015–16]

The other, Governal, in view of his 'armes vaires', must be a foreigner; they are both enchanted, 'gel sai sanz dote'. But in reality only Yseut 'bien les connut' (v. 4033).

These two perfect knights ('Tant bel portent lor garnement Conme s'il fusent né dedenz', vv. 4023–4), who conform so closely in everything, even in the impression they create, to the conventional model, have not come, as they seem to have, 'por los aquerre', and do not stick to the regulations of the tournament, but content themselves with killing Andret and the forester, strangely included in such select company, and are then pursued by all the others, who 'Virent laidier lor conpaignons' (v. 4059).[50] Thus the tournament turns into a matter of hit and run, and the intervention of Tristran and Governal is never explained. They remain for ever 'fantosmes' (vv. 4062 and 4072). Like the preceding burlesques, this scene is also underlined by Yseut's secret laugh:

> Yseut, qui ert et franche et sinple,
> S'en rist doucement soz sa ginple. [vv. 4055–6]

But the ambiguous scene closes with further touches of courtly convention and the description of the barons' magnificent encampment is completed with the verse

> Maint chevalier i out sa drue. [v. 4086]

And there are further details—the knights' generosity:

> Qui out devices n'est pas lenz,
> Li uns a l'autre fait presenz, [vv. 4091–2]

the opulence of clothing and the taste for music:

> Maint calemel, mainte troïne,
> Qui fu la nuit en la gaudine
> Oïst an pavellon soner. [vv. 4111–13]

What conclusion is to be drawn from all this? For one thing, any quantitative calculation seems to become less and less defensible. What meaningful purpose could there be in this episode for distinguishing, listing and weighing the courtly and non-courtly features? What counts is their simultaneous presence, or rather the manner in which they are combined.

It is even impossible to establish the greater sincerity of one tendency and dismiss the other as affectation. Certainly Artu's knights do not really seem to come alive: all they can do is 'bohorder' at every opportunity and seem to exist only as 'bohordanz' (vv. 3712, 3779, 3810, 3984 and 4074), even at the least suitable moments. But even these are only secondary features and it should be realised that courtly habits tend by their very nature to become stylised. In a sense it is true that both courtliness and non-courtliness give the impression of affectation in Beroul, since neither has independent existence for him. Therefore, as thematic and cultural systems they are bound to become nothing more than stylised material in his poem. This makes it all the more true that Beroul cannot be pinned down in terms of these two opposite poles. In the Blanche Lande episode the two tendencies are both simultaneously stronger than elsewhere, but the impression is that their opposing forces balance each other and cancel each other out, providing further confirmation of the substantial originality of the narrative *pastiche* in which they are combined. This allows us to regard Beroul as perfectly familiar with the tendencies which to us seem to contain the vital sap of French narrative literature at the turn of the twelfth century, but at the same time we must recognise that he is endowed with a different and more personal character.

4
The mingling of styles

Before trying to use the conclusions we have reached to place Beroul accurately in the literary panorama of his time,[51] it is necessary briefly to summarise the medieval position with regard to uniformity of tone. We should be mistaken if we were to regard Beroul as exposed to two corresponding and opposing tendencies, the one favouring the mixing of tones and the other inclining towards selection. In reality, flexibility of style and tone is not confined to the *sermo humilis* of the Christian tradition[52] but fully covers the whole field of the epic, including even the most controlled of all, the *Roland*. None of the earliest texts hesitates to juxtapose heroic sublimity and the crudest, most shameless realism, often without even attempting an organic fusion (and thus provoking many suspicions as to the unity of the tales). One need think only of *Gormont*, certainly not one of the later *chansons*: the standard-bearer Hugon is anything but a clownish figure, and yet it is he who smugly tells his enemy Gormont,

> C'est Huëlin qui vos meisele,
> qui, l'autrir, fut a voz herberges
> le message Lowis faire.
> Si vos servi come pulcele;
> le poun mis en l'asquiele:
> unkes n'en mustes la maissele.[53]

Auerbach accurately wrote that 'the lofty tone of the *chanson de geste* breaks with the classical tradition by its impurity, that is, the constant admixture of grotesque and farcical elements'.[54] This means that the second half of the twelfth century is characterised not so much by a conflict between two traditions, but rather by a demand for consistency of tone in certain circles, though these thus remained distinct from the generally predominant taste. The two traditions are therefore not parallel: one, which might be called the 'purist' tendency, is active, while the other is more passive.[55] The demand for homogeneity of form had considerable difficulty in asserting itself and did so only with occasional lack of rigour[56] and even inconsistency within the output of a single writer.[57] These uncertainties on the part of individual writers precisely symbolise the struggle towards a formal ideal which was not fully formed at birth, like a second Athena springing from the head of Zeus, as we seem to believe when we speak of courtliness in abstract terms, but the result and sum of tendencies which were varied, complex and at times even contradictory because of the different personalities of the authors who aspired to the epithet 'courtly'.

The hope of tying up courtly ideals in precise, convenient formulas is too enticing not to have attracted many scholars. In Germany the trend reached the point of a systematic codification which claimed to be based on the *Moralium dogma philosophorum* of Guillaume de Conches, but the attempt did not stand up, as we now know, to the examination of Curtius,[58] who accurately wrote: 'The peculiar charm of the chivalric ethos consists precisely in fluctuation between many ideals, some of them closely related, some diametrically opposed. The possibility of this free interplay, of freedom to move within a rich and manifold world of values, must have been an inner stimulus to the courtly poets.'[59] If we relate these last observations to what was said above on the search for stylistic uniformity, it is obvious that the two processes are parallel and at least in part interrelated, the one as the formal aspect and the other as the ideological aspect of a critical phase in the formation of new cultural standards.

When this situation is referred back to the case of Beroul, the conclusion which must be drawn is that it is impossible to qualify his version of the Tristram tale in purely social terms. One need think only of the *rendez-vous épié* episode, the enormous popularity of which we have noted. Taken on its own, even when attenuated in the courtly versions, it has an undeniably unrefined tone, so that the preference of the public (and of the richest public, which could afford to commission the works of art we are referring to) provides the proof that in the twelfth and thirteenth centuries that selection of tastes which the most refined poets were suggesting had not yet taken place, and that preference was generally given to quite eclectic standards.[60]

5
Love and the motivation of the action

Thus Beroul does not emerge as a popular narrator, or at least the data in our possession do not permit such a conclusion, but on the other hand he is affected to only a limited extent by the new cultural demands. He is not ignorant of these but, in the case of both subject matter and form, accepts only an echo of them; this is totally insufficient evidence to prove any close adherence to them.[61] Instead, he exploits the vast range of tones offered by the more conservative narrative taste, and by applying it to a subject which in its traditional outlines is perfectly suited to such an exercise he obtains strikingly powerful effects from it.

But before concluding it is perhaps necessary to ask oneself if there is not some single point which might serve on its own to clarify Beroul's position in relation to the literature which is most consciously and rigorously courtly. This is without doubt the conception of love, which was raised to a 'paragon of human experience'[62] by all the lyric poets and also by the more recent narrative tradition, transcending all personal divergence of interpretation on the part of individual poets. In terms of love the courtly ideal becomes an individual exercise of perfection, but of this, as we know, only the occasional inconspicuous echo appears in Beroul. This exercise takes the form, in the protagonist of a romance (or in a lyric poet), of minute attention to psychology, resolved in a verbal and dialectical translation of feelings,[63] but again we find virtually nothing of this in Beroul, since he has very few introspective dialogues. As part of the exercise it is love, or rather a particular capacity for, and manner of, loving, which qualifies the hero and makes him worthy of the *aventure*, but neither was this the case in the traditional Tristram tale nor did Beroul do anything to introduce it.[64] Certainly love is the principal motive force behind the action in all the Tristram poems including Beroul's, but here again in a completely different sense from the way it works in courtly literature, because here love remains something undergone and suffered and becomes the instrument of a quite different form of ennoblement, that of man in suffering. Hence Beroul's reaction to such a central point in courtly ideology fully confirms the conclusions we have reached from a different direction.[65]

We could also examine the particular synthesis between individual and social considerations found in courtly literature. Like the epic hero before him, though in a quite different way, the courtly hero has a mission which is, in a sense, of collective interest and for which he is singled out; in fact he struggles not against personal adversaries but against the enemies of Arthur's court, and therefore of courtliness itself, and no action on his part which conflicts with the interests of the court is ever remotely considered.[66] The courtly world is surrounded by an incomprehensible and indefinable series of unknown quantities which every so often break into it and dominate it, necessitating action on the part of the hero, who restores peace by reaffirming with his exploits the victorious superiority of his ideals. This cycle of problems is completely alien to Beroul, whose protagonists are neither embodiments nor defenders of any endangered ideal. Their struggle therefore has no goal outside themselves and their individual happiness, nor does it seem that the events can be raised to the level of an example so that lovers 'aveir em poissent grant confort'.[67] In view of this lack of a transcendental dimension, the punishment of the traitors is limited to their function as personal enemies: neither is there any question of converting them to the ideal of the protagonists (as often occurs in romances) nor is there any attempt to assure the audience of their eternal damnation.

Furthermore, we should note how the action of Beroul's romance is also differently motivated from the action of the epic. Not only is there no similarity with the *chansons* based on a national, religious cause, those in which the combat is fought for *douce France* or to *essaucier Crestientez*, but we are also a long way from the rebellious baron cycle, in which the hero is bound to society by clearly defined legal bonds, violation of which sets the action in motion. The difference is that figures such as Raoul de Cambrai and Girart de Roussillon are at first in the right and if they lose their legal justification it is because their actions go beyond the permitted limits, whereas Beroul's hero, although he seeks to save the formal legitimacy of his actions, is from the outset and always substantially in the wrong because, however involuntarily, he has breached both his moral and his feudal duties. Thus in the rebellious baron *chansons* the juridical problems are of primary importance and provide the motivation, while in Beroul they determine only the forms of the action.

Beroul's is a tale of sufferings and vengeances which are absolutely individual. This does not, however, mean that his hold over the audience is therefore weaker, because the listener does not hear it as a member of feudal society defended against the infidel or against evil, nor as a courtly individual, perfectly convinced of his ideals, but as a man who is sensitive to human suffering.

Beroul's characterisation should be further considered. His protagonists do not evolve as chivalric heroes like Erec or, above all, Perceval. Their identity is static, precisely because what is essential to the tale is not the maturing of the individual but the fact that he finds himself in a dramatic situation; this constitutes an additional reason why the romance should lack a linear unity comparable to that of the examples by Chrestien. On the other hand, while the maturing of the courtly hero is a process of progressive refinement and therefore both of a deepening and a restricting of his personality, Beroul's characters have very wide margins of flexibility and can adapt themselves to varying situations with much greater disregard for an absolute standard.[68] We have seen how Beroul's characters have no internal dialectic and are almost without remorse or problems; this is precisely because he does not have to reckon with any absolute standard. In other words, for Beroul there would be no question, as regards either style or even content, of any uncertainty on Tristram's part regarding the most appropriate behaviour to adopt with Yseult of the White Hands;[69] such uncertainty is wholly based on courtly casuistry. As is not the case with Thomas's protagonists, the force against which Beroul's lovers are struggling is only occasionally and incidentally something inside themselves; generally it is something external and clearly definable, and is wholly personified in the traitors.

But Beroul's poetry does not lie only, as it does in some *chansons de geste*, in the overcoming of an external obstacle, but above all in the suffering which the struggle inexorably imposes. Unlike an epic hero, Beroul's protagonists, although so superficially characterised and analysed, have a touching spirituality of their own because they are single, isolated individuals oppressed by the whole of society, with its suspicions and precepts. This results in a slowing down of the narrative flow, a certain disregard for the tale as a complete cycle of events and a corresponding attention to the pictured scene, which, as a figurative synthesis of the problematic and dramatic feeling for life, is thus designed to contain in itself all the expressiveness, if not all the richness, of the tale.

In order to attain these aims Beroul never resorts to revolutionary means. As we have seen in the course of this study, the formulation of the tale, its ideological structure, and its transposition into formal terms, correspond to clear choices between the possibilities offered by tradition but never break with tradition; on the contrary, Beroul is on the whole quite a conservative writer. His art is not so much an innovation (and in fact it did not attract imitators) as the translation of a personal feeling for life and poetry which is neither new nor original in its components, but elevated and sincere in the poetic synthesis: it is not a landmark of cultural importance but certainly a high point in the history of poetry. Beroul did not write literature which opened up fertile vistas, for the main direction of future development was certainly the courtly one,[70] at least in the field of romance; but he did leave passages of great and moving poetry.

Beroul's position with respect to the narrative tradition does not allow us to isolate new currents or new programmes in the literature of the second half of the twelfth century. It does, however, show that this literature cannot simply be reduced to two poles, the epic and the courtly narrative. In fact in the sphere of the romance there exist positions which are irreducible to these schemes—one need only mention *Horn*—and above all there is a continuous flow of positive solutions which are new and different. An attentive examination of these will no doubt permit the reconstruction of a much more varied and attractive panorama than is generally thought to be possible.

Notes

1 *Le Moyen Age*, p. 64.
2 *Les Personnages Féminins*, on which cf. Wind's 'Les Eléments Courtois' and Lejeune's 'Les "Influences Contemporaines" '.
3 In Beroul each of the lovers realises this independently, as is clear from vv. 3-4, in which Yseut hastens to speak first so that her tone will warn Tristran, and vv. 97-8, where Tristran gathers from Yseut's words that she too has seen the king.
4 This scene is one of the best known in the romance. Besides being contained in all the versions, it also appears as an isolated tale in the *Novellino, nouvelle* 65 (Di Francia's edition, pp. 127-30, or in Segre

and Marti's *La prosa del Duecento*, pp. 854-6). Above all, it was a favourite with illustrators, as can be seen from Loomis and Loomis's *Arthurian Legends in Medieval Art*, pp. 50-69 and corresponding plates. There is a monographic study of this episode based on a comparative approach, Newstead's 'The tryst beneath the tree'.

5 Cf. pp. 34-5.
6 Why it should be a pine tree has been clarified by Del Monte in his *Civiltà e poesia romanze*, pp. 82-8.
7 Published in Cohen's *La 'Comédie' Latine*, vol. 1, pp. 211-46.
8 Published in Montaiglon and Raynaud's *Recueil . . . des fabliaux*, vol. 3, pp. 54-7.
9 Another tale of this kind, in the *Directorium vitae humanae*, John of Capua's translation of *Calila and Dimna*, is examined by Newstead, 'The tryst beneath the tree', pp. 279-80.
10 *Lidia*, vv. 533-4, 537-8 and 549-50.
11 Ed. Warnke, pp. 145-7.
12 All that it needs to convince the peasant that he must distinguish between the evidence of the senses and truth is to make him observe that his reflection in water is unreal. The atmosphere of the fable allows paradoxical schematism of this kind, and redeems it with the irony of the conclusion, exemplary in its own way: 'Dist li vileins: "Jeo me repent! Chescuns deit mielz creire e saveir Ceo que sa femme dit pur veir Que ceo que si malvais ueil veient, Ki par veüe le foleient".' Here, moreover, there is an obvious echo of Ovid's *Amores*, II, 2, vv. 57-8 (Loeb edition, p. 386), already used by Peire Rogier, I, vv. 8 *et seq.* (Appel's edition, p. 37).
13 The husband is active only in *Lidia*, where it is he who suggests that Pyrrus climb the tree (vv. 508-9), and he who decides to climb it in his turn (vv. 527-8). But even here he only anticipates his wife's schemes. Boccaccio eliminates these maladroit initiatives.
14 In Boccaccio the woman loses her temper at what she pretends to regard as an unpardonable lack of trust on the part of her husband. In the end, 'Nicostratus then craving her pardon, she graciously granted it him, bidding him never again to suffer himself to be betrayed into thinking such a thing of her, who loved him more dearly than herself' (*Decameron*, Everyman translation, vol. 2, p. 142). ['a Nicostrato, che di ciò la pregava, benignamente perdonò, imponendogli che più non gli avvenisse di presumere, di colei che più che sè l'amava, una così fatta cosa giammai' (Branca's edition, vol. 2, p. 286).]
15 See Micha's article '*Le Mari Jaloux*', though to me it does not seem entirely convincing.
16 I have followed the last, partial, edition by Ranke, p. 45, vv. 14916-14941. For an assessment of Gottfried, cf. Amoretti's *Il 'Tristran' di Gottfried von Strassburg*.

17 Penguin translation, p. 238. Even more succinct is the *Tavola ritonda* (in Arese's *Prose di romanzi*, p. 318, or in Bédier's edition of Thomas, vol. 1, p. 203): 'E lo re avendo ascoltato loro parlamento, dismonta del pino, dicendo infra sé ched e' non fu già mai la verità che infra Tristano e Isotta fosse mai niuno rio pensamento' ['And the king, having heard their conversation, descends from the pine-tree, saying to himself that it was never true that there was ever a single sinful intention between Tristram and Yseult']. The *Novellino* (Segre and Marti, *op. cit.*, p. 855, or Di Francia's edition, p. 129) has 'E lo re Marco, che era sopra loro, quando udì questo, molto si rallegrò di grande allegrezza' ['And when king Mark, who was above them, heard this, he was much cheered with great joy']. The prose romance, which has Mark climb the tree armed with a bow and arrows with the intention of killing Tristram, resolves the situation thus: 'Car li rois Marc n'i pensera ore mie a si grant mal comme il fesoit devant; la roïne en sera mains gardee, et Tristanz en sera mieus amez du roi Marc, et li traïtor en seront mainz creü; por ce ne leroit il pas que il n'en menast demain ou pois demain hors de Cornoaille la royne Yseult, s'il en venoit en leu, car la royne le voudroit trop bien' (Bédier's edition of Thomas, vol. 2, p. 351).

18 Penguin translation, p. 239.

19 Edition of Thomas, vol. 1, p. 201.

20 Bédier's edition of Thomas, vol. 2, p. 352. In his reconstruction of the original poem (*ibid.*, p. 247) he has, 'le lendemain matin, Marc interroge la reine, et lui avoue comment il a été rassuré. Il rappelle Tristan auprès de lui et lui rend toute sa confiance (*OBTR*)'. Among the variants he points out that in *R* the king banishes Audret. This example serves to illustrate the relationship between the 'reconstruction' and surviving texts.

21 Cf. the brazenly equivocal words of Lidia: 'Nec Pirrus me mouet, immo pirus' (*Lidia*, v. 548).

22 I think it should be recorded that Pauphilet thought otherwise: 'Le poète ne lui prête ni regret d'abuser ainsi le meilleur des hommes, ni honte de la vie menteuse où l'amour la condamne. Son retour est d'un réalisme étonnant: pâle d'émotion, elle résume l'affaire à sa confidente Brangain et conclut: *Le Roi ne s'est douté de rien, je me suis débrouillée. Partie me sui du tripot*, expression d'une vulgarité frappante' (*Le Legs du moyen âge*, p. 129).

23 Cf., in the prose romance, 'Li rois fet mander por Tristan, et *cil i vient liez et joianz*, car bien pensse que il orra noveles qui li pleront' (Bédier's edition of Thomas, vol. 2, p. 352).

24 Boccaccio's Lidia reasons the other way round: 'Foul fall thee, if thou knowest so little of me as to suppose that, if I were minded to do thee such foul dishonour as thou sayst thou didst see me do, I would come

hither to do it before thine eyes! Rest assured that for such a purpose, were it ever mine, I should deem one of our chambers more meet, and it should go hard but I would so order the matter that thou shouldst never know ought of it' (*trans. cit.*, p. 142) ['Sia con la mala ventura, se tu m'hai per sì poco sentita, che, se io volessi attendere a queste tristezze che tu di' che vedevi, io le venissi a fare dinanzi agli occhi tuoi. Sii certo di questo, che qualora volontà me ne venisse, io non verrei qui, anzi me crederrei sapere essere in una delle nostre camere, in guisa e in maniera che gran cosa mi parrebbe che tu il risapessi giammai' (*ed. cit.*, p. 285)].

25 Cf. Eilhart, vv. 3636–764, where there is nothing of all this and only an extremely rough sketch of personalities (cf. also Jonin's *Les Personnages Féminins*, pp. 22–4), which reduces Marc, with his dull-witted, contented credulity, to the same level as his fellow cuckolds.

26 Vv. 6114–17.

27 Ed. Roques, vol. 1, vv. 652–5.

28 Cf. Hoepffner's second edition of the Berne *Folie Tristan*, p. 123.

29 Bédier's edition of Thomas, vol. 2, p. 359.

30 'Ainz par moi n'en fu un desdit, Mes Governal, cui Deus ait! Lor dona teus cous des bastons Ou s'apooient des moignons' (vv. 456–9). This seems to be one of the strongest factors suggesting the dependence of this *Folie* on Beroul: cf. Hoepffner's introduction, pp. 15–16.

31 This discussion of courtliness and baseness remains extraneous to any sociological assessment. An upper-class audience would certainly have enjoyed the parody of the epic, just as a lower-class audience would have admired the ideal consistency constantly demanded of their hero and would not have felt identifiable with the vile band of lepers, alien to any stratum of civilised society at that time.

32 Cf. Frappier's *Le Roman Breton*, p. 69.

33 Cf. 'merci vos crie, Conme la vostre chiere amie' (vv. 3437–8).

34 Just as in the archaic *Lai du Cor*, vv. 144–8, Arthur says to the messenger who has brought him the horn, 'Mangiez e si bevez. Quant jo mangié avrai Chevalier vos ferrai, E cent livres d'or fin Vos dorrai le matin.'

35 Cf. Beszard's *Les Larmes dans l'épopée*. Courtly kings, unlike epic kings, do not usually weep—for instance, Arthur never weeps in Chrestien. Characters of a lower social status, and even Cligés and Yvain, weep more freely.

36 Note that the order of the challenges, apparently reflecting the prominence given to the individual wicked barons (especially since the first to make his challenge is Gauvain), is the opposite of that of their subsequent deaths, which seem to be deliberately graduated. Note too that the same trio of Arthurian knights figures in the *Lai du Cor* (vv. 169–70 and 295–7).

37 Cf. 'Se j'ai de toi l'otrise' (v. 3459). In the *Chanson de Roland* (v. 866)

Marsile's nephew asks his uncle, 'Dunez m'un feu, ço est le colp de Rollant.'

38 Later Tristran, too, says to Governal, 'Cil chevalier d'estrange terre Bohorderont por los aquerre; Et, por l'amor Yseut m'amie, I ferai tost une esbaudie' (vv. 3599–602).

39 On the other hand, Guillaume d'Orange had had no scruples about clownishly disguising himself as a merchant to get into Nîmes (*Charroi de Nîmes*, laisse 40) and at the same time Bertran had put on such crude shoes of ox-hide that he could no longer move and had fallen in the mud, to the playful taunts of his friends (*ibid.*, laisse 39).

40 Similarly Guillaume, too, is abused and has his beard pulled, but immediately gets his revenge (*Charroi de Nîmes*, laisse 51) by killing Harpin and giving the signal for the conquest of the city.

41 'fabliau truculent' (Pauphilet, *Le Legs du moyen âge*, p. 120).

42 Where, predictably, the treatment is quite different. Cf. Bédier's edition, vol. 1, pp. 208–9.

43 A parallel is to be found in Horn, who disguises himself as a pilgrim, clashes with the traitor, enters the king's castle and speaks with Rigmel, at first without her recognising him (*Horn*, laisses 189 *et seq.*); later he and his followers disguise themselves as *jongleurs* in order to rescue Rigmel (*laisses* 241 *et seq.*). But, once again, greater similarities of tone are found in the scene where Guillaume is questioned on his circumstances by King Otran (*Charroi*, laisse 44).

44 This could suggest an intoxication with vice, again similar to that of Guillaume, who passes himself off as a thief (*Charroi*, vv. 1234 *et seq.*). We should not overlook the irony of v. 3777, similar to that of v. 527.

45 'Seignors, la roïne est venue Por fere son aresnement; Allez oïr cel jugement' (vv. 3834–6).

46 'A certain, Ja ne seront mais net sanz bain; Voiant le pueple, se despollent, Li dras laisent, autres racuellent' (vv. 3861–4). On the comic and dishonourable light in which nudity was seen, cf. Curtius's *European Literature*, pp. 433–4.

47 The intention is identical in the *Charroi de Nîmes*.

48 *Cligés*, vv. 4614 *et seq.*: 'Cligés, qui ce ot et escote, Sist sor Morel, s'ot armeüre Plus noire que more meüre; Noire fu s'armeüre tote.' No one recognises him; the following day he appears in green arms and later in red arms.

49 The story of a *noir chevalier* is told both in Wauchier's continuation of *Perceval* and in the *Didot 'Perceval'* (Roach's edition, pp. 213 *et seq.*): cf. Paton's *Studies in the Fairy Mythology of Arthurian Romance*, pp. 208–9. In the *Didot 'Perceval'* he is unnamed, but in Wauchier he is called the Noir Chevalier de l'Arcel de la Sepouture en la Lande.

50 Note that universal solidarity is not here maintained against the wicked barons.

51 I do not think there is any support for the view that the romance was not written at the end of the century, even if, after Whitteridge's clarification ('The date of the *Tristran* of Beroul'), we regard the correction of v. 3849, 'mal dagres', to 'mal d'Acre', which would give a dating after 1191, as mistaken. It should also be mentioned that the manuscript has a large number of errors even in the transcription of proper names (cf. Ewert's 'On the text of Beroul's *Tristran*', p. 96), which makes the conjecture more probable; in any case v. 4285, 'Tristran set molt de Malpertis', does not suggest a much earlier dating, and it is perhaps no coincidence that the cloth of Regensburg (v. 3722) occurs in *Tydorel*, v. 45, and in the *Escoufle*, v. 6704, which led Foulet ('Marie de France et la légende de Tristan', p. 264n.) to assert that it was in fashion for only a short time, approximately 1190–1200.

52 Cf. Auerbach's *Literary Language and its Public*, pp. 25–66, and also, on the inevitable influence on hagiography, Curtius's *European Literature*, pp. 425–8.

53 Vv. 241–6 (cf. also vv. 257 *et seq.* and Bayot's introduction, pp. x–xi). De Vries ('La Chanson de *Gormont et Isembart*', p. 42) claims that these are 'injures, lors de son embassade', but in view of the fact that the 'ambassador' is disguised it is more likely that what we have here is a particularly daring and animated reconnaissance, perhaps only thinly veiled as an embassy, as occurs in the *Aspremont*. The feature clearly comes straight out of the *nouvelle* tradition. Thus Becker was quite wrong to begin his paragraph on the *chanson* (*Grundriss*, vol. I, p. 36) with the words 'The earliest *chansons de geste* in our possession are a succession of genuine historical epics, serious in purpose and of patriotic, martial inspiration.' This would be shown even by a brief glance at what Curtius wrote in his *European Literature*, pp. 429–31 and his *Gesammelte Aufsätze,* p. 156.

54 *Literary Language*, p. 202.

55 It would not, however, be correct to transpose this difference into chronological terms and assume that the courtly tradition superseded the epic. A sizeable number of the surviving epic texts were composed at the end of the twelfth century; they are certainly more or less tinged with courtliness, but demonstrate that for the epic this is a period of full flowering and great popularity.

56 Cf. Auerbach, *Literary Language,* p. 216.

57 Cf. an observation in Jauss's *Untersuchungen*, p. 28: 'In the sphere of Old French literature the heyday of courtly literature does not by any means coincide with the supremacy of the elevated style, which would exclude the *vulgares fabellae*. Marie herself, the contemporary of Chrestien, demonstrates that the boundary between the elevated and low *genres* can run right through the middle of the *œuvre* of a given author.'

58 Now in *European Literature, excursus* XVIII, pp. 519–37.
59 *Ibid.*, p. 535. Cf. also Lazar's *Amour Courtois et Fin'Amors*, p. 23: 'La *Fin'Amors* des troubadours, l'*amour conjugal courtois* de Chrétien, l'*amour-passion* (enrichi de certains éléments de la *fin'amors*) du *Tristan et Iseut* de Thomas et des contes poétiques de Marie de France, ce sont là autant de conceptions qui ne se laissent pas réduire à un dénominateur commun, à une seule et même formule.'
60 On the public of the time and its taste cf. Auerbach's *Literary Language*, pp. 235–338, and pp. 283–6 of my 'I *fabliaux* e la società'.
61 As regards Beroul's culture, besides what we have already said in passing, see the elements gathered together by Novati on p. 399 n. of 'Un nuovo e un vecchio frammento del *Tristan* di Tommaso', and another added by Curtius in his *Gesammelte Aufsätze*, p. 159n.
62 'fiore dell'umana esperienza' (Battaglia in *La coscienza letteraria*, p. 419).
63 'What is distinctive about *Minne* as found in the courtly romance is the detailed analysis of the inmost processes of thought and feeling of which it consists. The novelty lies in the explanation and justification of the intentions and actions of the lovers' (Heyl, *Die Theorie der Minne*, p. 205).
64 Cf. pp. 74 *et seq.*
65 Conversely, the adoption of this approach in the case of Thomas confirms that there too Jonin's procedure is not conducive to convincing conclusions. Far more reliable was the earlier examination by Novati (*art. cit.*), whose conclusion I think can be regarded as completely valid: 'I confess that I would not know where to find a more exquisitely refined conception than this; if this work is not actually imbued with a considerable aura of the chivalric spirit, then I do not have sufficiently clear ideas about what that spirit is' (p. 415). See too the study, which could even be called over-meticulous, by Fourrier in *Le Courant Réaliste*, pp. 43–109. Those characteristics which Jonin regarded as non-courtly must obviously be related to what we said earlier about the flexibility of the system and the personal uncertainties in individual choices of themes and tones. But this does not affect our principal discussion.
66 There is perhaps an exception when Keu confronts Meleagant at the beginning of the *Charrette*, but in fact Keu strikes a discordant note in the Arthurian circle.
67 Thomas, ed. Wind, Sneyd fragment 2, v. 836.
68 The observations of Jauss (*op. cit.*, p. 234), who claims that Beroul does not fall short of the ideal standard, do not seem to me to be persuasive, and are above all limited to only a few points of the complex question. The only absolute standard in Beroul is the social and religious code, 'la loi de Rome' (v. 2194): cf. Frappier's 'Vues sur les conceptions courtoises', p. 144.

69 Thomas, ed. Wind, Sneyd fragment 1.
70 Even if affected by the 'revolution' of Jean Renart (anticipated, moreover, by the unknown author of the French original of *Moriz von Craûn*), which in my view was implicit in the courtly tradition and perfectly unobjectionable, with the result that it does not break away from the path leading to the extremely stylised prose romance.

Postscript, 1971

Returning to something one wrote ten years ago (although this book appeared in Italian in 1963, it was written in 1961) always presents difficult problems, especially if it is not a piece of erudite research or an enquiry of a textual character. In such cases it is generally sufficient to bring the information up to date, to revise what seems to have been objectively proved deficient; but in the case of a critical reading, one's discomfort is much greater, because one's views on methodology, the way in which one approaches the text and the way in which one presents one's conclusions have often changed. In addition, the last decade has brought a great acceleration in the development of new critical notions, which we owe to structuralism and semeiology. And finally, since only a small part of my activity has been devoted to Old French literature (in fact I have concerned myself more with linguistics and Spanish philology), I return to these pages with distinct detachment and therefore with a great desire for such a profound revision as would amount to a new book. But for this very reason, as always happens in such cases, I prefer to leave the original text untouched.[1] What I do, however, propose to do briefly here is to discuss the observations of the reviewers and the principal conclusions reached in Tristram criticism during the last decade.

I am acquainted with the following reviews of the 1963 edition (subsequent references to them will be made simply by mentioning the name of the author):

M. Antunes in *Broteria*, LXXVIII, 1964, p. 520.
V. Bertolucci in *Studi Francesi*, VIII, 1964, pp. 492–5.
A. Ewert in *French Studies*, XVIII, 1964, pp. 145–6.
J. M. Ferrante in *Romanic Review*, LV, 1964, p. 283.
J. Frappier in *Cahiers de Civilisation Médiévale*, VII, 1964, pp. 353–9.
R. Hitze in *Romanische Forschungen*, LXXX, 1968, pp. 177–81.

U. T. Holmes in *Speculum*, XLIII, 1968, pp. 196–8.
M. D. Legge in *Medium Aevum*, XXXIV, 1965, pp. 55–8.
J. Marx in *Etudes Celtiques*, XI, 1964–7, p. 553.
J. C. Payen in *Le Moyen Age*, LXXI, 1965, pp. 600–7.
J. M. Ferrante in *Romance Philology*, XXIV, 1971, pp. 651–6.[2]

I must thank all these scholars for the generosity of their judgements and for the information and ideas which put me in their debt. Almost all of them acknowledge the legitimacy of my aim to work out a reading of the text for what it is (see particularly Payen, p. 602). It is here fitting to quote the words with which Eugène Vinaver defines a similar method: 'Dépouillées de tout parti pris de "décadence" ou de "progrès", elles [les réflexions qu'on va lire] procèdent d'un effort pour découvrir au niveau même des œuvres, *au ras des textes*, comme disait Péguy, ce qui leur confère leur existence propre. [. . .] . . . le domaine propre de toute poétique historique, où règnent à la fois le sentiment de l'intégrité de l'œuvre e la conscience de tout ce qui la relie à nous. On ne saurait y pénétrer qu'au prix d'un double effort de compréhension tendant à situer l'œuvre poétiquement et à nous situer en même temps vis-à-vis d'elle; effort qui ne peut tout d'abord s'exercer que sur des événements poétiques perçus isolément, en dehors de tout contexte collectif.'[3]

Frappier (p. 353), although acknowledging the legitimacy and necessity of the method, remarks that 'sans doute [m']est-il arrivé . . . de trop *m*'enfermer dans *mon* examen particulier sans jeter un coup d'oeil utile et révélateur sur la version parallèle'. I am willing to admit that today I would make wider use of Eilhart and also of the other texts of the legend, though still seeking to preserve a clear distinction between the examination of Beroul and the examination of the tradition of which he is a part. The correct identification of the message certainly involves fitting it into its context and, just as I sought to take the social, emotional and literary context into account, it is necessary to give due weight to the more immediate context, which is precisely the tradition of the Tristram poems.[4]

Similar, but different, is Hitze's objection (pp. 177 *et seq.*): taking 'tradition' to be not that of content but that of technique, she accuses me of making everything the responsibility of a mythical author, Beroul; she also condemns me for being pathetically subjective, and for employing an insidious *a priori* kind of reasoning, both these weaknesses being unconscious ones. It is not difficult to document criticisms of this kind, selecting impeachable sentences and quoting them with opportune excisions, and Hitze does this with an ironic tone. I can share her irony in as much as I feel I have moved away from the style of writing I employed then (which other reviewers, e.g. Holmes, p. 196, and Frappier, p. 353, have remarked upon, but which seems to have been considerably attenuated in the English translation); however, with regard to the basic problem I stand by my opinions. Hitze is one of those who believe that that which is not new, that which is traditional or conventional, has no expressive value of its own. This ingenuous position of hers is contradicted, to make but a simple reply, by the functioning of language, which is conventional by definition and yet capable of extremely varied forms of expressiveness. What we must do is develop instruments capable of measuring expressive efficacy in relation to the type of code which the writer is using. This will certainly need to be done better than I have been able to do it,[5] but it is unpardonable to think all the problems are cleared up when one has found a few parallels for a theme, or a commonplace, or a stylistic device, or a syntagma: when this has been done, only the premisses for the interpretation have been established, and there is nothing to suggest that critical qualification is impossible.[6] As to whether my judgements are *a priori* or born of a meticulous examination of the text, I leave the reader to decide.

The indispensable starting point for an analysis of the text is a decision as to whether and to what extent it is unitary. This has been the most debated problem of recent years. Among the reviewers, Frappier (pp. 358–9) expressed several doubts (cf. also p. 354, on the subject of internal contradictions), though not completely rejecting the hypothesis that Beroul combined several sources into a single work; instead, he suggests (p. 359) the parallel of the *Chanson de Guillaume* and puts forward the hypothesis that Beroul reworked a canvas which Eilhart also used, but with different innovations from those of the German poet.[7] This possibility is to me all the more acceptable in that it squares perfectly with my idea of the Tristram tradition as a whole (cf. my article on 'La teoria dello archetipo tristaniano'). The discussion of the poem's unity has continued to be most lively. Raynaud de Lage has defended his views against Hanoset's criticisms (in 'Faut-il attribuer . . . ?'), but it does not seem to me that he has achieved his purpose. Another front of attack has been opened by T. B. W. Reid ('The *Tristran* of Beroul'), who has sought to re-state the proof that the language of the two authors is not identical; despite Reid's easy success (in 'A further note') against the feeble objection of A. Holden ('Note sur la langue de Béroul'), I do not think his evidence is at all decisive and I stand by my opinion of the text as a unitary work, comforted by the assent of Ewert (*The Romance of Tristran*, vol. 2, pp. 1–3) and by the substantial agreement of Whitteridge ('The *Tristran* of Béroul'). Exponents of the opposite view are Loomis (in *The Development of Arthurian Romance*, p. 83) and Lecoy ('L'Episode du harpeur d'Irlande', p. 544).

A part of the new material concerns the date of the romance. Dominica Legge, who, strangely, accused me (p. 57) of never mentioning this point (she must have missed n. 51 in chapter 6, with which Frappier agrees on p. 358, n. 19, and p. 359, n. 22), has recently maintained (in 'Place names and the date of Beroul') that the romance was written in 1160; but the references to the contemporary situation in Scotland (according to her, Beroul, a Norman-speaking Briton, was patronised by King Conan IV) are extremely insubstantial. At the same time E. M. R. Ditmas ('King Arthur in Béroul's *Tristran*') put forward the theory that the poet's patrons were William of Gloucester and Reginald of Cornwall, which would place the work between 1147 and 1183; in order to be convinced by this we should need at least the full text of her study, which is available for the time being only in summarised form. Whitteridge (*art. cit.*, p. 350) seems to be thinking of the years 1160–75. Of course, the terms of the problem are different for those who admit two authors: even if one retains the late date for the second (cf. Reid, 'The *Tristran* of Beroul': end of the twelfth century or beginning of the thirteenth), the first can easily be placed earlier: Lecoy (*art. cit.*, pp. 544–5) thinks in terms of approximately 1170–5; Raynaud de Lage ('Trois Notes', pp. 524–6) allows that *Erec* quotes the first part; Reid (*art. cit.*) thinks it was written in the third quarter of the century.

On the question of the poem's structure (chapter 1), there seems to be no disagreement, except on minor details. Frappier (pp. 354–5) observes that the autonomy of the episodes is not absolute and does not obliterate their overall connection: this is perfectly fair, and it is opportune to remember, while on the subject, that it is above all the affective constant factors, e.g. the hatred for the lovers' enemies, which bind the text together with their stability. As could have been predicted, opinions on the relationship between the contradictions and the autonomy of the episodes show considerable variation:

Frappier (p. 356) maintains that the most significant indication of the autonomy of the episode, and thus the most striking example of the consequent contradictions, is probably the statement that the effect of the potion has worn off, after which the love does not, however, come to an end; he says I was wrong not to take account of the contradiction from this point of view. It seems to me that this is too debatable an element (cf. *infra*) to bring into play when dealing with a problem which already in itself is none too clear. On the other hand, I would incorporate the contradiction noted by Raynaud de Lage ('Trois Notes', pp. 523–4), who goes on to give a functional explanation which does not differ from my own.

Frappier (p. 355) raises another interesting point when he says it is unconvincing to regard the reminiscence of Orri's *celier* as an improvised image which symbolically explains Yseut's state of mind; he is right in saying that anything can be explained in this way and therefore that it explains nothing, but all I was saying was (see p. 35) that the reminiscence becomes, not a symbol, but the expression, the vehicle, the external sign, of her state of mind. What I would say now is that the text may contain two kinds of reminiscence and perhaps of prophecy (our ignorance of the beginning and end of the romance makes it difficult to be certain): one internal both to the Tristram tradition and to Beroul, the other internal to the former but reaching outside the latter. Of this second type the reminiscence of the *celier* is an example. To me (cf. chapter 9, n. 23), this is not 'a confused recollection of something in Thomas', as Legge calls it (p. 57), but simply a reference to a traditional element not taken up by Beroul, though it was taken up by Thomas (cf. Ewert, vol. 2, pp. 214–15). The case of the relationship between Yseut and Artu could be similar (vv. 3546–9; cf. Ewert, vol. 2, pp. 235–6, and, for other cases, Delbouille, 1959, pp. 420 and 422).

To conclude the discussion of chapter 1 with one further point, I believe that my differentiation between Beroul's method of composition and that of the epic, on which Bertolucci entertains doubts (p. 493) and Hitze waxes ironical (p. 178), is defensible, as Frappier agrees (p. 355). On the function of the lack of continuity, I record the dissent of Payen (pp. 603–4), who, on the one hand, regards it as conditioned by the fragmentary material Beroul was using (but in that case how is one to explain the cases of discontinuity within a single episode?), and, on the other, thinks that the medieval audience was prepared for a story to have alternative developments and had a baroque sensibility which was open to the implausible.

I must confess to not sharing this broad view of what a twelfth-century audience was ready to hear, and, above all, I must admit a diffident attitude towards the use of concepts such as those of *nouveau roman* and baroque in the study of medieval texts, so that I do not disagree with Payen himself when (p. 603) he regards as over-bold my mention of the Way of the Cross (p. 34). Instead, these words of Vinaver's (*op. cit.*, p. 85) seem to me to have considerable relevance: 'A un système de successivité dans l'agencement des épisodes et des descriptions, s'oppose ici un complexe de motifs et de thèmes *toujours présents*; à la conscience du contexte immédiat s'ajoute et parfois se substitue celle d'un contexte thématique.'

On chapter 2 it may be said that there have been no reservations other than that of Hitze (pp. 178–9), who is always ready to confuse what is repeated with what is identical, poetry or oral creation and/or tradition with lettered poetry intended for recitation, such as were all the contemporary romances, including Beroul's.[8] Bertolucci (p. 439) would allow (against my p. 58) that the appeal to the audience is equally intense at least in the *Roland*; it is a question of nuances, but, if nothing else, there is at least a striking difference in the values on which the solidarity between narrator and audience is based.

Chapter 3 is much more controversial. Perhaps Holmes is not wrong when he writes (p. 197): 'We cannot say that Dr Vàrvaro has explained consistently these problems; perhaps no one can.' Frappier (p. 356n.) has observed that I seem to attribute (pp. 75–6) to Beroul alone the invention of the potion; this was not my intention, but certainly I omitted to note that in Eilhart too the love is born exclusively of the potion.[9] Marx stresses the relatively late appearance of this causation of the love,[10] though it is found both in Thomas[11] and in the prose romance.[12]

If the potion is the sole cause of the love, do the lovers have any moral responsibility? Caulkins[13] resolutely states that they do not, so that *pechiez* (v. 1415) means not 'sin' but 'misfortune'. It is more prudent, however, to remain uncertain between the two meanings, as does Ewert (vol. 2, p. 165). Whatever one makes of *pechiez*, it seems to me that, until the end of the three years, one can speak, with Frappier (p. 356), of innocence towards God and guilt towards Marc.[14] I thus agree with Payen (pp. 604–6) that Beroul was influenced by the moral ideas of Abelard.

As regards my analysis of the second meeting with Ogrin, I have been made to think again by a personal communication from the same scholar, in which he throws doubt on the fact that Ogrin is a priest. The implication of this would be that the reason why the confession is omitted is that it could never take place, rather than that it was rejected by the narrator, as I thought.[15] Payen's position differs from mine above all because we set ourselves different problems: what mattered to me was to see whether Ogrin's behaviour was correct or not. None the less, it seems to me impossible to deny that Yseut repents: the promise to sin no more (vv. 2323–4) seems to involve repentance, or at least an admission that she has sinned previously (whatever may be the interpretation of v. 1415).

Nevertheless, the crucial point is that the love continues. Ewert (vol. 2, pp. 194–5) thinks Beroul 'neglects to say that the potion continues to act with diminished power, in the same way as he had neglected to mention the three years' term in the first instance'; Frappier is of more or less the same opinion (p. 356 and 'Structure et sens du *Tristan*', pp. 269 *et seq.*). Delbouille (*art. cit.*, pp. 423–4) thinks that when the three years are up the love remains indissoluble but with a lesser degree of passion. There is no doubt that the attenuation of the potion existed before Beroul (cf. Eilhart), but, unlike the information concerning the duration of the effect of the drink, that concerning its implied continuance is withheld not only at the critical moment, that is, at the end of the three years, but also afterwards, when there should presumably be some explanation of why the lovers continue to meet. Curtis (*Tristan Studies*, pp. 28–35) has sought to explain 'The abatement of the magic in Beroul's *Tristan*' not as an expedient to facilitate the lovers' return from the Morrois (though in fact nothing permits us to say, as she does, that they had reached the limit of their resistance and would therefore have returned anyway), but as a means of marking a turning point in their lives, in the sense that from this moment onwards they can know physical and moral separation. This may be true, but in the part of the poem we still possess there is nothing authorising us to think in terms of either a moral or a physical separation, because the two lovers remain just as united as they were before going to live in the Morrois. However this may be, whether extinguished or attenuated, the effect of the potion no longer justifies the lovers' irresponsibility, and in fact they are conscious of their sin (cf. again vv. 2323–4 and Curtis, *op. cit.*, p. 34), but this does not lead to the slightest change in their situation or in the sympathy they enjoy: this is a decisive proof of the poet's lack of interest in the moral problem, which is compensated for by his interest in problems of a social character.

On these intricate points the most original opinion is that of S. G. Nichols ('Ethical criticism and medieval literature'). Going against all the evidence, Nichols claims that we too share Marc's doubts on the lovers' sin,[16] that the end of the effect of the potion is to be understood as a sign of the maturity of the love (which therefore not only continues, but only now becomes mature), that Ogrin is lax, and that the romance proves that it is possible for a love such as this to exist without threatening social harmony (provided the lovers make a few concessions to society, especially that of concealing the relationship), thus (he says) realising the ideal of *harmonia discors*, to which the twelfth century aspired. It would be a waste of time to reject point by point such extravagant ideas.

I note with surprise that Legge (pp. 56–7) thinks I am convinced of the moral nature of the work. I should have thought, on the contrary, that chapter 4 was wholly dedicated to showing the importance of social problems, which at that time could be none other than feudal ones. To be quite accurate, Frappier (p. 357) has pointed out that the juridical aspects and the religious aspects are inseparable, because the *escondit* and the *deraisne* are judgements by God (cf. my p. 98).[17] As regards the function of Marc's gestures in the hut of leaves, Marx defends his interpretation, and Frappier (p. 357) thinks the juridical values can be seen as complementary to the affective values: in fact I allowed this integration (pp. 116–17), though regarding the affective values as the more important. Vinaver, to whom we owe a perceptive study of the forest episode (*A la Recherche d'une poétique médiévale*, pp. 75–104), thinks the scene 'ne fait qu'affirmer sa [Marc's] présence dans la vie des amants' (pp. 92–3), but he denies that the King's gestures are born of affection (p. 93, n. 29). In his interpretation I notice too that he considers the 'vie aspre et dure' to be 'à l'abri de toute souffrance' (p. 102); it seems to me, on the contrary, that one must distinguish between the material sufferings, on which the poet places great emphasis, and the fact that the love makes them bearable, though without annulling them: cf. Legge, p. 57; Lazar, p. 154; Curtis, *op. cit.*, p. 31; and above all Delbouille, *art. cit.*, p. 421. On the naked sword between the lovers see now pp. 157–9 of 'Isolt of the white hands' by Helaine Newstead, who sees in it the twin influence of the story of Diarmaid and Grainne and that of Amis and Amile. For the text of vv. 1991 *et seq.* I originally followed a suggestion by Henry, but now consider Ewert to be completely convincing (cf. his vol. 2, pp. 186–7).

As for the wicked barons, Bertolucci (p. 494) has rightly observed that they cannot be put on the same level as Ganelon, whose nobility is admired by everyone at the beginning of the *Roland*. Needless to say, the pages on the *felon*, too, failed to satisfy Hitze (p. 179), who observes among other things that to speak of an obsession with the number three, as I did on p. 106, can be explained only as a manner of conceiving philology which is stuck in the Curtius rut without even realising it—a serious defect into which Frappier has also slipped (p. 359, n. 24). On the progressive individualisation of the enemies see now Ewert, vol. 2, pp. 119 and 223; Bertolucci (p. 495) suggests that we have here the figure of speech known as *retardatio nominis*. Perhaps Frappier is right in saying (p. 357) that it is going too far to think the wicked barons disrupt social harmony: but it is not easy to attribute other crimes to them, apart from the arrogance of innate evil.

On the subject of pp. 107-8, it should be added that the backcloth to this situation is quite old and goes back at least as far as a pseudo-etymology quoted by Horace: 'Rex eris . . . si recte facias' (*Epist.*, I, 1, 59-60), and then by Isidore (ed. Lindsay), I, xxix, 3: ' "reges" a regendo et recte agendo'; Isidore writes again later (IX, III, 4): 'Non autem regit, qui non corrigit, Recte igitur faciendo regis nomen tenetur, peccando amittitur. Vnde et apud veteres tale erat proverbium: "Rex eris, si recte facias: si non facias, non eris".' The principle was widely known: cf. Schultz's 'Bracton on kingship', pp. 41-3. A sign of a different situation occurs in Iago's words in *Othello*, IV, 1: 'If you be so fond over her iniquity, give her patent to offend; for, if it touch not you, it comes near nobody.'

In chapter 5, according to Hitze (p. 180), I am too generous towards Beroul's rhetoric and under-emphasise the banal nature of the examples; according to Bertolucci (p. 495), on the other hand, Beroul is a *dictator* who knows and applies all the rules.[18] I would accept Frappier's middle course (p. 357): not all my examples are significant, and perhaps Beroul is even further removed from scholastic rhetoric than I thought. In a word, the conclusions of Raynaud de Lage ('Du Style de Béroul') find me in complete agreement. On the concrete nature of Beroul's imagination see now Rigolot's 'Valeur figurative du vêtement'; important, too, are Vinaver's observations in *op. cit.*, pp. 85 and 99.

In relation to chapter 6, the decisive problem is that of Beroul's assumed *courtoisie*. Jonin's thesis found two other dissenters, neither of whom had read what I had written: Noble ('L'Influence de la courtoisie') uses arguments which are a little crude but none the less accurate; more subtle is D. Stone Jnr. ('El realismo y el Béroul real'), who also gives an excellent analysis of the scene at the Mal Pas[19] and shows clearly how confusing it is to refer *courtoisie* either to love psychology or to the external forms of gallantry. Cf. what Frappier has to say on the subject (p. 358), rightly referring to his well known distinction between *amour courtois* and *courtoisie* (cf. also his 'Structure et sens du *Tristan*', pp. 260 and 263–4).

Köhler[20] judges Thomas to be non-courtly partly because Chrestien de Troyes opposes him in his *Cligés*;[21] thus he regards as synonymous not only Chrestien and courtliness but also sociality and courtliness (and hence extra-sociality and anti-courtliness). In reply to this reasoning, I can only say again that if *courtoisie* is given an interpretation which is rigid, or anchored to fixed parameters, and if individual works are not seen against the background of a quite coherent field of aspirations, which must be analysed in their ever-shifting combinations and juxtapositions, then the discussion of *courtoisie* will always remain abstract. In Köhler's analysis the fixed parameters are Chrestien and the social nature of his work: but is not the love of the troubadours often extra- or anti-social? The aspirations which make up the background include the ethical, the psychological, the thematic, the formal, etc, and exist on distinct levels which must not be confused. What matters is not to establish whether Beroul or Thomas is courtly or not, but *how* he is courtly, or, better still, how he relates to the problems current in contemporary literary culture. Problems such as Legge's (p. 58) ('The story of Tristan and Iseult is one of uncourtly passion and neither Beroul nor Thomas was capable of making it fit the Procustean beds of their own devising. Why they tried is one of the great mysteries of literature.') are exemplarily ill-formulated, because the fact is that they did try and that their work met with great success. Thus it remains to be explained what they did and how they did it, which is what I have tried to do for Beroul, though of course running into the disapproval of Hitze (pp. 180–1), who finds the method completely unsuitable; perhaps this is because she has not realised that my whole discussion leads to the same conclusion as that defended by her, that Beroul represents a stage in the evolution of French literature from epic forms to the forms of the more mature romance, and perhaps also because she confuses the evolution of *genres* with chronological evolution. In the case of epic and romance the two parabolas do not coincide, and the result is a phase displacement which it was my purpose to illustrate, not in abstract terms but through concrete analyses.[22]

Notes

1 The only modifications in the text are the updating of bibliographical references in notes 55 (p. 17), 3 (p. 68), 3 (p. 91), 43 (p. 132), 61 (p. 134), 59 (p. 195) and 62 (p. 195), and a change in the title of chapter 4, which was rightly criticised by Frappier on p. 356 of the review mentioned immediately below; the correction of the numerical data on pp. 8–9 is to be credited to the translator.
2 By the time I was able to read Ferrante's second review it was too late to take account of it in this Postscript.
3 *A la Recherche d'une poétique médiévale*, pp. 10 and 12.
4 This is what I tried to do in my article 'L'utilizzazione letteraria'.
5 It has been noted, e.g. by Frappier (p. 357), that the examples in chapter 5 are not completely convincing, and this is certainly true; it does not follow, however, that the conclusions of that chapter are erroneous.
6 Moreover, between Hitze's neo-traditionalist position and that of Curtius, which she attacks so harshly, there is much greater similarity than she believes, precisely in this lack of sensitivity to the individual quality of every context, a fact to which Lionel Friedman has drawn her attention in *Romance Philology*, XXII, 1969, p. 336. The placing of my method beside that of such a great scholar as Curtius is a compliment to me, but it seems that Hitze missed note 3 in chapter 2.
7 Delbouille, in 'Le Premier roman de Tristan', p. 420, thinks the text is all the work of one writer who reworked several sources.
8 Cf. Gallais, 'Recherches sur la mentalité des romanciers français'.
9 Cf. Frappier, 'Structure et sens du *Tristan*', pp. 266 *et seq*.
10 *Nouvelles Recherches*, pp. 282–3n.
11 Cf. Frappier, *art. cit.*, pp. 273 *et seq*., though he rejects Marx's proposal to assume that in the archetype the love existed before the potion; cf. also Beyerle's 'Der Liebestrank im Thomas-Tristan' and Jodogne's 'Comment Thomas d'Angleterre a compris l'amour'; on Gottfried cf. Schröder's 'Der Liebestrank in Gottfrieds *Tristan und Isolt*'.
12 In opposition to what Fedrick attempted in 'The love potion', Curtis's *Tristan Studies*, pp. 19–23, is perfectly convincing.
13 'Beroul's concept of love', a note which, starting from reasonable premisses, arrives at exaggerated conclusions.
14 On the divine protection of the lovers, often affirmed in the text but never certain, cf. the very perceptive comments in Frappier's 'Structure et sens du *Tristan*', pp. 447–9.

15 Payen has returned to these problems in his book *Le Motif du repentir*.
16 For the opposite view, see Lazar's *Amour Courtois et Fin'Amors*, p. 153. According to this scholar (pp. 154–5), the lovers' positions in the hut of leaves and the first conversation with Ogrin are a pretence, but this is unproved, as is also the statement (p. 156) that they repent insincerely after the end of the three years; also, the conception of Marc as a *fabliau* husband (p. 154) is unsubtle.
17 On the connection between Tristran's challenges and his faith in God's help see Frappier's 'Structure et sens du *Tristan*', pp. 445–6; but perhaps Bédier was not completely wrong when he threw doubt on the lovers' confidence in the triumph of justice.
18 Conversely, and with reference to the same passage, Vinaver rightly observes that there is also such a thing as non-scholastic rhetoric (*op. cit.*, p. 82); cf. also Curtis, *op. cit.*, pp. 54–7.
19 Cf. also Newstead's 'The equivocal oath', which has some good observations on Beroul (p. 1081), but also has the mistaken conviction that Artu appears there in the quality of a judge (p. 1084).
20 In his review of Fourrier's *Le Courant Réaliste*, and again in his *Ideal und Wirklichkeit* (pp. 267–71).
21 But on this cf. Bertolucci's 'Di nuovo su *Cligés* e *Tristan*'.
22 See also Hackett's observations on Beroul's syntax in her 'Syntactical features common to *Girart de Roussillon* and Beroul's *Tristan*'.

Bibliography

Reviews of the Italian edition of this book are listed on pp. 197–8

Arese, F. (ed.), *Prose di romanzi: il romanzo cortese in Italia nei secoli XIII e XIV*, Turin, 1950.
Benedeit, *Voyage of St Brendan*, ed. E. G. R. Waters, Oxford, 1928.
Beroul, *Roman de Tristan*, ed. E. Muret, Paris, 1903.
— *Roman de Tristan*, ed. E. Muret, Paris, 1913.
— *Roman de Tristan*, ed. E. Muret, Paris, 1927.
— *Roman de Tristan*, ed. E. Muret and L. M. Defourques, Paris, 1947.
— *The Romance of Tristran*, ed. A. Ewert, two vols, Oxford, 1939–70.
Biket, Robert, *Lai du Cor*, ed. F. A. Wulff, Lund, 1888.
Boccaccio, Giovanni, *Decameron*, ed. V. Branca, two vols, Florence, 1952.
— *Decameron*, trans. E. Hutton, Everyman's Library, two vols, London, 1955.
Cantar de mio Cid, ed. R. Menéndez Pidal, three vols, Madrid, 1908–11.
Chanson d'Aspremont, ed. L. Brandin, two vols, second edition, Paris, 1923–24.
Chanson de Guillaume, ed. D. McMillan, two vols, Paris, 1949–50.
Charroi de Nîmes, ed. J.-L. Perrier, Paris, 1931.
Charroi de Nîmes (ms D), ed. E. Lange-Kowal, Berlin, 1934.
Chastelaine de Vergi, ed. F. Whitehead, second edition, Manchester, 1931.
Chrestien de Troyes, *Cligés*, ed. A. Micha, Paris, 1957.
Cohen, G. (ed.), *La 'Comédie' Latine en France au XIIe siècle*, two vols, Paris, 1931.
Couronnement de Louis, ed. E. Langlois, second edition, Paris, 1925.
Didot 'Perceval', ed. W. Roach, Philadelphia, 1941.
Eilhart von Oberge, *Tristan*, ed. F. Lichtenstein, Strasbourg, 1877.
Folie Tristan (Berne), ed. E. Hoepffner, second edition, Paris, 1949.
Garin le Loheren, ed. J. E. Vallerie, Ann Arbor, Mich., 1947.
Gormont et Isembart, ed. A. Bayot, second edition, Paris, 1921.
Gottfried von Strassburg, *Tristan und Isold*, ed. F. Ranke, Berne, 1946.
— *Tristan*, trans. A. T. Hatto, Penguin Books, 1967.
Guillaume le Clerc, *Fergus*, ed. E. Martin, Halle, 1872.
Lai du Conseil, ed. A. Barth, *Romanische Forschungen*, XXXI, 1912, pp. 799–872.
Marie de France, *Fables*, ed. K. Warnke, Halle, 1898.
— *Lanval*, ed. J. Rychner, Geneva, 1958.
Moniage Guillaume, ed. W. Cloëtta, two vols, Paris, 1906.
Montaiglon, A., and Raynaud, G. (eds.), *Recueil Général et complet des fabliaux des XIIIe et XIVe siècles*, six vols, Paris, 1872–90.

Morawski, J. (ed.), *Proverbes Français Antérieures au XVe siècle*, Paris, 1925.
Mort le Roi Artu, ed. J. Frappier, Geneva and Lille, 1954.
Novellino, ed. L. di Francia, Turin, 1945.
Ovid, P. N., *'Heroides' and 'Amores'*, ed. and trans. G. Showerman, Loeb Classical Library, London, 1925.
Pèlerinage Charlemagne, ed. E. Koschwitz, third edition, Leipzig, 1895.
Prise d'Orenge, ed. B. Katz, New York, 1947.
Quatre Fils Aymon, ed. F. Castets, Montpellier, 1909.
Roman de Renart, ed. M. Roques, six vols, Paris, 1948-63.
Segre, C., and Marti, M. (eds.), *La prosa del Duecento*, Milan and Naples, 1959.
Thomas, *Le Roman de Tristan*, ed. J. Bédier, two vols, Paris, 1902-05.
— *Les Fragments du Roman de Tristan*, ed. B. H. Wind, Leiden, 1950.
— *Romance of Horn*, ed. M. K. Pope, two vols, Oxford, 1955-64.
Wace, Robert, *Brut*, ed. I. D. O. Arnold, two vols, Paris, 1938-40.

Amoretti, G. V., *Il 'Tristan' di Gottfried von Strassburg*, Pisa, 1934.
Appel, C., *Das Leben und die Lieder des Trobadors Peire Rogier*, Berlin, 1882.
Auerbach, E., *Mimesis*, trans. W. Trask, New York, 1957.
— *Literary Language and its Public in Late Latin Antiquity and in the Middle Ages*, trans. R. Manheim, London, 1965.
Battaglia, S., *La coscienza letteraria del medioevo*, Naples, 1965.
Bayrav, S., *Symbolisme Médiéval (Béroul, Marie, Chrétien)*, Paris, 1957.
Becker, P. A., *Grundriss der altfranzösischen Literatur*, vol. 1, Heidelberg, 1907.
Bédier, J., *Les Légendes Epiques: recherches sur la formation des chansons de geste*, four vols, third edition, Paris, 1917-29.
Bernheimer, R., *Wild Men in the Middle Ages: a Study in Art, Sentiment and Demonology*, Cambridge, Mass., 1952.
Bertolucci, V., 'Di nuovo su *Cligés* e *Tristan*, *Studi Francesi*, VI, 1962, pp. 401-13.
Beszard, L., *Les Larmes dans l'epopée,* Halle and Strasbourg, 1903.
Beyerle, D., 'Der Liebestrank im Thomas-Tristan', *Romanistisches Jahrbuch*, XIV, 1963, pp. 17-86.
Biller, G., *Etude sur le style des premiers romans français en vers (1150-1175)*, Göteborg, 1916.
Bolelli, T., 'La leggenda del Re dalle Orecchie di Cavallo in Irlanda', in *Due studi irlandesi*, Pisa, 1950, pp. 43-98.
Bossuat, R., *Le Moyen Age*, Paris, 1955.
Bréhier, E., *La Philosophie du moyen âge*, second edition, Paris, 1949.
Brugger, E., review of J. Loth, *op. cit.*, *Zeitschrift für französische Sprache und Literatur*, XLVII, 1925, pp. 218-39.

Burger, A., 'Le Rire de Roland', *Cahiers de Civilisation Médiévale*, III, 1960, pp. 2–11.
Carlyle, R. W. and A. J., *A History of Mediaeval Political Theory in the West*, six vols, Edinburgh and London, 1915.
Castro, A., *La realidad histórica de España*, Mexico, 1954.
Caulkins, J. H., 'Béroul's concept of love as revealed in *Tristan et Iseult*', *Bulletin Bibliographique de la Société Internationale Arthurienne*, XXI, 1969, p. 150.
Curtis, R. L., *Tristan Studies*, Munich, 1969.
Curtius, E. R., *European Literature and the Latin Middle Ages*, trans. W. Trask, New York, 1953.
— *Gesammelte Aufsätze zur romanischen Philologie*, Berne and Munich, 1960.
Delbouille, M., 'Les Chansons de Geste et le livre', in *La Technique littéraire des chansons de geste (actes du Colloque de Liège)*, Paris, 1959, pp. 295–408.
— 'Le Premier roman de Tristan', *Cahiers de Civilisation Médiévale*, V, 1962, pp. 273–86 and 419–36.
Del Monte, A., *Tristano*, Naples, 1952.
— *Civiltà e poesia romanze*, Bari, 1958.
Dessau, A., 'L'Idée de la trahison au moyen âge et son rôle dans la motivation de quelques chansons de geste', *Cahiers de Civilisation Médiévale*, III, 1960, pp. 23–6.
De Vries, J., 'La Chanson de *Gormont et Isembart*', *Romania*, LXXX, 1959, pp. 34–62.
Ditmas, E. M. R., 'King Arthur in Béroul's *Tristran*', *Bulletin Bibliographique de la Société Internationale Arthurienne*, XXI, 1969, p. 161.
Eberwein, E., *Zur Deutung mittelalterlicher Existenz (nach einigen altromanischen Dichtungen)*, Bonn and Cologne, 1933.
Esmein, A., *Cours Elémentaire d'histoire du droit français*, fifth edition, Paris, 1925.
Ewert, A., 'On the text of Beroul's *Tristran*', in *Studies in French Language and Mediaeval Literature presented to Professor Mildred K. Pope*, Manchester, 1939, pp. 87–98.
Faral, E., *Les Arts Poétiques du XIIe et du XIIIe siècle: recherches et documents sur la technique littéraire du moyen âge*, Paris, 1958.
Fedrick, A., 'The love potion in the French prose *Tristan*', *Romance Philology*, XXI, 1967–68, pp. 23–34.
Foulet, L., 'Marie de France et la légende de Tristan', *Zeitschrift für romanische Philologie*, XXXII, 1908, pp. 161–83 and 257–89.
Foulon, C., 'Le Conte des oreilles du roi Marc dans le *Tristan* de Béroul', *Bulletin Philologique et Historique*, 1951–52, pp. 31–40.
Fourrier, A., *Le Courant Réaliste dans le roman courtois en France au moyen âge*, vol. I, *Les Débuts (XIIe siècle)*, Paris, 1960.

Frappier, J., *Le Roman Breton: les origines de la légende arthurienne: Chrétien de Troyes*, Paris, 1950.
— *Les Chansons de Geste du cycle de Guillaume d'Orange*, two vols, second edition, Paris, 1967.
— 'La Composition du *Conte du Graal*', *Le Moyen Age*, LXIV, 1958, pp. 67–102.
— 'Vues sur les conceptions courtoises dans les littératures d'oc et d'oïl au XIIe siècle', *Cahiers de Civilisation Médiévale*, II, 1959, pp. 135–56.
— 'Structure et sens du *Tristan*: version commune, version courtoise', *Cahiers de Civilisation Médiévale*, VI, 1963, pp. 255–80 and 441–54.
Gallais, P., 'Recherches sur la mentalité des romanciers français du moyen âge', *Cahiers de Civilisation Médiévale*, VII, 1964, pp. 479–93, and XIII, 1970, pp. 333–47.
Ganshof, F. L., *Feudalism*, trans. P. Grierson, third edition, London, 1964.
Gautier, L., *Les Epopées françaises*, four vols, second edition, Paris, 1878–92.
Giese, W., 'König Markes Pferdeohren', *Zeitschrift für romanische Philologie*, LXXV, 1959, pp. 493–506.
Gilson, E. H., *The Spirit of Medieval Philosophy*, trans. A. H. C. Downes, second edition, London, 1950.
Golther, W., *Die Sage von Tristan und Isolde. Studie über ihre Entstehung und Entwicklung im Mittelalter*, Munich, 1887.
— *Tristan und Isolde in den Dichtungen des Mittelalters und der neuen Zeit*, Leipzig, 1907.
Graf, A., *Roma nella memoria e nelle immaginazioni del medio evo*, two vols, Turin, 1883.
Guerrieri Crocetti, C., *La leggenda di Tristano nei più antichi poemi francesi*, Genoa and Milan, 1950.
Hackett, W. M., 'Syntactical features common to *Girart de Roussillon* and Beroul's *Tristan*', in *Medieval Miscellany presented to Eugène Vinaver*, ed. F. Whitehead, A. H. Diverres and F. E. Sutcliffe, Manchester, 1965, pp. 157–66.
Hanoset, M., 'Unité ou dualité du *Tristran* de Béroul?', *Le Moyen Age*, LXVII, 1961, pp. 503–33.
Heinzel, R., 'Gottfrieds von Strassburg *Tristan* und seine Quelle', *Zeitschrift für deutsches Alterthum*, XIV (N.F. II), 1869, pp. 272–447.
Heller, B., 'L'Epée symbole et gardienne de chasteté', *Romania*, XXXVI, 1907, pp. 36–49, and XXXVII, 1908, pp. 162–3.
Henry, A., *Etudes de syntaxe expressive*, Paris, 1960.
Heyl, K., *Die Theorie der Minne in den ältesten Minneromanen Frankreichs*, Marburg, 1911.
Hofer, S., 'Das Verratsmotiv in den Chansons de Geste', *Zeitschrift für romanische Philologie*, XLIV, 1924, pp. 594–609.

Hofer, S., 'Die Komposition des Tristanromans', *Zeitschrift für romanische Philologie*, LXV, 1949, pp. 257–88.
Holden, A., 'Note sur la langue de Béroul', *Romania*, LXXXIX, 1968, pp. 387–99.
Hollyman, K.-J., *Le Développement du vocabulaire féodal en France pendant le haut moyen âge (étude sémantique)*, Geneva and Paris, 1957.
Jauss, H. R., *Untersuchungen zur mittelalterlichen Tierdichtung*, Tübingen, 1959.
Jodogne, O., 'Comment Thomas d'Angleterre a compris l'amour de Tristan et Iseut', *Lettres Romanes*, XIX, 1965, pp. 103–19.
Jonin, P., *Les Personnages Féminins dans les romans français de Tristan au XIIe siècle. Etude des influences contemporaines*, Gap, 1958.
— 'Le Songe d'Iseut dans la forêt du Morois', *Le Moyen Âge*, LXIV, 1958, pp. 103–13.
Kelemina, J., *Geschichte der Tristansage nach den Dichtungen des Mittelalters*, Vienna, 1923.
Kienast, W., *Untertaneneid und Treuvorbehalt in England und Frankreich*, Weimar, 1952.
Köhler, E., review of A. Fourrier, *Le Courant Réaliste*, *Zeitschrift für romanische Philologie*, LXXVIII, 1962, pp. 529–36.
— *Ideal und Wirklichkeit in der höfischen Epik*, second edition, Tübingen, 1970.
Langfors, A., *Les Incipit des poèmes français antérieures au XVIe siècle*, Paris, 1917.
Lazar, M., *Amour Courtois et Fin'Amors dans la littérature du XIIe siècle*, Paris, 1964.
Lecoy, F., review of G. Raynaud de Lage, 'Faut-il attribuer ... ?' *Romania*, LXXX, 1959, pp. 88–9.
—'L'Episode du harpeur d'Irlande et la date des *Tristan* de Beroul et de Thomas', *Romania*, LXXXVI, 1965, pp. 538–45.
Le Gentil, P., 'La Légende de Tristan vue par Béroul et Thomas. Essai d'interprétation', *Romance Philology*, VII, 1953–54, pp. 111–29.
— 'L'Episode du Morois et la signification du *Tristan* de Béroul', in *Studia philologica et litteraria in honorem L. Spitzer*, ed. A. G. Hatcher and K. L. Selig, Berne, 1958, pp. 267–74.
Legge, M. D., review of P. Jonin, *Les Personnages Féminins*, *Cahiers de Civilisation Médiévale*, III, 1960, pp. 510–12.
— 'Place-names and the date of Beroul', *Medium Aevum*, XXXVIII, 1969, pp. 171–4.
Lejeune, R., 'Les "Influences Contemporaines" dans les romans français de Tristan au XIIe siècle. A propos d'un livre récent', *Le Moyen Âge*, LXVI, 1960, pp. 143–62.
Loomis, R. S., 'Breton folklore and Arthurian romance', *Comparative Literature*, II, 1950, pp. 289–306.

Loomis, R. S., *The Development of Arthurian Romance*, London, 1963.
Loomis, R. S. and L. A., *Arthurian Legends in Medieval Art*, London and New York, 1938.
Loth, J., *Contributions à l'étude des romans de la Table Ronde*, Paris, 1912.
Marx, J., *Nouvelles Recherches sur la littérature arthurienne*, Paris, 1965.
Menéndez Pidal, R., 'Leyenda de la condesa traidora', in *Historia y epopeya*, Madrid, 1934, pp. 1–27.
— 'La épica española y la *Literaturästhetik des Mittelalters* de E. R. Curtius', in *Castilla, la tradición, el idioma*, Madrid, 1945, pp. 75–94.
— *La España del Cid*, fourth edition, Madrid, 1947.
— *Poema de mio Cid*, seventh edition, Madrid, 1955.
— 'Fórmulas épicas en el *poema del Cid*', in *Los godos y la epopeya española*, Madrid, 1956, pp. 241–55.
— *Flor Nueva de romances viejos*, eleventh edition, Madrid, 1958.
Mergell, B., *Tristan und Isolde. Ursprung und Entwicklung der Tristandichtung des Mittelalters*, Mainz, 1949.
Micha, A., 'Le Mari Jaloux dans la littérature romanesque des XIIe et XIIe siècles', *Studi Medievali*, XVII, 1951, pp. 303–20.
Muret, E., 'Eilhart d'Oberg et sa source française', *Romania*, XVI, 1887, pp. 288–363.
— review of W. Röttiger, *op. cit.*, *Romania*, XXVII, 1898, pp. 608–19.
Murrel, S. E., *Girart de Roussillon and the Tristan Poems*, Chesterfield, 1926.
Newstead, H., 'The tryst beneath the tree: an episode in the Tristan legend', *Romance Philology*, IX, 1955–56, pp. 269–84.
— 'King Mark of Cornwall', *Romance Philology*, XI, 1957–58, pp. 240–53.
— 'Isolt of the white hands and Tristan's marriage', *Romance Philology*, XIX, 1965–66, pp. 155–66.
— 'The equivocal oath in the Tristan legend', in *Mélanges offerts à Rita Lejeune*, Gembloux, 1969, vol. 2, pp. 1077–85.
Nichols, S. G., 'Ethical criticism and medieval literature: *Le Roman de Tristan*', in *Medieval Secular Literature: Four Essays*, ed. W. Matthews, Berkeley and Los Angeles, Cal., 1965, pp. 68–89.
Niermeyer, J. F., *Mediae latinitatis lexicon minus*, twelve vols, Leiden, 1954–65.
Noble, P., 'L'Influence de la courtoisie sur le *Tristan* de Béroul', *Le Moyen Age*, LXXV, 1969, pp. 467–77.
Nolting-Hauff, I., *Die Stellung der Liebeskasuistik im höfischen Roman*, Heidelberg, 1959.
Novati, F., 'Un nuovo ed un vecchio frammento del *Tristan* di Tommaso', *Studj di filologia romanza*, II, 1887, pp. 369–515.
Paton, L. A., *Studies in the Fairy Mythology of Arthurian Romance*, second edition, New York, 1960 (first edition 1903).

Pauphilet, A., *Le Legs du moyen âge*, Melun, 1950.
Payen, J. C., *Le Motif du repentir dans la littérature française médiévale*, Geneva, 1967.
Pellegrini, S., *Studi rolandiani e trobadorici*, Bari, 1964.
Pope, M. K., 'Note on the dialect of Beroul's *Tristan* and a conjecture', *Modern Language Review*, VIII, 1913, pp. 189–92.
Raynaud de Lage, G., 'Faut-il attribuer à Béroul tout le *Tristan*?', *Le Moyen Age*, LXIV, 1958, pp. 249–70.
— 'Postscriptum', *Le Moyen Age*, LXVII, 1961, pp. 167–8.
— 'Trois Notes sur le *Tristan* de Béroul', *Romania*, LXXXIII, 1962, pp. 522–6.
— 'Du Style de Béroul', *Romania*, LXXXV, 1964, pp. 518–30.
— 'Faut-il attribuer à Béroul tout le *Tristan*?' *Le Moyen Age*, LXX, 1964, pp. 33–8.
Reid, T. B. W., 'The *Tristran* of Beroul: one author or two?', *Modern Language Review*, LX, 1965, pp. 352–8.
— 'A further note on the language of Beroul', *Romania*, XC, 1969, pp. 382–90.
Rigolot, F., 'Valeur Figurative du vêtement dans le *Tristan* de Béroul', *Cahiers de Civilisation Médiévale*, X, 1967, pp. 447–53.
Robson, C. A., 'The technique of symmetrical composition in medieval narrative poetry', in *Studies in Medieval French presented to A. Ewert*, Oxford, 1961, pp. 26–75.
Röttiger, W., *Der heutige Stand der Tristanforschung*, Hamburg, 1897.
Rychner, J., *La Chanson de Geste. Essai sur l'art épique des jongleurs*, Geneva and Lille, 1955.
— *Contributions à l'étude des fabliaux*, two vols, Neuchâtel and Geneva, 1960.
Sauerland, E., *Ganelon und seines Geschlecht im altfranzösischen Epos*, Marburg, 1886.
Schoepperle, G., *Tristan and Isolt: a Study of the Sources of the Romance*, Frankfurt and London, 1913; reprinted New York, 1951.
Schröder, W. J., 'Der Liebestrank in Gottfrieds *Tristan und Isolt*', *Euphorion*, LXI, 1967, pp. 22–35.
Schultz, F., 'Bracton on kingship', in *L'Europa e il diritto romano: studi in memoria di P. Koschaker*, Milan, 1954, vol. I, pp. 41–3.
Schultz-Gora, O., 'Zur französischen Metapher und ihrer Erforschung', *Germanisch-Romanische Monatsschrift*, IV, 1912, pp. 217–33.
Schürr, F., *Das altfranzösische Epos. Zur Stilgeschichte und inneren Form der Gotik*, Munich, 1926.
Stauffer, M., *Der Wald. Zur Darstellung und Deutung der Natur im Mittelalter*, Berne, 1959.
Stone, D., Jr., 'El realismo y el Béroul real', *Anuario de estudios medievales*, III, 1966, pp. 457–63.

Tobler, A., 'Methodik der philologischen Forschung', in *Grundriss der romanischen Philologie*, ed. G. Grober, second edition, Strasbourg, 1904–06, vol. 1, pp. 318–60.
Tobler, A., and Lommatzsch, E., *Altfranzösisches Wörterbuch*, eight vols, Berlin, 1925–69.
Van Dam, J., 'Tristanprobleme', *Neophilologus*, xv, 1930, pp. 18–34.
Varvaro, A., 'I *fabliaux* e la società', *Studi mediolatini e volgari*, viii, 1960, pp. 275–99.
— 'La teoria dell'archetipo tristaniano', *Romania*, LXXXVIII, 1967, pp. 13–58.
— 'L'utilizzazione letteraria di motivi della narrativa popolare nei romanzi di Tristano', in *Mélanges de langue et de littérature du moyen âge et de la renaissance offerts à Jean Frappier*, Geneva, 1970, vol. 2, pp. 1057–75.
Vinaver, E., *A la Recherche d'une poétique médiévale*, Paris, 1970.
Waremann, P., 'Spielmannsdichtung. Versuch einer Begriffsbestimmung' (dissertation), Amsterdam, 1951.
Warren, F. M., 'Some features of style in early French narrative poetry (1150–70)', *Modern Philology*, III, 1905, pp. 179–209 and 513–39.
Whitehead, F., 'Tristan and Isolt in the forest of the Morrois', in *Studies in French Language and Mediaeval Literature presented to Professor Mildred K. Pope*, Manchester, 1939, pp. 393–400.
Whitteridge, G., 'The date of the *Tristan* of Beroul', *Medium Aevum*, XXVIII, 1959, pp. 167–71.
— 'The *Tristan* of Béroul', in *Medieval Miscellany presented to Eugène Vinaver*, ed. F. Whitehead, A. H. Diverres and F. E. Sutcliffe, Manchester, 1965, pp. 337–56.
Wilmotte, M., 'Corrections: *Chanson de Roland* (ed. Jenkins)', *Romania*, LI, 1925, pp. 122–8.
Wind, B. H., 'Les Eléments Courtois dans Béroul et dans Thomas', *Romance Philology*, XIV, 1960, pp. 1–13.

Index

Figures in italics indicate references in the notes

Abelard, 80, 202
Alexis (Chanson de), 48–9
Amis et Amile, *134*, 204
Amoretti, G. V., *190*
Antunes, M., 197
Appel, C., *190*
Arese, F., *191*
Aristotle, 91
Arnold, I. D. O., *161*
Aspremont (Chanson de), 16, *132*, *134*, *135*, *194*
Aucassin et Nicolette, 122
Auerbach, E., 48–9, 185, *194*, *195*
Augustine (Saint), 80

Battaglia, S., 69, *195*
Bayot, A., *194*
Bayrav, S., 43
Becker, P. A., *194*
Bédier, J., 10, *14*, *46*, 91, *134*, 170, *191*, *192*, *193*, *208*
Bernheimer, R., 122
Bertolucci, V., 197, 201, 202, 205, *208*
Beszard, L., *192*
Beyerle, D., *207*
Bible, 82
Biller, G., 141, *161*
Boccacio, G., 166, *190*, *191*
Bolelli, T., *46*
Bossuat, R., *162*
Branca, V., *190*
Bréhier, E., 92
Brendan, Voyage St, 92
Brugger, E., *15*
Bueve d'Hamtone, *134*
Burger, A., *132*

Calila and Dimna, *190*

Carlyle, A. J., *132*
Carlyle, R. W., *132*
Cassiodorus, 116
Castro, A., *17*
Caulier, L., *128*
Caulkins, J. H., 202
Charroi de Nîmes, 45, 46, *134*, *135*, *193*
Chrestien de Troyes, 43, 111, 137, 162, *192*, 206
  Charrette, 168, *195*
  Cligés, *135*, 182, 206
  Erec, 200
Cicero, 138
Cid, Cantar de mio, 69, 116
Cohen, G., *190*
Conan IV, King, 200
Condesa traidora, Cantar de la, *132*
Conseil, Lai du, 93
Cor, Lai du, *135*, *192*
Couronnement de Louis, 46, 108, *133*
Curtis, R. L., 203, 204, *207*, *208*
Curtius, E. R., 48, 68–9, 185, *193*, *194*, *195*, 205, *207*

Defourques, L. M., 92
Delbouille, M., *46*, 201, 203, 204, *207*
Del Monte, A., *131*, *190*
Dessau, A., *132*
De Vries, J., *194*
Diarmaid and Grainne, 204
Di Francia, L., *189*, *191*
Ditmas, E. M. R., 200

Eberwein, E., 60–1, 71–2, *135*
Eilhart von Oberg, 3, 5, 8, 9–10, 13, *46*, 68, *71*, 115, *134*, 164, 170, 175, 179, *192*, 198, 199, 202, 203

Enéas, Roman de, 162
Esmein, A., *128, 129*
Ewert, A., *17, 46, 92, 194,* 197, 200, 201, 202, 203, 204, 205

Faral, E., *45*
Fedrick, A., *207*
Fergus, 92
Ferrante, J. M., 197, 198
Flamenca, 168
Folie Tristan, Berne, 115, 175, 179, *192*
Foulet, L., *194*
Foulon, C., *46*
Fourrier, A., *16, 17, 91, 160–1, 195, 208*
Frappier, J., 43, *48,* 67, *91, 93, 192, 195,* 197, 198, 199, 200, 201, 202, 203, 204, 205, 206, *207, 208*
Friedman, L., *207*
Fulbert of Chartres, *131*

Gallais, P., *207*
Ganshof, F. L., *131, 134*
Garin, 166
Garin le Loheren, 15, *45,* 111, *129, 135, 136,* 174
Gautier, L., *46*
Geoffroi de Vinsauf, *45*
Gerineldo, Romance de, 134
Giese, W., *46*
Gilson, E. H., *91,* 92
Girart de Roussillon, 92
Golther, W., *3, 4, 8, 9,* 11, *16, 47*
Gormont et Isembart, 184
Gottfried von Strassburg, 1, *14,* 122, 123, 168–70, 173, *207*
Graf, A., *47*
Guerrieri Crocetti, C., *93, 135*
Gui de Nanteuil, 133
Guillaume, Chanson de, 43, 67, 71, 199
Guillaume de Conches, 185
Guillaume de Palerne, 122

Hackett, W. M., *208*
Hanoset, M., *15, 16,* 199
Heinzel, R., *1–3, 7,* 10–11, 12, 13, 24, *161*
Heller, B., *134*

Henry, A., *134,* 204
Heyl, K., *195*
Hitze, R., 197, 198–9, 201, 202, 205, 206
Hoepffner, E., *192*
Hofer, S., *16, 46, 133*
Holden, A., 200
Hollyman, K.-J., *132*
Holmes, U. T., 198, 199, 202
Horace, 205

Isidore of Seville, 205

Jauss, H. R., *47, 194, 195*
Jean Renart, *196*
    Escoufle, 115, *194*
    Guillaume de Dole, 111
Jodogne, O., *207*
John of Capua, *190*
Jonin, P., *17, 45,* 92, *93,* 103, 111, *128, 129, 130, 134,* 162-3, *192, 195,* 205

Kelemina, J., *15, 44, 47,* 49
Kienast, W., *130*
Köhler, E., 206

La Fontaine, J. de, 166
Lange-Kowal, E., *45*
Langfors, A., *46*
Lazar, M., *195,* 204, *208*
Lecoy, F., 12, *15,* 200
Le Gentil, P., *16, 17, 91, 93*
Legge, M. D., *16, 131,* 198, 200, 201, 204, 206
Lejeune, R., *45, 128, 189*
Lidie, Comedia, 166, *190, 191*
Lindsay, W. M., 205
Lommatzsch, E., 92, *130*
Loomis, L. A., *190*
Loomis, R. S., *46, 190,* 200
Loth, J., 15

Marie de France, 60
    Chaitivel, 60
    Dous Amanz, 60
    fables, 166
    Lanval, 88–9, 92, 111, *131, 133*
    Laostic, 168
    Yonec, 60

Index

Marti, M., *190, 191*
Marx, J., *91,* 115, 198, 202, 204, 207
Matthieu de Vendôme, *45*
Menéndez Pidal, R., *16, 69, 130, 132, 134*
Mergell, B., *131*
Micha, A., *190*
Moniage Guillaume II, 48, 67, *134*
Montaiglon, A., *190*
Morawski, J., *93*
Moriz von Craûn, 196
Mort Artu, 93, 109
Muret, E., 2–5, 9, 11, 12, *17, 46, 92*
Murrel, S. E., *92*

Newstead, H., *46, 190,* 204, *208*
Nichols, S. G., 204
Niermeyer, J. F., *127*
Noble, P., 205
Nolting-Hauff, I., *48*
Novati, F., *15, 195*
Novellino, 189–90, 191

Orlando furioso, 69
Othello, 205
Ovid, *190*

Paris la Duchesse, 133
Paton, L. A., *193*
Pauphilet, A., *17, 71, 91, 93, 94, 191, 193*
Payen, J. C., *198,* 201, 202, 203
Peire Rogier, 190
Pèlerinage Charlemagne, 16
Pellegrini, S., *132*
Perceval, Didot, 193
Perrier, J.-L., *45, 135*
Poire, Roman de la, 114
Pope, M. K., *17*
Prise d'Orenge, 45, 46, 48, 135
Pulci, L., 12

Quatre fils Aymon, 132

Ranke, F., *190*
Raynaud, G., *190*
Raynaud de Lage, G., 5–10, 11, 13, 199, 200, 201, 205
Reginald of Cornwall, 200
Reid, T. B. W., *199–200*

Renart, Roman de, III, *134,* 174
Rigolot, F., 205
Roach, W., *193*
Robson, C. A., *49*
Roland, Chanson de, 49, 92, 109, III, 116, *134, 192–3,* 202, 205
Roques, M., *134, 192*
Rose, Roman de la, 16
Röttiger, W., 3
Rychner, J., *17,* 24, *47, 131, 161*

Sauerland, E., *133*
Schoepperle, G., *16*
Schröder, W. J., 207
Schultz, F., 205
Schultz-Gora, O., *71*
Schürr, F., *48, 161*
Segre, C., *189, 191*
Sept Sages, Roman des, 134
Stauffer, M., 122
Stone, D., 206

Tavola Ritonda, 170, *191*
Thèbes, Roman de, 69
Thomas, 1, 6, 10, *14, 46, 47, 75, 91, 94,* 114, 115, 123, *135,* 156, 158, 162, 168, 175, 179, *188, 191, 195, 196,* 201, 202, 206
 Horn, Romance of, 128, 132, 134, 189, 193
Tobler, A., *16, 92, 130*
Tristan en prose, Roman de, 46, 170, 175, 179, *191,* 202
Trois boçus, Fabliau des, 46
Tydorel, 194

Van Dam, J., *15*
Vinaver, E., *198,* 202, 204, 205, *208*

Wace, *15,* 138
Waremann, P., *68, 69, 70*
Warnke, K., *190*
Warren, F. M., *161*
Waters, E. G. R., *92*
Wauchier de Dinant, *193*
Whitehead, F., 121, *132*
Whitteridge, G., *194,* 200
William of Gloucester, 200
Wilmotte, M., *134*
Wind, B. H., *135, 189, 195, 196*